T0383221

THE COLLECTED POEMS OF
Ai

Ai

THE COLLECTED POEMS OF

INTRODUCTION BY YUSEF KOMUNYAKAA

W. W. NORTON & COMPANY • NEW YORK • LONDON

For information about permission to reproduce selections from this book,
write to Permissions, W. W. Norton & Company, Inc.,
500 Fifth Avenue, New York, NY 10110

For information about special discounts for bulk purchases, please contact
W. W. Norton Special Sales at specialsales@wwnorton.com or 800-233-4830

Manufacturing by Courier Westford
Book design by JAM Design
Production manager: Louise Mattarelliano

Library of Congress Cataloging-in-Publication Data

ISBN 978-0-393-07490-1 (hardcover)

W. W. Norton & Company, Inc.
500 Fifth Avenue, New York, N.Y. 10110
www.wwnorton.com

W. W. Norton & Company Ltd.
Castle House, 75/76 Wells Street, London W1T 3QT

1 2 3 4 5 6 7 8 9 0

CONTENTS

Dread

No Surrender

THE METHOD OF AI

*Infect your partner! Infect the person you are concentrating on! Insinu-
ate yourself into his very soul, and you will find yourself the more
infected for doing so. And if you are infected everyone else will be even
more infected.*

—Konstantin Stanislavski

I REMEMBER SITTING IN my Greystone apartment in Colorado Springs,
gazing out over Monument Park, Pikes Peak looming there, as I turned
from Ai on the cover of the *American Poetry Review** back to the poems
printed in those pages, poems that would appear in her first book, *Cruelty*.
Ai's poetry found me when I was repeatedly reading Ted Hughes's *Crow*,
momentarily taken by the poetic strangeness of this mythic bird; but her
raw imagery and the stripped-down music of her voice seemed even
stranger, more foreboding. Ai's poems are grounded in this world—
naturally telluric—even when her characters are almost totemic. And
back then her poems seemed like scenes from nightmarish movies
imprinted on the eyeballs, yet the images were revealed so matter-of-
factly, so damn casually. Upon reading a poem or two, I'd flip back to the
APR cover and take another look at Ai. From the outset, she knew how
to infect her reader through insinuation. There was an air of innocence
or coquettishness in her, and this seemed incongruous to the bold, raw,
sensuous, bloody imagery entering my psyche that summer afternoon.

I searched literary magazines for other poems by Ai. She was born
Florence Anthony, and I learned that Ai means "love" in Japanese.
Each monologue I discovered made me feel that her speakers were
tinged with an unusual, rural reality. They haunted me, and never
again would I think of poetry quite the same way.

When *Cruelty* was published in 1973, I read the collection repeat-
edly, transported by the mystery in the poems and by the politics of
gender on almost every page. The way the first poem in the collec-
tion, "Twenty-Year Marriage," opens is a clue to this poet's psychol-
ogy: "You keep me waiting in a truck / with its one good wheel

---

*July–August 1973, volume 2, number 4.

stuck in a ditch, / while you piss against the south side of a tree. / Hurry. I've got nothing on under my skirt tonight." The speaker's insinuation is calculated. The intentional, invented tension breathes on the page. She has our attention. But Ai knows—like any great actor—that language and pace are also crucial. Sometimes a poem may seem like personalized folklore, a feeling culled from the imagination. The characters hurt each other out of a fear of being hurt, and often they are doubly hurt. Do we believe her characters because they seem to evolve from some uncharted place beyond us but also inside us? They are of the soil, as if they've always been here; but they also reside on borders—spiritually, psychologically, existentially, and emotionally—as if only half-initiated into the muscular terror of ordinary lives. All the contradictions of so-called democracy live in her speakers. Most of the characters in Ai's poetry are distinctly rural, charged in mind and belly with folkloric signification, always one step or one trope from homespun violence and blasphemy.

What first deeply touched me in *Cruelty* is this: Ai's images—tinctured by an unknown folklore—seemed to arise from some deep, unsayable place, translated from a pre-language of knowing or dreaming with one's eyes open, as if something from long ago still beckoned to be put into words. Let's look at the third stanza of "Warrior":

> When you are standing in the river,
> you grab a fish,
> tear its flesh with your teeth, and hold it,
> until the bones in your fingers buck up
> and fly about you like moths.

Is the warrior African, Native American, an unnamed aboriginal, or some mythical citizen of an unknown place from the misty mountains of the imagination?

We believe Ai's various speakers even when we don't wish to. The speaker in "The Rivals" is a perfect example of such an aversion, highlighted by the poem's ending: "Just try it. Fall! I don't give a damn. / You're hurting, so am I, / but I'm strong enough to let you cry alone." If we believe this speaker, do we also possess a similar capacity for malice? In a sense, we enter into a dialogue with each character that she's created; and we argue not only for our own humanity but also for the speaker's. Such a discourse through the unsaid does the job of poetry. Silence, pace, rhythm—the whole tonal shape of a poem is important to Ai.

The power in her poetry isn't rancor, but the terrifying beauty of pure candor. The second stanza from the last poem in *Cruelty*, "New Crops for a Free Man," underscores Ai's ability to create characters that challenge us morally:

> Behind me, another fire, my woman,
> under sheets wrinkled and stiff from heat and sweat,
> throws them back and rises.
> She cracks her knuckles, leans from the window and yells,
> but I keep my head turned toward the thing I understand.
> She's hot from a match I never lit
> and strokes her breasts, cone-shaped candles,
> whose wicks, her nipples, aflame, burn holes in her hands, in me.

Ai's characters uncover their senses of self as they speak, baring themselves physically, psychologically, and spiritually, and the music of telling seems to bring them to the cusp of being transformed. Each poem is a confession.

Could she be for real? Even if Ai hadn't personally experienced what she conveyed in her poetry directly, image after image, character by character, I believed and felt every word on the page. I thought I knew the violence and terror humans perfected and exacted on one another, but reading Ai's poems that afternoon so long ago, I felt that I had only tiptoed to the perimeter of a terror Ai depicted with such graphic ease. Many of her most memorable characters exist in the heart of an American frontier situated in a static passage of time that seems slanted. And, thus, she knew how to be in this world by existing out of this world through a supreme candor and honed toughness that approach transcendence.

Six years later I cracked the spine of Ai's second collection of poems, *Killing Floor*, and I encountered the same provocative passion as in *Cruelty*; I already knew she was singing a deep, instinctual blues, but not because the book's title made me think of Skip James. She could carry her own tune. It wasn't just a tune plucked on the gut string that made one's teeth chatter; her blues didn't rise out of fear or the rage of unrequited love, but by brushing up against more expansive moments of universal truths. Ai's title poem, "Killing Floor," isn't located in the Mississippi delta or the Chicago stockyards, but in an extended nightmare in Russia (1927) and Mexico (1940), and it ends with the speaker facing his wife's mirror in a dream as a cross-dresser, saying:

> I lean forward and see Jacques's reflection.
> I half-turn, smile, then turn back to the mirror.
> He moves from the doorway,
> lifts the pickax
> and strikes the top of my head.
> My brain splits.
> The pickax keeps going
> and when it hits the tile floor,
> it flies from his hands,
> a black dove on whose back I ride,
> two men, one cursing, the other blessing all things:
> *Lev Davidovich Bronstein,*
> *I step from Jordan without you.*

Some poems in *Killing Floor* are for Yukio Mishima, Yasunari Kawabata, Marilyn Monroe, Ira Hayes; the poet even dedicates "Pentecost"—a poem with Emiliano Zapata at its center—to herself, ending with these two lines: "If you suffer in the grave, / You can kill from it." A frontier philosophy seems to touch all sides and angles of the poet's vision.

For Ai, the page was always her stage, and the voices in her poems were hers and they weren't hers. She mastered the shape-shifter's voice not as a form of ventriloquism, but through a unique personification where the most unspeakable acts still speak to us and where we are frightened by our own most secret thoughts and daydreams through acts of imaginative participation. She created characters that earned our attention. The voices were mainly rural but also tonally antipastoral; her characters are at home in the silence of the landscape but always have something to say about life-and-death matters. We believe Ai's voice because it transports us to a place shaped by the old brain, that terrain located in the right hemisphere.

There are battles beyond the mind and flesh, yet purely of the flesh. Ai's images refuse to let us off the hook; she keeps us fully situated in the dynamics of modern life, holding a magnifying glass up to our most wounded moments, as she does so expertly in "The Kid" (he's not Billy the Kid—our antihero of the Wild West—but just as vicious).

After the speaker kills his father, mother, sister, and two horses, the poem ends with these lines:

> Yeah. I'm Jack, Hogarth's son.
> I'm nimble, I'm quick.
> In the house, I put on the old man's best suit
> and his patent leather shoes.
> I pack my mother's satin nightgown.
> and my sister's doll in the suitcase.
> Then I go outside and cross the fields to the highway.
> I'm fourteen. I'm a wind from nowhere.
> I can break your heart.

This character comes out of the brutal silence of America. The word *your* in the last line makes us the speaker's accomplice.

I think it was Stanislavski who said, "If an actor thinks he is the character, the director should fire him." In many ways, Ai is a proxy actor in the various characters she creates through the agency of the monologue, but she also remains the conjurer, the maker of the most tantalizing imagery in American poetry. Her work has always had an audience. The voices she creates are of her and also outside of her. Though she once created a voice for Jimmy Hoffa that she read in a few times, Ai was always the poet, first and most importantly.

Recently, as I reread Adrienne Rich's smart, compact, little book *Poetry and Commitment*, I thought of Ai, especially in the following paragraph:

> If to "aestheticize" is to glide across brutality and cruelty, treat them merely as dramatic occasions for the artist rather than structures of power to be revealed and dismantled—much hangs on the words "merely" and "rather than." Opportunism isn't the same as committed attention. But we can also define the "aesthetic" not as a privileged and sequestered rendering of human suffering, but as news of an awareness, a resistance, that totalizing systems want to quell: art reaching into us for what's still passionate, still unintimidated, still unquenched.

Ai's *news of an awareness* is what corners the reader. She lets her characters betray themselves by what they say and don't say—imagistic and brutally honest.

Ai was a believer, in the old-fashioned sense of good and evil, and this seems to have directed the unmitigated passion in her poems. One only has to look at the titles of her eight collections to glimpse the moral equation of Ai's work: *Cruelty, Killing Floor, Sin, Fate, Greed, Vice: New and Selected Poems, Dread*, and *No Surrender*. Some of her poems at times seem like excerpted passages or facsimiles gleaned from the Book of Revelation. Hidden in the praises are curses—from the mouths of seers, soothsayers, and shape-shifting prophets posing as everyday citizens. She also gives us the voices of J. Edgar Hoover, James Dean, Jack Ruby, Lenny Bruce, General George Armstrong Custer, Jimmy Hoffa, Walt Whitman, Richard Nixon, Joe McCarthy, and the Good Shepherd. And some of the voices let us in on secretive thoughts, on moments that betray the speaker and the listener (reader). But some of the most political moments are in the unsaid. Ai mastered signification because she knew our history, what we are truly made of.

The complexity of her own lineage perhaps shaped her outlook—privately and publicly—on the reality of American culture. She embodied both conflict and harmony, as conveyed in the title of her 1978 essay "On Being 1/2 Japanese, 1/8 Choctaw, 1/4 Black, and 1/16 Irish."* In an interview for *Standards*,† it becomes clear that race and skin color formed the psychological axis of Ai's most intimate feelings and thoughts. Speaking about her unpublished novel, she says, "The novel is called *Black Blood*, and it turns on how much Black blood these people have, in the novel. [laughs] So how did they get mixed? By having sex with somebody in another race; that's how! But I think my memoir is really gonna be good. [laughs] If she ever finishes her research!" Ai seems taunted and haunted by Blackness in her life and her work. Elsewhere in that same interview, she says, "I told one reporter that night, 'Well, score one for mixed race!'"

"Passing Through," the last poem in *Vice* (which won the 1999 National Book Award), shows Ai overtly addressing race and skin color. The monologue opens with these lines:

> "Earth is the birth of the blues," sang Yellow Bertha,
>   as she chopped cotton beside Mama Rose.
>   It was hot as any other summer day,

New York Times, March 27, 2010.
†Spring–Summer 2001.

when she decided to run away.
Folks say she made a fortune
running a whorehouse in New Orleans,
but others say she's buried somewhere out west,
her grave unmarked,
though you can find it in the dark
by the scent of jasmine and mint,
but I'm getting ahead of myself.

The story the poet gives us is woven from blues shaped out of American history. The voice is so clear and layered that it seems the story has been lived. And we believe these lines when the poem ends, after the twists and turns of a rueful, relentless life:

When I got off the bus,
a hush fell over the people waiting there.
I was as white as my mother,
but my eyes were gray, not green.
I had hair down to my waist and braids so thick
they weighed me down.
Mother said, my father was a white musician
from another town,
who found out her secret
and left her and me to keep it.
Mama Rose knew me, though, blind as she was.
"What color are you, gal?" She asked
and I told her, "I'm as black as last night."
That's how I passed, without asking permission.

This moment of passing in reverse says much about the poet's sense of politics and history.

In the end, Ai becomes a pronoun, but remains a one-of-a-kind voice that refuses to plead for mercy. In the last section of "The Cancer Chronicles" she says, "Her thoughts clattering around in her head like marbles, / Their sound echoing down the long road of suffering / She must have chosen, / Although she couldn't remember doing so. . . ." The slanted directness in this poem is vintage Ai. And, of course, this posture of resistance and acceptance echoes through everything she's written. Ai is still a hard act to follow, and her illuminating poems accentuate her true identity and presence. She has created a body of work that endures, that questions who we are and what borders we cross.

I believe Ai will continue to engage readers who are brave enough to face her vision. Her "method" was being alive. Giving us numerous hints along the way, she instinctively captured the nature of being in this world. She gave us clues to her spirit—as a human, as a poet, as a woman—sometimes with only a few lines. Ai, the method actor-poet who superbly insinuated through a passionate language of the frontier, may find a home with actors who are searching for unique monologues to hone their voices with truth solid as whetstone. I can still see Ai stepping from the page to the stage. There's no voice like hers in American poetry; her unusual characters bear multiple truths.

THE COLLECTED POEMS OF

Ai

Cruelty

TWENTY-YEAR MARRIAGE

You keep me waiting in a truck
with its one good wheel stuck in the ditch,
while you piss against the south side of a tree.
Hurry. I've got nothing on under my skirt tonight.
That still excites you, but this pickup has no windows
and the seat, one fake leather thigh,
pressed close to mine is cold.
I'm the same size, shape, make as twenty years ago,
but get inside me, start the engine;
you'll have the strength, the will to move.
I'll pull, you push, we'll tear each other in half.
Come on, baby, lay me down on my back.
Pretend you don't owe me a thing
and maybe we'll roll out of here,
leaving the past stacked up behind us;
old newspapers nobody's ever got to read again.

ABORTION

Coming home, I find you still in bed,
but when I pull back the blanket,
I see your stomach is flat as an iron.
You've done it, as you warned me you would
and left the fetus wrapped in wax paper
for me to look at. My son.
Woman, loving you no matter what you do,
what can I say, except that I've heard
the poor have no children, just small people
and there is room only for one man in this house.

THE COUNTRY MIDWIFE: A DAY

I bend over the woman.
This is the third time between abortions.
I dip a towel into a bucket of hot water
and catch the first bit of blood,

as the blue–pink dome of a head breaks through.
A scraggy, red child comes out of her into my hands
like warehouse ice sliding down the chute.

It's done, the stink of birth, Old Grizzly
rears up on his hind legs in front of me
and I want to go outside,
but the air smells the same there too.
The woman's left eye twitches
and beneath her, a stain as orange as sunrise
spreads over the sheet.
I lift my short, blunt fingers to my face
and I let her bleed, Lord, I let her bleed.

THE UNEXPECTED

As I wipe the dust off my face,
you sweep the kitchen floor
for the third time today
and I wonder if we are having some special guest.
I don't feel like company,
but I know it doesn't bother you, woman,
pregnant walnut of flesh,
waiting for birth to crack you open
with her sharp, brown teeth
and force you to give up your white meat.

You sweep the dirt into a pile.
I get the dustpan and kneel down,
so you can push the dirt onto it,
but before you've finished,
I reach under your skirt and stroke your ankle.
It's wet. Frightened, I stand up.
Go on, just give me the broom
and let me finish sweeping up for you,
you never know who might stop by
and everything's got to be clean, clean.

BUT WHAT I'M TRYING TO SAY MOTHER IS

You are barely able to walk,
sewn up between your legs, bleeding,
and slumped over from the weight
of six months of pregnancy,
although it *is* all over.
You wear your green chenille robe
and carry a picture of the dead child, the fifth one.
Mother, why don't you stop looking at me?
Let me wash you, please.
And yes, I go to the cemetery.
I cry, I pray for his soul,
I pour milk on his grave,
and I do it because I loved you once, I did
and it was good.

THE ESTRANGED

I lay peeled potatoes in the iron pot,
beside the meat, as it strains a tongue of fat
to lick its own blood,
just as I strain at keeping you with me.
I am the needle, woman,
let me pierce your camel eye
and sew you to me with iron thread,
let my ovaries, the potatoes,
give you a bridge of babies' heads
to cross back into yourself
and my monthly blood, mixed with water,
will be a blanket of gravy to cover you
from one icy night to the next.

CRUELTY

The hoof-marks on the dead wildcat
gleam in the dark.
You are naked, as you drag it up on the porch.

That won't work either.
Drinking ice water hasn't,
nor having the bedsprings snap fingers
to help us keep rhythm.
I've never once felt anything
that might get close. Can't you see?
The thing I want most is hard,
running toward my own teeth
and it bites back.

THE TENANT FARMER

Hailstones puncture the ground,
as I sit at the table, rubbing a fork.
My woman slides a knife across her lips,
then lays it beside a cup of water.
Each day she bites another notch in her thumb
and I pretend relief is coming
as the smooth black tire, Earth,
wheels around the sun without its patch of topsoil
and my mouth speaks: *wheat, barley, red cabbage,*
roll on home to Jesus,
it's too late now you're dead.

STARVATION

Rain, tobacco juice, spit from the sky
shatters against your body,
as you push the pane of glass through the mud.
The white oak frame of the house shakes
when I slam the door and stand on the porch,
fanning myself with a piece of cardboard,
cut in the shape of a ham.

There's a pot of air on the stove.
You drove seventy miles, paid for that glass
and I can't remember the last good meal I had,
but bring it up here. I'll help you. I'm not angry.
We'll paint the sun on it from the inside,

so if we die some night, a light will still be on.
It's hell to starve in the dark.
I don't know why. I'm just your woman,
like you, crazy to lose all I've got.
It's rotten, you know, rotten.
The table's set. What time is it?
Wash your hands first. You're late.

PROSTITUTE

Husband, for a while, after I shoot you,
I don't touch your body,
I just cool it with my paper fan,
the way I used to on hot nights,
as the moon rises, chip of avocado

and finally, too bored to stay any longer,
I search your pockets, finding a few coins.
I slip your hand under my skirt
and rub it against my chili-red skin,
then I put on your black boots.
I stick the gun in my waistband,
two beaded combs in my hair.

I never cost much,
but tonight, with a gun, your boots . . .

POSSESSIONS

You sit on the porch steps,
rubbing your knuckles on your pants.
I press the hen against my skirt
and go into the kitchen.
As I slice through the right wing,
I hear you come inside, and soon, your mouth is on my arm.
I wait for you to ask me how it was with the other man,
but you don't need to.
You have it all now, even what was his.

WHY CAN'T I LEAVE YOU?

You stand behind the old black mare,
dressed as always in that red shirt,
stained from sweat, the crying of the armpits,
that will not stop for anything,
stroking her rump, while the barley goes unplanted.
I pick up my suitcase and set it down,
as I try to leave you again.
I smooth the hair back from your forehead.
I think with your laziness and the drought too,
you'll be needing my help more than ever.
You take my hands, I nod
and go to the house to unpack,
having found another reason to stay.

I undress, then put on my white lace slip
for you to take off, because you like that
and when you come in, you pull down the straps
and I unbutton your shirt.
I know we can't give each other any more
or any less than what we have.
There is safety in that, so much
that I can never get past the packing,
the begging you to please, if I can't make you happy,
come close between my thighs
and let me laugh for you from my second mouth.

I HAVE GOT TO STOP LOVING YOU

So I have killed my black goat.
His kidney floats in a bowl,
a beige, flat fish, around whom parasites, slices of lemon,
break through the surface of hot broth, then sink below,
as I bend, face down in the steam, breathing in.
I hear this will cure anything.

When I am finished, I walk up to him.
He hangs from a short wooden post,

tongue stuck out of his mouth,
tasting the hay-flavored air.
A bib of flies gather at his throat
and further down, where he is open
and bare of all his organs,
I put my hand in, stroke him once,
then taking it out, look at the sky.
The stormclouds there break open
and raindrops, yellow as black cats' eyes, come down
each a tiny river, hateful and alone.

Wishing I could get out of this alive, I hug myself.
It is hard to remember if he suffered much.

YOUNG FARM WOMAN ALONE

What could I do with a man? —
pull him on like these oxhide boots,
the color of plums, dipped in blue ink
and stomp hell out of my loneliness,
this hoe that with each use grows sharper.

RECAPTURE

When you run off, I start after you,
as the sun rolls overhead
and rocks in the sky's blue hands.

As always, I find you, beat you.
The corner of your mouth bleeds
and your tongue slips out, slips in.
You don't fight me, you never do.

Going back, you stumble against me
and I grab your wrist, pulling you down.
Come on, bitch of my love, while it is still easy.

WOMAN TO MAN

Lightning hits the roof,
shoves the knife, darkness,
deep in the walls.
They bleed light all over us
and your face, the fan, folds up,
so I won't see how afraid
to be with me you are.
We don't mix, even in bed,
where we keep ending up.
There's no need to hide it:
you're snow, I'm coal,
I've got the scars to prove it.
But open your mouth,
I'll give you a taste of black
you won't forget.
For a while, I'll let it make you strong,
make your heart lion,
then I'll take it back.

THE ANNIVERSARY

You raise the ax,
the block of wood screams in half,
while I lift the sack of flour
and carry it into the house.
I'm not afraid of the blade
you've just pointed at my head.
If I were dead, you could take the boy,
hunt, kiss gnats, instead of my moist lips.
Take it easy, squabs are roasting,
corn, still in husks, crackles,
as the boy dances around the table:
old guest at a wedding party for two sad-faced clowns,
who together, never won a round of anything but hard times.
Come in, sheets are clean,
fall down on me for one more year
and we can blast another hole in ourselves without a sound.

1931

I bend to kiss your breasts, but you push me away
and I go to the bedroom to look at my son.
His irises, two blue, baby onions
come apart as he wakes.
I take him to you and walk into the street.
I can't blame you for not wanting me.
Before you only gave yourself out of boredom
and with this hunger, even that is gone.
I hear the screen door slam and keep walking.
I know you'll follow, always behind or ahead of me,
never at my side.

TIRED OLD WHORE

This is my property, I laid for it, paid for it, you know,
and I just want to build a cement walkway
right up to my front door.
I'll be the only whore within fifty miles
who can claim she did something with her hands
that didn't get a man hard.

What? — but I'm so tired. Can't you wait a while?
I'm forty-five, my breath's short, I like to sleep alone.
Yeah, yeah, I rolled in my jelly and it felt good,
but this belly isn't wood, or steel.
Man, turn your butt to my face.
But wait, I need a little help, help me, sweet thing.
Pull down your pants.
I like to see what I'm getting now,
before it gets into me.

FORTY-THREE-YEAR-OLD WOMAN, MASTURBATING

I want to kill this female hand —
its four centipede fingers;
the thumb, cricket, that lags behind,

digging its nail into me, until I move my legs apart;
the palm, body of a tarantula,
that sinks down over my clitoris,
as the fingers inch into my vagina —
but each time, after it happens,
the fingers, moist and flaccid, crawl up to my mouth,
my grasshopper tongue, darting out, licks them
and I am grateful for a small taste of anything.

OLD WOMAN, YOUNG MAN

He thrusts his arms in the barrel of grain,
takes them out
and rubs them across his bare chest
because I love the gritty feel of it
and wear it on each breast like a bracelet.

Unashamed, I part my legs.
As always he says, *look there's a rose,*
yes, but it's lost its teeth.
He eats without tasting
and I reach to scratch my name
on the damp face rising
with a few crinkled gray hairs
shoving their white-tipped heads
against his scarred and frightened lips.

ONE MAN DOWN

Your brother brings you home from hunting,
slung over your horse, dead,
with the wild boar tied down beside you.
I ask no questions.

He throws the boar at my feet,
hands me the red licorice he promised.
I drop my shawl
and his hands cover my breasts.

He whispers of a dress in town,
while I unbutton my skirt.

I sit on the ground, waiting,
while he loosens his belt.
He smiles, swings it across my face,
then pushes me back. I keep my eyes open.
The hound's paws bloody the tiles
lining the flower bed.
The bitch walks behind him, licking his tracks.
I scratch the flesh above me.
The odor of fresh meat
digs a finger in my nostrils.
The horse rears,
your body slides from the black saddle
like a bedroll of fine velvet.
I laugh, close my eyes, and relax.

AFTER A LONG TIME

the halves of the egg, impotence,
slide into each other on waxed feet
and the wait is over.
The seam between my legs
basted with hair tears apart,
as your blue, flannel spoon slips inside,
digs out the pieces of cracked shell
and lays them on my thighs,
like old china plates made too thin
for holding anything but love.

HANGMAN

In the fields, the silos open their mouths
and let the grain dribble down their sides,
for they are overflowing.
The farmers swing their scythes, brows dripping blood.
They have had the passion ripped out of their chests
and share no brotherhood with the wheat,

while far across the open land,
the Hangman mounts an empty scaffold.
He slides his hands over the coarse-grained cedar
and smells the whole Lebanese coast
in the upraised arms of Kansas.
The rope's stiff bristles prick his fingers,
as he holds it and lifts himself above the trap door.

He touches the wood again.
This will be his last hanging
and anyway he has seen other fields,
workmen nailing brass spikes into the scaffolds
and rope which coiled and uncoiled
in the laps of farm women.
He places his foot on the step going down
and nearby, a scarecrow explodes,
sending tiny slivers of straw into his eyes.

THE SWEET

The man steps in out of the blizzard with his Klootch,
his Eskimo prostitute and the room heats up, as they
cross the floor. I know he is dying and I spin a half
dollar around on the bar, then slide my eyes over the woman.
She has a seal's body. Her face is a violet in the center
of the moon. The half dollar falls over, I remind myself
that to love a Klootch is always to be filled with emptiness,
turn and lift my glass.

I shake my head, drink. When I hear retreating footsteps,
I turn. The man stands at the door, facing me. His hand
gropes out, as the woman backs off and I see the Northern
Lights flare up in his eyes, before he stumbles and falls.
The woman leans back against the wall. I pick up the half
dollar, spin it around again and go to her. We walk out
into the darkness and I am cold as I squeeze her buttocks,
her blue, dwarf stars.

THE COLOR THIEF

I enter your room,
with my purple face moist from excitement.
The black straw basket I carry
in my yellow arms cracks softly,
in tune with the brittle snap of my blue legs,
as I sneak to your bed.
Little girl, have you got a pink buttock to lend,
or a cream-colored navel
that darkens to brown as it spirals inward?

Or breasts? Yes.
They are swelling now
for the first time.
I touch them.
I take the nipples in my hands.
They are hard
and almost as magenta as plums.
I drop them into my basket
and leave quickly.
The light bulbs I've stuck in the tips of your breasts
shine far into your middle age,
the clearest white I've ever seen.

THE CORPSE HAULER'S ELEGY

Beside the river, I stop the wagon,
loaded with the plague dead
and have a drink.
I fill my mouth and swallow slowly,
then climb back into my seat.
The old horse drops one turd, another.
Corpses, I give you these flowers.

THE HITCHHIKER

The Arizona wind dries out my nostrils
and the heat of the sidewalk burns my shoes,
as a woman drives up slowly.
I get in, grinning at a face I do not like,
but I slide my arm across the top of the seat
and rest it lightly against her shoulder.
We turn off into the desert,
then I reach inside my pocket and touch the switchblade.

We stop, and as she moves closer to me, my hands ache,
but somehow, I get the blade into her chest.
I think a song: "Everybody needs somebody,
everybody needs somebody to love,"
as the black numerals 35 roll out of her right eye
inside one small tear.
Laughing, I snap my fingers. Rape, murder, I got you
in the sight of my gun.

I move off toward the street.
My feet press down in it,
familiar with the hot, soft asphalt
that caresses them.
The sun slips down into its cradle behind the mountains
and it is hot, hotter than ever
and I like it.

THE ROOT EATER

The war has begun
and I see the Root Eater bending,
shifting his hands under the soil
in search of the arthritic knuckles of trees.
I see dazed flower stems
pushing themselves back into the ground.
I see turnips spinning endlessly
on the blunt, bitten-off tips of their noses.
I see the Root Eater going home on his knees,

full of the ripe foundations of things,
longing to send his seed up through his feet
and out into the morning

but the stumps of trees heave themselves forward
for the last march
and the Root Eater waits,
knowing he will be shoved, rootless,
under the brown, scaly torso of the rock.

THE WIDOW

After I burn the boar's carcass,
I fill the slop bucket
and the old sow gets up,
grunting from deep inside,
where the piglets, just beginning to wake,
are already smelling the sour food,
and stretching their pink toes toward me.

As I dump the slop into the trough,
the sow rubs her snout against my leg
and I kneel, pushing my head through
to the muddy side of her body.
I touch her teat with my tongue.
She grunts and I climb over the fence.
I sink down on my side
in the mud, the wet, black cotton of the earth,
as my wife calls. No, not my wife, the woman.
I don't say anything.
How can I tell her he will never come?

THE DESERTER

Through the hole in the hut's wall,
I watch the old woman who put me up,
leaning against a wooden tub, elbow deep in wash water.
I go to her, feeling an itch somewhere inside my mouth,

knowing I've got to leave everything of myself here.
I raise the rifle, as she presses a white shawl
far down in the water, and fire.
She dies quietly; even her heart spits blood
through clenched teeth.

I take bread, onions, radishes and set out,
leaving my rifle behind, while the wind is down
and stillness, with its knives of powdered lead,
slashes the coarse, brown hair from my arms
as I hold them, empty, at my sides.

CUBA, 1962

When the rooster jumps up on the windowsill
and spreads his red-gold wings,
I wake, thinking it is the sun
and call Juanita, hearing her answer,
but only in my mind.
I know she is already outside,
breaking the cane off at ground level,
using only her big hands.
I get the machete and walk among the cane,
until I see her, lying face-down in the dirt.

Juanita, dead in the morning like this.
I raise the machete —
what I take from the earth, I give back —
and cut off her feet.
I lift the body and carry it to the wagon,
where I load the cane to sell in the village.
Whoever tastes my woman in his candy, his cake,
tastes something sweeter than this sugar cane;
it is grief.
If you eat too much of it, you want more,
you can never get enough.

SUNDAY

changeling, props a coffin against my door,
stains the windows with its brown curtains,
floats, belly-up in my glass of water.
I see its back in my mirror,
its hand walking in my shoes.
I smell its piss odor in my underwear
and when it peels off the sheet onto my body,
I yell, grab for its throat
and get its mud heart, shaped like a box,
and just full of things
you can't quite put your finger on.

INDECISION

seamstress, you sew a screen door to my mouth
and it slams back against my cheek, soundlessly,
when I try to speak,
leaving only a question mark
that wheels around on its period,
its one leg, yelling, go ahead,
ask me anything, ask me anything,
but don't make me decide what to do.

THE CRIPPLE

I pull my legs from the floor,
as I would two weeds, gently,
pretending my roots have remained
in the soil that once held me upright
in the palm of its hand,
in the roads of black thread,
I walked, sowing years.
Instead, the itch deep in my heel
cries from its mouth one thorn after another.

THE SUICIDE

The street coughs blood
in a linen handkerchief,
as I strut down to the river,
where the oil ships, black bars of soap,
float upright on steel spines.
The wharf has a tight, deep vagina of water
and I'm going to fuck it until it novas,
just to let everybody see
how I cut through life like a diamond
in a sack of glass, with no regrets,
and a what's it to you
to shove up your ass.

DISREGARD

Overhead, the match burns out,
but the chunk of ice in the back seat
keeps melting from imagined heat,
while the old Hudson tiptoes up the slope.
My voile blouse, so wet it is transparent,
like one frightened hand, clutches my chest.
The bag of rock salt sprawled beside me wakes, thirsty
and stretches a shaky tongue toward the ice.

I press the gas pedal hard.
I'll get back to the house, the dirt yard, the cesspool,
to you out back, digging a well
you could fill with your sweat,
though there is not one reason I should want to.
You never notice me until the end of the day,
when your hand is on my knee
and the ice cream, cooked to broth,
is hot enough to burn the skin off my touch.

CHILD BEATER

Outside, the rain, pinafore of gray water, dresses the town
and I stroke the leather belt,
as she sits in the rocking chair,
holding a crushed paper cup to her lips.
I yell at her, but she keeps rocking;
back, her eyes open, forward, they close.
Her body, somehow fat, though I feed her only once a day,
reminds me of my own just after she was born.
It's been seven years, but I still can't forget how I felt.
How heavy it feels to look at her.

I lay the belt on a chair
and get her dinner bowl.
I hit the spoon against it, set it down
and watch her crawl to it,
pausing after each forward thrust of her legs
and when she takes her first bite,
I grab the belt and beat her across the back
until her tears, beads of salt-filled glass, falling,
shatter on the floor.

I move off. I let her eat,
while I get my dog's chain leash from the closet.
I whirl it around my head.
O daughter, so far, you've only had a taste of icing,
are you ready now for some cake?

THE DWARF

From where I stand, Fat Lady,
I can see you winding the radium clock
in your vagina,
while your half-life, already caught in the lymph nodes
is burning out.
I can see the pimples on your knees growing red,
hairs sprouting, split at the tips, each a great antenna,

your toes wiggling in despair
and there in your eyes, my own shoe-like face,
laced with the same uncontrollable laughter.

WARRIOR

You sharpen the tip of spear
with your teeth,
while your wife plows the ground
with jawbone of an ox.
She is a great, black fire.

The old blood is drifting up your throat
and the witch-men sing all night
of melon-breasted women in rival villages,
but the spear is wilting in your hands.

When you are standing in the river,
you grab a fish,
tear its flesh open with your teeth, and hold it,
until the bones in your fingers break up
and fly about you like moths.

The river, a fish, your fingers, moths,
the war song churning in your belly.

WOMAN

The adobe walls of the house
clutch the noon heat in tin fists
and while bathing, I fan my breasts,
watching the nipples harden.
I pinch them, feeling nothing, but wanting to,
and shift my weight from left buttock to right,
while the water circling my waist tightens,
as if you had commanded it.
I stand up, spreading my legs apart,
ready to release the next ribbon of blood.

All right. You want me now, this way.
I haven't locked the door.
My swollen belly feels only its heaviness,
you would weigh less than the pain
chipping away at my navel with an ice pick of muscle.
I can carry you.
The blood, halved and thinned, rolls down my legs,
cupping each foot in a red stirrup
and I am riding that invisible horse,
the same one my mother rode.
It's hungry, it has to be fed,
the last man couldn't, can you?

THE RIVALS

You swat flies with your hand, cursing,
calling them the names of our sons.
Forget them, we don't need them to help us.
On days when you drive the wagon into town
I wear the harness myself and keep plowing.
Some nights, too, while sleeping, I dream you young again,
shoving your snake up me, hissing the love
you can never say you feel
and wake to find your fingers
combing the snarled hair between my legs,
until I rise up on one arm, twenty years your junior,
moan for more and get a back turned to my eyes.
I take the old, smoked sausage from under my pillow
and push it inside me, before I tell you
how much of a woman I still am.

I go out to the wagon,
where I am painting roses; ten on two sides,
one for the pencil, each year,
that drew a black line across my face
since you first laid me beneath you.
It's true my back's bent, my breasts smell like buttermilk.
You used to love that, but I understand.
I'm the first woman you had,

I've got the saw mark across my leg
where you brought it down on me, when I was heavy-bellied,
unable to help you with the chores.

Now you kill flies, your body rains sweat, you wet your pants
if I don't get them down in time.
Holding the bucket of paint, I dance and sing.
You think you can walk a step without stumbling, you
                                                    sonofabitch?

Just try it. Fall! I don't give a damn.
You're hurting, so am I,
but I'm strong enough to let you cry alone.

EVERYTHING: ELOY, ARIZONA, 1956

Tin shack, where my baby sleeps on his back
the way the hound taught him;
highway, black zebra, with one white stripe;
nickel in my pocket for chewing gum;
you think you're all I've got.
But when the 2 ton rolls to a stop
and the driver gets out,
I sit down in the shade and wave each finger,
saving my whole hand till the last.

He's keys, tires, a fire lit in his belly
in the diner up the road.
I'm red toenails, tight blue halter, black slip.
He's mine tonight. I don't know him.
He can only hurt me a piece at a time.

BEFORE YOU LEAVE

I set the bowl of raw vegetables on the table.
You know I am ripe now.
You can bite me, I won't bleed;
just take off my kimono. Eat, then go ahead, run.

I won't miss you, but this one hour
lift me by the buttocks
and press me hard against your belly.
Fill my tunnel with the howl
you keep zipped in your pants
and when it's over, don't worry, I'll stand.
I'm a mare. Every nail's head
in my hooves wears your face,
but not even you, wolf, can bring me down.

NEW CROPS FOR A FREE MAN

I drop the torch of rags in a bucket of water,
then watch the field burn.

Behind me, another fire, my woman,
under sheets wrinkled and stiff from heat and sweat,
throws them back and rises.
She cracks her knuckles, leans from the window and yells,
but I keep my head turned toward the thing I understand.
She's hot from a match I never lit
and strokes her breasts, cone-shaped candles,
whose wicks, her nipples, aflame, burn holes in her hands, in me.

Go back to sleep, I don't need you now.
I just want the dirt under my fingernails to become mountains,
to listen to my heartbeat inside the rocks
and scream as my own death slides into bed
with her ass bloody and sweet when I lick it,
one stalk of wheat no man
can pull from the ground and live to eat.

Killing Floor

KILLING FLOOR

1. Russia, 1927

On the day the sienna-skinned man
held my shoulders between his spade-shaped hands,
easing me down into the azure water of Jordan,
I woke ninety-three million miles from myself,
Lev Davidovich Bronstein,
shoulder-deep in the Volga,
while the cheap dye of my black silk shirt darkened the water.

My head wet, water caught in my lashes.
Am I blind?
I rub my eyes, then wade back to shore,
undress and lie down,
until Stalin comes from his place beneath the birch tree.
He folds my clothes
and I button myself in my marmot coat,
and together we start the long walk back to Moscow.
He doesn't ask, *what did you see in the river?,*
but I hear the hosts of a man drowning in water and holiness,
the castrati voices I can't recognize,
skating on knives, from trees, from air
on the thin ice of my last night in Russia.
Leon Trotsky. Bread.
I want to scream, but silence holds my tongue
with small spade-shaped hands
and only this comes, so quietly

Stalin has to press his ear to my mouth:
I have only myself. Put me on the train.
I won't look back.

2. Mexico, 1940

At noon today, I woke from a nightmare:
my friend Jacques ran toward me with an ax,
as I stepped from the train in Alma-Ata.
He was dressed in yellow satin pants and shirt.
A marigold in winter.

When I held out my arms to embrace him,
he raised the ax and struck me at the neck,
my head fell to one side, hanging only by skin.
A river of sighs poured from the cut.

3. Mexico, August 20, 1940

The machine-gun bullets
hit my wife in the legs,
then zigzagged up her body.
I took the shears, cut open her gown
and lay on top of her for hours.
Blood soaked through my clothes
and when I tried to rise, I couldn't.

I wake then. Another nightmare.
I rise from my desk, walk to the bedroom
and sit down at my wife's mirrored vanity.
I rouge my cheeks and lips,
stare at my bone-white, speckled egg of a face:
lined and empty.
I lean forward and see Jacques's reflection.
I half-turn, smile, then turn back to the mirror.
He moves from the doorway,
lifts the pickax
and strikes the top of my head.
My brain splits.
The pickax keeps going
and when it hits the tile floor,
it flies from his hands,
a black dove on whose back I ride,
two men, one cursing,
the other blessing all things:
Lev Davidovich Bronstein,
I step from Jordan without you.

NOTHING BUT COLOR

For Yukio Mishima

I didn't write Etsuko,
I sliced her open.
She was carmine inside
like a sea bass
and empty.
No viscera, nothing but color.
I love you like that, boy.
I pull the kimono down around your shoulders
and kiss you.
Then you let it fall open.
Each time, I cut you a little
and when you leave, I take the piece,
broil it, dip it in ginger sauce
and eat it. It burns my mouth so.
You laugh, holding me belly-down
with your body.
So much hurting to get to this moment,
when I'm beneath you,
wanting it to go on and to end.

At midnight, you say *see you tonight*
and I answer *there won't be any tonight,*
but you just smile, swing your sweater
over your head and tie the sleeves around your neck.
I hear you whistling long after you disappear
down the subway steps,
as I walk back home, my whole body tingling.
I undress
and put the bronze sword on my desk
beside the crumpled sheet of rice paper.
I smooth it open
and read its single sentence:
I meant to do it.
No. It should be common and feminine
like *I can't go on sharing him,*
or something to imply that.
Or the truth:

that I saw in myself
the five signs of the decay of the angel
and you were holding on, watching and free,
that I decided to go out
with the pungent odor
of this cold and consuming passion in my nose: death.
Now, I've said it. That vulgar word
that drags us down to the worms, sightless, predestined.
Goddamn you, boy.
Nothing I said mattered to you;
that bullshit about Etsuko or about killing myself.
I tear the note, then burn it.
The alarm clock goes off. 5:45 A.M.
I take the sword and walk into the garden.
I look up. The sun, the moon,
two round teeth rock together
and the light of one chews up the other.
I stab myself in the belly,
wait, then stab myself again. Again.
It's snowing. I'll turn to ice,
but I'll burn anyone who touches me.
I start pulling my guts out,
those red silk cords,
spiraling skyward,
and I'm climbing them
past the moon and the sun,
past darkness
into white.
I mean to live.

LESSON, LESSON

I draw a circle on a paper bag
with the only crayon you've ever had
and hold it above the cot.
You laugh. So the sun ain't green.
You not supposed to know yet.
Just pretend maybe won't be
another little gimme-fill-my-belly

next year while you out in the fields.
Hear me. You imagine real good
because your daddy a hammer.
Hard-time nail in his pants.
He feel wood beneath him,
he got to drive it home.

JERICHO

The question mark in my belly kicks me
as I push back the sheet, watching you undress.
You put on the black mask and lie on your side.
I open the small sack of peppermint sticks
you always bring and take one out.
I suck it as you rub my shoulders, breasts,
then with one hand, round the hollow beneath,
carved by seven months of pregnancy,
stopping when your palm covers my navel.
You groan as I slide the peppermint across my lips.

So I'm just fifteen, but I've seen others like you:
afraid, apologizing because they need something
maybe nobody else does.
You candy man, handing out the money, the sweets,
ashamed to climb your ladder of trouble.
Don't be. Make it to the top.
You'll find a ram's horn there.
Blow it seven times, yell goddamn
and watch the miniature hells below you
all fall down.

THE MORTICIAN'S TWELVE-YEAR-OLD SON

Lady, when you were alive
I'd see you on the streets,
the long green dress with the velvet flower
sewn dead center between your breasts
so tightly I could never get a look inside.

Now the gas lamps half-light the table,
washing the sheet that covers you with shadows.
A few strands of your dyed red hair
hang nearly to the floor,
as if all your blood had run there to hide.

I lift the sheet, rub the mole on your cheek
and it comes off black and oily on my hand.
I bend over your breasts and sing,
love, sister, is just a kiss away.
I cover each nipple with my mouth.
Tonight, just a kiss away.

THE GERMAN ARMY, RUSSIA, 1943

For twelve days,
I drilled through Moscow ice
to reach paradise,
that white tablecloth, set with a plate
that's cracking bit by bit
like the glassy air, like me.
I know I'll fly apart soon,
the pieces of me so light they float.
The Russians burned their crops,
rather than feed our army.
Now they strike us against each other like dry rocks
and set us on fire with a hunger
nothing can feed.
Someone calls me and I look up.
It's Hitler.
I imagine eating his terrible, luminous eyes.
Brother, he says.
I stand up, tie the rags tighter around my feet.
I hear my footsteps running after me,
but I am already gone.

TALKING TO HIS REFLECTION IN A SHALLOW POND

For Yasunari Kawabata

Chrysanthemum and nightshade:
I live on them,
though air is what I need.
I wish I could breathe like you,
asleep, or even awake,
just resting your head
on the pillow wrapped in black crepe
that I brought you from Sweden.
I hoped you'd die,
your mouth open, lips dry and split,
and red like pomegranate seeds.
But now, I only want you to suffer.
I drop a stone in the pond
and it sinks through you.
Japan isn't sliding into the Pacific
this cool April morning, you are.
Yasunari Kawabata, I'm talking to you;
just drop like that stone
through your own reflection.
You stretch your lean hands toward me
and I take them.
Water covers my face, my whole head,
as I inhale myself:
cold, very cold.

Suddenly, I pull back.
For a while, I watch you struggle,
then I start walking back to my studio.
But something is wrong.
There's water everywhere
and you're standing above me.
I stare up at you from the still, clear water.
You open your mouth and I open mine.
We both speak slowly.
Brother, you deserve to suffer,
You deserve the best:
this moment, death without end.

29 (A DREAM IN TWO PARTS)

1.

Night, that old woman, jabs the sun
with a pitchfork,
and dyes the cheesecloth sky blue-violet,
as I sit at the kitchen table,
bending small pieces of wire in hoops.
You come in naked.
No. Do it yourself.

2.

I'm a nine-year-old girl,
skipping beside a single hoop of daylight.
I hear your voice.
I start running. You lift me in your arms.
I holler. The little girl turns.
Her hoop rolls out of sight.
Something warm seeps through my gown onto my belly.
She never looks back.

SHE DIDN'T EVEN WAVE

For Marilyn Monroe

I buried Mama in her wedding dress
and put gloves on her hands,
but I couldn't do much about her face,
blue-black and swollen,
so I covered it with a silk scarf.
I hike my dress up to my thighs
and rub them,
watching you tip the mortuary fan back and forth.
Hey. Come on over. Cover me all up
like I was never here. Just never.
Come on. I don't know why I talk like that.
It was a real nice funeral. Mama's.
I touch the rhinestone heart pinned to my blouse.
Honey, let's look at it again.
See. It's bright like the lightning that struck her.

I walk outside
and face the empty house.
You put your arms around me. Don't.
Let me wave goodbye.
Mama never got a chance to do it.
She was walking toward the barn
when it struck her. I didn't move;
I just stood at the screen door.
Her whole body was light.
I'd never seen anything so beautiful.

I remember how she cried in the kitchen
a few minutes before.
She said, *God. Married.*
I don't believe it, Jean, I won't.
He takes and takes and you just give.
At the door, she held out her arms
and I ran to her.
She squeezed me so tight:
I was all short of breath.
And she said, *don't do it.*
In ten years, your heart will be eaten out
and you'll forgive him, or some other man, even that
and it will kill you.
Then she walked outside.
And I kept saying, I've got to, Mama,
hug me again. Please don't go.

ICE

breaks up in obelisks on the river,
as I stand beside your grave.
I tip my head back.
Above me, the same sky you loved,
that shawl of cotton wool,
frozen around the shoulders of Minnesota.
I'm cold and so far from Texas
and my father, who gave me to you.
I was twelve, a Choctaw, a burden.

A woman, my father said, raising my skirt.
Then he showed you the roll of green gingham,
stained red, that I'd tried to crush to powder
with my small hands. I close my eyes,

and it is March 1866 again.
I'm fourteen, wearing a white smock.
I straddle the rocking horse you made for me
and stroke the black mane cut from my own hair.
Sunrise hugs you from behind,
as you walk through the open door
and lay the velvet beside me.
I give you the ebony box
with the baby's skull inside
and you set it on your work table,
comb your pale blond hair with one hand,
then nail it shut.
When the new baby starts crying, I cover my ears,

watching as you lift him from the cradle
and lay him on the pony-skin rug.
I untie the red scarf, knotted at my throat,
climb off the horse and bend over you.
I slip the scarf around your neck,
and pull it tight, remembering:
I strangled the other baby,
laid her on your stomach while you were asleep.
You break my hold and pull me to the floor.
I scratch you, bite your lips, your face,
then you cry out,
and I open and close my hands
around a row of bear teeth.

I open my eyes.
I wanted you then and now,
and I never let you know.
I kiss the headstone.
Tonight, wake me like always.
Talk and I'll listen,
while you lie on the pallet

resting your arms behind your head,
telling me about the wild rice in the marshes
and the empty .45 you call *Grace of God* that keeps you alive
as we slide forward, without bitterness, decade by decade,
becoming transparent. Everlasting.

THE RAVINE

I wake, sweating, reach for your rosary and drop it.
I roll over on the straw and sit up. It's light out.
I pull on my pants, slip into my rope sandals
and go outside, where you sit
against a sack of beans.
I touch the chicken feathers
stuck to the purple splotches of salve on your stomach.
Your eyes, two tiny bowls of tar
set deep in your skull, stare straight ahead
and your skin is almost the color of your eyes,
because Death pressed his black face against yours.
I put our daughter in your lap,
lift you both and walk to the ravine's edge.
I step over —

— the years fly up in my face like a fine gray dust.
I'm twenty. I buy you with matches, a mirror and a rifle.
You don't talk. While I ride the mule downhill,
you walk beside me in a blue cotton dress.
Your flat Indian face shines with boar grease.
Your wide feet sink deep in the spring mud.
You raise your hands to shade your eyes
from the sudden explosion of sunlight
through the umber clouds.
In that brightness, you separate into five stained-glass women.
Four of you are floating north, south, east and west.
I reach out, shatter you in each direction.

I start to fall, catch myself,
get off the mule and make you ride.
You cry silently, ashamed to let me walk.

At bottom, you look back.
I keep going. Up a few yards,
I strip two thin pieces of bark off a tamarisk tree,
and we chew on them, sweetening the only way home.

GUADALAJARA CEMETERY

You sort the tin paintings
and lay your favorite in my lap.
Then you stroke my bare feet
as I lean against a tombstone.
It's time to cross the border
and cut your throat with two knives:
your wife, your son.
I won't try to stop you.
A cow with a mouth at both ends
chews hell going and coming.
I never asked less.
You, me, these withered flowers,
so many hearts tied in a knot,
given and taken away.

GUADALAJARA HOSPITAL

I watch the orderly stack the day's dead:
men on one cart, women on the other.
You sit two feet away, sketching
and drinking tequila.
I raise my taffeta skirt above the red garter,
take out the pesos
and lay them beside you.
I don't hold out on you.
I shove my hand under my skirt,
find the damp ten-dollar bill.
You're on top. You call the shots.
You said we'd make it here and we have.
I make them pay for it.

Later, we walk close,
smoking from one cigarette
until it's gone. I take your arm.
Next stop *end of the line.* You pull me to you
and push your tongue deep in my mouth.
I bite it. We struggle. You slap me.
I lean over the hood of the car.
You clamp a handkerchief between your teeth,
take the pesos and ten-dollar bill from your pocket
and tear them up.
Then you get in the car
and I slide in beside you.

When we finally cross the border,
I stare out the back window.
The Virgin Mary's back there
in her husband Mendoza's workroom.
She's sitting on a tall stool,
her black lace dress rolled up above her knees,
the red pumps dangling from her feet,
while he puts the adz to a small coffin;
a psalm of hammer and emptiness
only the two of them understand.
You say, *sister, breathe with me.*
We're home, now, home.
But I reach back, back through the window.
Virgin Mary, help me. Save me.
Tear me apart with your holy, invisible hands.

THE KID

My sister rubs the doll's face in mud,
then climbs through the truck window.
She ignores me as I walk around it,
hitting the flat tires with an iron rod.
The old man yells for me to help hitch the team,
but I keep walking around the truck, hitting harder,
until my mother calls.
I pick up a rock and throw it at the kitchen window,

but it falls short.
The old man's voice bounces off the air like a ball
I can't lift my leg over.

I stand beside him, waiting, but he doesn't look up
and I squeeze the rod, raise it, his skull splits open.
Mother runs toward us. I stand still,
get her across the spine as she bends over him.
I drop the rod and take the rifle from the house.
Roses are red, violets are blue,
one bullet for the black horse, two for the brown.
They're down quick. I spit, my tongue's bloody;
I've bitten it. I laugh, remember the one out back.
I catch her climbing from the truck, shoot.
The doll lands on the ground with her.
I pick it up, rock it in my arms.
Yeah. I'm Jack, Hogarth's son.
I'm nimble, I'm quick.

In the house, I put on the old man's best suit
and his patent leather shoes.
I pack my mother's satin nightgown
and my sister's doll in the suitcase.
Then I go outside and cross the fields to the highway.
I'm fourteen. I'm a wind from nowhere.
I can break your heart.

ALMOST GROWN

I swing up on the sideboard of the old car. I'm wearing
the smell of hay better than I do these starched coveralls,
my dead father's shirt, patched under each arm, and the
underwear I bought especially for today. Mother says nothing
just watches me and sucks on her unlit pipe. My sister,
still too young to get away, wipes away a few tears with the end
of her blue apron. The red bitch runs behind yapping, then
veers into the charred field, where she chases her tail
and, building speed, makes wider and wider circles, until
she is just a streak of fire, finally burning herself to a quick stop.

I get off at the feed store. The old men playing cards ignore me.
It's Saturday afternoon. I carry the cardboard box that holds my
things under one arm, swinging the other. I see Jake the Bootlegger
car, parked in front of the café. When I'm close, the sun
strikes its gray steel with a hammer and I have to shade my eyes
from the glare. I grope for the door, then stagger inside. The
cooler rattles a welcome. Mae, the waitress, hollers from the
kitchen, but I can't make out what she says. I sit on a stool with
the box propped up beside me.

Suddenly, Jake comes out and Mae follows him. He winks at me.
I stare through Mae's sheer nylon blouse at her lace bra. She
takes my order and I watch her as she walks to the far end of the
counter, where Jake sits, waiting, twisting the long gold chain
of his watch. I grunt with satisfaction. Good I moved, left the
farm to finish dying without me. I take out my ten-dollar bill,
rub it, feeling all the things I can buy with it: a striped tie,
one more box of cigars, a room for a week at the hotel. Hell!
It's great. Two more days and I start work at the gas station.
I take a big bite out of the hamburger Mae has set on the counter.

Jake gets up, Mae reaches for him. He shakes his head and
walks outside. She goes into the kitchen, and soon I hear her crying.
I hesitate, then follow her. She's lying on a cot, jammed against
the wall. I bend over her and she lifts her hand and touches me
the way no one ever has. I'm clumsy, but it gets done, same as
anything, I guess. She shoves me, cursing. Money, she wants
money. I'm nervous, I clutch the ten, then throw it at her. I run,
grabbing my box. In the street again, the heat, my empty pockets
heavy, as if filled with coins. At the gas station, I slip into the
Men's room and bolt the door. I sit on the dusty toilet and lean
back against the tank. Shit! I'm not through yet. I heard this
somewhere and it's true, it's got to be: you can't tell a shotgun
or a man what to do.

THE EXPECTANT FATHER

The skin of my mouth, chewed raw, tastes good.
I get up, cursing, and find the bottle of Scotch.
My mouth burns as darkness, lifting her skirt,

reveals daylight, a sleek left ankle.
The woman calls. I don't answer.
I imagine myself coming up to my own door,
holding a small reed basket in my arms.
Inside it, there is a child,
with clay tablets instead of hands,
and my name is written on each one.
The woman calls me again and I go to her.
She reaches for me, but I move away.
I frown, pulling back the covers to look at her.
So much going on outside;
the walls could cave in on us any time, any time.
I bring my face down
where the child's head should be and press hard.
I feel pain, she's pulling my hair.
I rise up, finally, and back away from the bed,
while she turns on her side
and drags her legs up to her chest.
I wait for her to cry,
then go into the kitchen.
I fix a Scotch and sit down at the table.
In six months, it is coming, in six months,
and I have no weapon against it.

SLEEP LIKE A HAMMER

I rub the hammer I use to slaughter stock
with coconut oil,
while you sit, staring at your feet, clucking,
though you've bent your head
so I can't see your lips.
The night the barn burned down,
I was crazy for help,
but you just sat on the porch
with your shoes in your lap.
I grabbed them and ran
and when I threw them into the fire,
you went in after them.
I had to drag you out

and beat out the flames.
Now you just sit,
every so often lifting your hands
as if they were holding broken glass,
and I don't know what to do, father,
I know you're thinking about your shoes
and I go on oiling, oiling,
because it's not good to let blood
harden in the cracks,
though the cows, the hogs don't care,
even I don't. I just worry like a woman.
I need something to do.
When I was fifteen, you took the pregnant hound
hunting at flood time and she didn't come back.
You said she was no good anyway
and I kicked you hard.
You took the shovel from the barn
and smashed my leg. I still limp.
I raise the hammer.
I hear my wife yelling.
She's running toward me,
bucket in one hand, the eggs in it
sloshing over the top;
huge white drops of water.
But she's in another country.
There's only you. Me.
When I bring the hammer down,
your toes splay out, snap off like burned bacon.
Your lips pull back
and your tongue drifts over your teeth
and I'm moving up to your hands, shoulders, neck, face.
Lord, moving up.

FATHER AND SON

THE MAN:
The priest and the old women
drag themselves over the hill,
as if bearing up a tiny coffin.

I look at you and the boy,
stretched out on the ground,
then back at them.
Their feet catch fire in the sunset.
Night is coming, shouldering a sack of misdeeds
that glow in the dark. Night and the carnival.
Night and the Devil.
I wipe the sweat from my face
and put on my Devil costume:
red shirt, red pants and the cotton mask.
I get the whip I keep under the pile of rocks
and strike the air with it.
When you wake, turning over on your back,
you hiss and hit your chest three times.
Keep quiet, woman. I strike the air again;
its ten-year-old hands, genitals, feet.

THE WOMAN:
I get up, pull on my burlap dress
and lift the lid off the papier-mâché coffin
you've laid across two sawhorses.
In it lies a porcelain doll,
wearing a baptismal dress.
I was pregnant when I told you
burn a doll each year
and the tenth year the boy will catch fire,
will burn away, not even leaving smoke behind.
You believed it, the way you believe
misery's a clock nobody can't walk,
that it's half past I've got,
or a quarter to got to get a shoe, get a shoe,
before the price of leather goes up.
But I say misery's another man's child.
Like this one. Francisco's son, not yours.
Francisco I took to bed,
Francisco who left Villa in 1917
and left me, too, there in the camp
and who, when you finally caught him,
heard my name and turned his pockets inside out.
He's coming tonight, after confession,

one ride on the ferris wheel
and a few drinks. He'll come.

THE MAN:
I never believed anything you said.
You had two men who now are nothing but shadows,
and soon only black like this doll's sockets.
That's what I believe in, the black.
Only the black forgets, so I wait.
I tend your garden of evil and watch it ripen.
Wake the boy. Go on, call him: Baby Bones, Baby Bones.
When you shake him, his head twists,
fear's wood slides under his fingernails,
he turns his round face to me and I almost reach for him.
When he gets up, I give him his costume: red shirt,
red pants, a mask.
He puts them on and I start the fire.
I never believed anything you said.

THE WOMAN:
The boy's an ape. If you look at him all the time
like I do, you see there's nothing human about him.
Francisco knows: that's why he comes,
to see for himself how his little ape grows and grows
like an ear of rainbow-colored corn,
after twelve long months of invisible rain,
rain that burns.
Sin: eat with it, sleep with it,
dress it up like the Devil.
He's still an ape.

THE MAN:
You don't know, woman. You don't know.
Everyday he's here, another man's son,
calling me father, making mud bricks with me.
Honor thy father, they say, but I say curse him.
Son of a bitch and son of a bastard,
that's what a father is. I tell him that.
Don't call me father, I say. I'm not,
you know who is.

I used to have you beat him for it
Father, he'd cry, *help me.*
Always the same.
Francisco won't come.
I saw him yesterday, in the village,
spitting blood again. And there, at his throat
the eruption of hair you find so beautiful.
I wanted to press my face in it, to bite deep,
but I held back.
He spat one last time, right at my feet,
and he walked away with his donkey
and one chicken in a cage.
I could have killed him.
Instead, my rage stabs at his back
again and again, and misses,
because it is going into the black,
where nothing touches nothing.
It starts with a toe and crawls up,
eating the shadow,
its fragments of sentences, match-heads, hope.
Here's the coffin. Go ahead, burn it.
You throw it into the fire.
I laugh. The boy dances and I follow him,
'round and 'round, two black tops on fire,
spinning under a sky full of firecrackers and stars,
letting fall a few handkerchiefs of light.

I CAN'T GET STARTED

For Ira Hayes

1. Saturday Night

A coyote eats chunks of the moon,
the night hen's yellow egg,
while I lie drunk, in a ditch.
Suddenly, a huge combat boot
punches a hole through the sky
and falls toward me.
I wave my arms. Get back.
It keeps coming.

2. Sunday Morning

I stumble out of the ditch
and make it to the shack.
I shoot a few holes in the roof,
then stare at the paper clippings of Iwo Jima.
I remember raising that rag
of red, white and blue,
afraid that if I let go, I'd live.
The bullets never touched me.
Nothing touches me.

Around noon, I make a cup of coffee
and pour a teaspoon of pepper in it
to put the fire out.
I hum between sips
and when I finish, I hug myself.
I'm burning from the bottom up,
a bottle of flesh,
kicked across the hardwood years.
I pass gin and excuses from hand to mouth,
but it's me. It's me.
I'm the one dirty habit
I just can't break.

HE KEPT ON BURNING

1. Spain, 1929

In the café, the chandelier hangs from the ceiling
by a thick rope. I'm seventeen, still a boy.
I put my hand in my lap and twist my class
ring 'round and 'round the little finger. The Basque,
toad in torn breeches and burlap vest, plays the guitar.
I look toward the stairs. The man is there, his hand
on the wooden railing. He's naked, except for the white
kimono with black cranes painted on it, and the brown pumps
with taps on each heel. I take a slice of salami, swallow
without chewing much. He comes to me, shaking his hips
as the guitar grows louder, leans down and lets me rub

a glassful of wine across his hard, rose-colored nipples.
Then he turns, taps his feet and the others clap their hands.
I take the cheese knife, slap it down on the table. He stomps
right foot, left, one-two, one-two-three, back toward me on
third step. He laughs, touches my lips and I sing,
Und der haifisch der hat zahne. The others watch me.
Trembling, I move to the door. I'm not one of you.
I back into the street, cursing. I slam my fist against the wall.
It doesn't bleed. The door opens, the kimono is thrown outside
I pick it up, smell it. On the train back to Germany, that smell
and a voice whispering, dance with me baby,
all night long.

2. Buchenwald, 1945

Joseph, you move beneath the blankets. I uncover you
and hold the glass of brandy to your mouth. Your eyes open.
Wake up, Jew, drink with me, eat some of the fine German
cake my mother sent. You take the glass and drink.
I put a small piece of cake in my mouth. I taste something:
a man, a country, Schmuel Meyer, Jenny Towler, Alphonse
Glite, seven children, metal. I squeeze my eyes shut. We
leave today. Am I shaking? I do shake, don't I. I stare
through the window at the last group of prisoners,
patchwork quilt, embroidered with the letters *SS*.
It is drizzling now four days and each man, cloth dipped
in useless dye, is running into the mud at his feet.
I turn my hands up; the palms are almost smooth.
I hear the shots. I keep looking at my hands.
When I was seventeen, Joseph, when I was seventeen,
I put out a fire, but it kept on burning.

3. Peru, 1955

Midnight bleeds through the window
as you walk to the table
and drink warm beer from a tin mug.
I sniff the sausages you've laid beside the boiled eggs
and hard bread. Are they as old as that time
I told you *come with me*? You'd love me, you said.
Yes, you and guilt, tabernacle of gold teeth

and the cantor inside singing over and over, *thou shalt not.*
I take your wrist; so thin, Joseph. Suicide? — no.
There's always the boy, always,
and a kimono that smells like orange blossoms.
And hurting; twenty-six years on a razor's edge.
And I want more. More.

THE WOMAN WHO KNEW TOO MUCH

I plait Carmen's hair tightly,
smelling the odor of straw
she takes with her everywhere.
Then I fasten the earrings in her ears,
the ones I made
that are orange,
like the inside of her mouth
when she's been drinking rum.

When the killer comes for her,
because she won't fight,
because she knows too much —
our guns, our weakness —
she offers him rum.
His mustache of two cigars gleams.

Later, I bury her,
then slip down into the valley
to wait for reinforcements.
I eat the yams she fried for me
and when I'm done,
I feel as if I've been sleeping.

Near sunrise, I see them:
five men and two women.
They want freedom on their own terms.
But it isn't like that.

They'll find out as Carmen did.
I go to meet them.

They think they've brought me everything I need
and now I'll tell them like all the others
that they are right.
Line up, you bastards,
so I can take a closer look.
Tonight I let my woman die.
She also had arms, legs, fingers,
all the unimportant things.
I don't want to forget. I won't let you.
Go ahead, strut around,
talk, fire your guns.
But don't tell me about freedom.
Just let me see his face.

THE SINGERS

1.

You lift a piece of meat to your mouth
with the silver fork
you took from the burning house.
It glitters in your hand,
a sliver of light on mud.
Don't leave me, woman, not now.
I smell the shit odor of fear again
like the night five years ago
when I crossed the Rio Grande into Texas.
The Carranzistas had killed Zapata
and they'd kill me too, if I stayed in Chihuahua.
But half a mile in, I saw him:
Zapata on the ground in front of me.
He bowed and danced slowly around his sombrero,
and the bullet holes in his body,
black, eight-pointed stars,
gave off a luminous darkness.

Back in Mexico, I don't remember riding,
only standing beside my horse
outside a whitewashed house.

When I looked through the window,
I saw you and your father, Indian, like me,
sitting at a table, bare, except for a silver fork.
Help me, I said. *I rode with Zapata.*
But neither of you moved.
You started singing: *Zapata, Zapata, your blood is so red.*
Zapata, Zapata, you're dead.
Who's at the window, a ghost, a ghost, only a ghost.
And when I lifted my hands,
they were transparent,
my bones, colorless light.
I struck the window,
they shattered
and I smelled fear again. I could see it:
the black outline of a horse on its hind legs,
a zero burning on its belly,
burning for me, Rosebud Morales.
I screamed, screamed my name
until I came back to myself
and could see my hands, their russet skin,
wrapping some straw in a ball.
I set it afire and threw it into the house.
When you ran out, I grabbed you.
You stabbed me with the fork, but I held on.
You kept singing while your father burned.

2.

You wrap the Spanish Bible you can't read
in your shawl,
then you start running.
But I catch you by your braids,
drag you to the cooking fire and push your head in it.
When I let go, you stagger up
wearing a halo of flames.
Come on, sing with me: *Zapata, Zapata, your blood is so red.*
Sing, goddamnit. You fall.
The shadow of a train rises from your body
and lightning zigzags from the smokestack.
The smokestack is a man. Zapata. I raise my pistol.

I'm not afraid of any sonofabitch on two feet.
I fire, then jam the barrel in my mouth.
Not even you, motherfucker, not even you.

PENTECOST

For Myself

Rosebud Morales, my friend,
before you deserted,
you'd say anyone can kill an Indian
and forget it the same instant,
that it will happen to me, Emiliano Zapata.
But my men want more corn for tortillas,
more pigs, more chickens, more chilis
and land.
If I haven't got a gun or a knife,
I'll fight with a pitchfork or a hoe,
to take them from the bosses,
those high–flying birds,
with the pomade glistening on their hair,
as they promenade into their coffins.
And if I'm killed, if we're all killed right now,
we'll go on, the true Annunciation.

Rosebud, how beautiful this day is.
I'm riding to meet Guajardo.
He'll fight with me now,
against Carranza.
When I get to the hacienda, it's quiet.
Not many soldiers,
a sorrel horse, its reins held
by a woman in a thin, white American dress
and Guajardo standing on a balcony.

I get off my horse and start up the steps.
My legs burn, my chest,
my jaw, my head.
There's a hill in front of me;
it's slippery, I have to use my hands to climb it.

At the top, it's raining fire and blood
on rows and rows of black corn.
Machetes are scattered everywhere.
I grab one and start cutting the stalks.
When they hit the ground,
they turn into men.
I yell at them.
You're damned in the cradle,
in the grave, even in Heaven.
Dying doesn't end anything.
Get up. Swing those machetes.
You can't steal a man's glory
without a goddamned fight.
Boys, take the land, take it; it's yours.
If you suffer in the grave,
you can kill from it.

THE GILDED MAN

*In 1561, on an expedition down the Marañon and
Amazon to find El Dorado, Lope de Aguirre killed
Urzúa, the leader of the expedition, then scores of
others. He declared rebellion against Spain and set
out to conquer Peru,* con el alma en los dientes,
with his soul between his teeth.

1. The Orinoco, 1561

For a while today, the rafts almost float side by side.
The river is as smooth and soft
as the strip of emerald velvet
sewn around the hem of your dress, my daughter.
I call you Vera Cruz,
because you are the true cross
from which I hang by ropes of gold.
The word *father,* a spear of dark brown hair,
enters my side and disintegrates,
leaving me whole again,
smelling of quinces and gunpowder

and your stale, innocent breath.
What is it?
you whisper. I take your hand
and we walk into the jungle.
I watch you raise your dress, bend,
then tear your petticoat with your teeth.
You fold the torn cloth
and slide it between your legs.
Then you hold out your bloody hands
and I wipe them on my shirt,
already red from fighting.
Urzúa is dead. Guzmán is dead. There is no Spain.
I'm hunting El Dorado, the Gilded Man.
When I catch him, I'll cut him up.
I'll start with his feet
and give them to you to wear as earrings.
Talk to me.
I hear nothing but the monkeys squealing above me.
I point my arquebus at a silhouette in the trees, and fire.
For a moment, I think it's you falling toward me,
your dress shredding to sepia light.
I drop the arquebus and stretch out my hands.
Fall, darling, fall into me.
Lope de Aguirre. I hear my name
as I lift you in my arms.
Daughter. Beautiful.
You weigh no more than ashes.

2. Barquisimeto, Venezuela, October 27, 1561

Today it rained vengefully and hard
and my men deserted me.
My kingdom was as close
as calling it by name. Peru.
I braid your hair, daughter,
as you kneel with your head in my lap.
I talk softly, stopping to press your face to my chest.
Vera Cruz. Listen. My heart is speaking.
I am the fishes, the five loaves.
The women, the men I killed simply ate me.

There is no dying, only living in death.
I was their salvation.
I am absolved by their hunger.
El Dorado, the kingdom of gold,
is only a tapestry I wove from their blood.
Stand up. My enemies will kill me
and they won't be merciful with you.
I unsheathe my dagger. Your mouth opens.
I can't hear you. I want to. Tell me you love me.
You cover your mouth with your hands.
I stab you, then fall beside your body.
Vera Cruz. See my skin covered with gold dust
and tongues of flame,
transfigured by the pentecost of my own despair.
I, Aguirre the wanderer, Aguirre the traitor,
the Gilded Man.
Does God think that because it rains in torrents
I am not to go to Peru and destroy the world?
God. The boot heel an inch above your head is mine.
God, say your prayers.

Sin

TWO BROTHERS
A Fiction

1

Night tightens its noose.
You swim toward me out of sleep
like an eel,
as I put the glass canister
beside you on the bed.
Death, Bobby, hit me
like the flat of a hand.
Imagine you are made of crystal
and someone ice picks you
and you shatter,
all your cells coming
almost to despair
it is so good. Dallas. Dallas.
I turn toward the window,
then turn back to you.
Remember that Crayola drawing
of John-John's? —
the black smoke coming out the roof
of the White House
like curly black hair.
How Jackie spanked his hand
and drew him another
with angels lifting up?
Our own childhoods? —
days of ease and grace.
The good life sucking us deeper
and deeper in
toward its hot, liquid center,
where seasoned with the right diction,
schools, and politics
we would fry crisp and greaseless.
King for a day,
that's who I was.
I drove power,
the solid-gold Cadillac.

Go ahead, frown.
Tell me about the sin of pride
and I'll tell you
about the lie of forgiveness.
It wasn't Oswald killed me,
it was envy.

2

"I have this dream, Jack," you say.
"I'm at Arlington. It's twilight.
Thousands of funeral markers
rise from the ground
like dirty alabaster arms.
It's here, pilgrim,
they seem to say.
And then I'm in a room.
A man is counting green bills
sharp enough to cut,
while I pry the lid off a barrel
and peer down into it,
as if inside, there are dark green pickles
or steel-blue fish,
as if I were a boy
on a crowded street in Russia
with my hand around a coin
and the other in my brother's hand.
And while I scuff my shoe
and try to decide,
from far away I hear bugles, hoofbeats,
I see my brother's head
suddenly rise from his body
like a tiny pink ball
on a spout of dark red water,
clear past the rooftops
into the serene evening sky.
I am that boy, Jack,
dipping his hands
in the one standing barrel,
into water warm as blood,

with nothing to say to anybody,
except, 'My brother is the moon.'"

3

Riddles, I say,
lifting the lid off the canister.
I pull out a wet, gray mass,
stare at it, then put it back.
Some African tribes
eat the brains of their dead.
It brings them closer;
it kills them too.
But whatever it takes, Bobby, right?
I look out the window
at the deep rose welts of dawn,
streaking the sky's broad back,
then hand you the canister.
You lift out my brain.
When you bite down, I burn.
The air smells like creosote
and I stand before you,
my skin plump and pink,
my wounds healed.
I put my arms around you
and you disappear into me . . .

I stare at myself in the mirror:
Jack Kennedy,
thinner now, almost ascetic,
wearing the exhaust fumes of L.A.
like a sharkskin suit,
while the quarter moon
hangs from heaven,
a swing on a gold chain. My throne.
I step back and knot my tie.
Bobby, it's all a matter of showmanship.
You have to have the ability to entertain,
to stand like P. T. Barnum
in the enchanted center

of the public eye,
to drop your pants now and then
and have the crowd
cry for more,
to give it to them,
to take those encores,
till like the clown in Piaf's song
the show is all there is,
and the bravos, the bravos.
You give the people what they want, Bobby,
someone they can't help loving
like a father or an uncle,
someone who through his own magical fall
lifts them above the slime
of their daily lives.
Not God made man,
but man made God.
I step back to the mirror.
Break a leg, kid, I say to myself.
Give 'em a miracle.
Give 'em Hollywood.
Give 'em Saint Jack.

BLUE SUEDE SHOES
A Fiction

1

Heliotrope sprouts from your shoes, brother,
their purplish color going Chianti
at the beginning of evening,
while you sit on the concrete step.
You curse, stand up, and come toward me.
In the lamplight, I see your eyes,
the zigzags of bright red in them.
"Bill's shot up," you say.
"Remember how he walked
on the balls of his feet like a dancer,
him, a boxer and so graceful
in his blue suede shoes?

Jesus, he coulda stayed home, Joe,
he coulda had the world by the guts,
but he gets gunned,
he gets strips of paper
tumbling out of his pockets like confetti."

Is Bea here? I say
and start for the house.
"No," you say. "This splits us, Joe.
You got money, education, friends.
You understand. I'm talking about family
and you ain't it.
The dock is my brother."
Lou, I say and step closer,
once I was fifteen, celestial.
Mom and Pop called me sweetheart
and I played the piano in the parlor
on Sunday afternoons.
There was ice cream.
Your girl wore a braid down the center of her back.
The sun had a face and it was mine.
You loved me, you sonofabitch, everybody did.
In 1923, you could count the golden boys on your fingers
and I was one of them. Me, Joe McCarthy.
I gave up music for Justice,
divorce, and small-time litigation.
And you moved here to Cleveland —
baseball, hard work, beer halls,
days fishing Lake Erie,
more money than a man like you
could ever earn on a farm
and still not enough.
Pop died in bed in his own house
because of my money.
Share, he always said, *you share*
what you have with your family
or you're nothing. You got nobody, boys.
Will you cut me off now
like you did
when I could have helped my nephew,

when you hated the way he hung on to me,
the way he listened when I talked
like I was a wise man? Wasn't I?
I could already see a faint red haze
on the horizon;
a diamond-headed hammer
slamming down on the White House;
a sickle cutting through the legs
of every man, woman, and child in America.
You know what people tell me today,
they say, *You whistle the tune, Joe,*
and we'll dance.
But my own brother sits it out.

2

A man gets bitter, Lou,
he gets so bitter
he could vomit himself up.
It happened to Bill.
He wasn't young anymore.
He knew he'd had it
that night last July
lying on a canvas of his own blood.
After a few months, he ran numbers
and he was good at it, but he was scared.
His last pickup
he stood outside the colored church
and heard voices
and he started to shake.
He thought he'd come all apart,
that he couldn't muscle it anymore,
and he skimmed cream for the first time —
$10s, $20s.

You say you would have died in his place,
but I don't believe it.
You couldn't give up your whore on Thursdays
and Bea the other nights of the week,
the little extra that comes in off the dock.

You know what I mean.
The boys start ticking —
they put their hands in the right place
and the mouse runs down the clock.
It makes you hot,
but I just itch
and when I itch, I want to smash something.
I want to condemn and condemn,
to see people squirm,
but other times,
I just go off in a dream —
I hear the Mills Brothers
singing in the background,
Up a lazy river,
then the fog clears
and I'm standing at Stalin's grave
and he's lying in an open box.
I get down on top of him
and stomp him,
till I puncture him
and this stink rises up.
I nearly black out,
but I keep stomping,
till I can smell fried trout, coffee.
And Truman's standing up above me
with his hand out
and I wake up always with the same thought:
the Reds are my enemies.
Every time I'm sitting at that big table in D.C.
and so-and-so's taking the Fifth,
or crying, or naming names,
I'm stomping his soul.
I can look inside you, Lou,
just like I do those sonsofbitches.
You got a hammer up your ass,
a sickle in between your percale sheets?
Threaten me, you red-hearted bastard. Come on.
I'll bring you to heel.

3

Yesterday Bill comes by the hotel
and he sits on the bed, but he can't relax.
Uncle, he says, and points at his feet,
all I ever wanted was this pair of blue suede shoes,
and he takes out a pawn ticket,
turns it over in his hand, then he gets up,
and at the door holds it out to me
and says, *You keep it.*

Today I go down to the pawnshop
and this is what I get back — a .38.
Bill didn't even protect himself.
You have to understand what happened to him,
in a country like this,
the chances he had.

Remember Dorothy and the Yellow Brick Road?
There's no pot of gold at the end,
but we keep walking that road,
red-white-and-blue ears of corn
steaming in our minds: America,
the only thing between us
and the Red Tide.
But some of us are straw —
we burn up like Bill in the dawn's early light.
He didn't deserve to live.
This morning, when I heard he was dead,
I didn't feel anything.
I stood looking out the window at the lake
and I thought for a moment
the whole Seventh Fleet was sailing away beneath me
flags waving, men on deck,
shining like bars of gold,
and there, on the bow of the last ship,
Dorothy stood waving up at me.
As she passed slowly under my window,
I spit on her.
She just stared at me,

as if she didn't understand.
But she did.
She gave up the Emerald City
for a memory.
I'd never do that, never.
I'm an American.
I shall not want.
There's nothing that doesn't belong to me.

THE PRISONER

1

Yesterday, the man who calls himself "Our Father"
made me crawl on smashed Coke bottles.
Today, I sleep. I think I sleep,
till someone beats on the door, with what? —
sticks, pans — but I don't move.
I'm used to it.
Still, when Our Father rushes into the room
and drags me out, I feel the old fear.
In the interrogation room,
he knocks me to the floor,
then sits on the side of his desk,
his arms folded, that sad look on his face
I know so well. He shakes his head slowly,
stops, and smiles.
"I've got something special today," he says,
"for a fucking whore of a terrorist bitch."
I want to say nothing,
knowing how denial angers him,
but I can't stop myself.
I'm not a terrorist, I say.
"That's not what I heard," he replies, standing up.
"Aren't you the friend of a friend of a friend
of a terrorist son of a bitch
who was heard two years ago to say
that someone ought to do something
about this government?"

I don't answer.
Already, I've begun to admit that it must be true.
"I lack just one thing," he says, "the name."
"I know you think you're innocent,
but you aren't.
Everyone is guilty."
He slaps me, then pushes one side of my face
toward the green glass.

2

I've been stung by a swarm of bees.
I'm eight. I'm running for the pond
on my uncle Oscar's farm.
Oscar, I cry. Our Father sighs deeply,
lifts me up, and sets me down in a chair.
"This Oscar," he says, handing me a notebook and pen
"where can I find him?"
I don't hesitate, as I take the pen
and set it down
on the clean, blank paper.

3

Our Father lets me off
a block from my apartment.
He keeps the motor running,
but comes and leans
against the car beside me.
I try to guess the month. March, April? I say.
He tells me it's September,
to just take a look at the sky.
Then he tells me he was a prisoner once too.
I stare at his face,
the dry, sallow skin,
the long scar running from temple to chin.
"Oh this," he touches the scar gently,
"I got this playing soccer.
No, the real scars don't show.
You should know that.
You need time, though, to sort it all out.

I'm still a young man,
but sometimes I feel as old as the Bible.
But this is a celebration."
He takes a bottle of wine from the car
and we drink, while the stars glitter above us.
Done, he tosses the bottle into the street.
"Freedom," he says, "freedom is something you earn.
The others don't understand that, but we do."

CONVERSATION

For Robert Lowell

We smile at each other
and I lean back against the wicker couch.
How does it feel to be dead? I say.
You touch my knees with your blue fingers.
And when you open your mouth,
a ball of yellow light falls to the floor
and burns a hole through it.
Don't tell me, I say. I don't want to hear.
Did you ever, you start,
wear a certain kind of silk dress
and just by accident,
so inconsequential you barely notice it,
your fingers graze that dress
and you hear the sound of a knife cutting paper,
you see it too
and you realize how that image
is simply the extension of another image,
that your own life
is a chain of words
that one day will snap.
Words, you say, young girls in a circle, holding hands
and beginning to rise heavenward
in their confirmation dresses,
like white helium balloons,
the wreaths of flowers on their heads spinning,
and above all that,
that's where I'm floating,

and that's what it's like
only ten times clearer,
ten times more horrible.
Could anyone alive survive it?

MORE

For James Wright

Last night, I dreamed of America.
It was prom night.
She lay down under the spinning globes
at the makeshift bandstand
in her worn-out dress
and too-high heels,
the gardenia
pinned at her waist
was brown and crumbling into itself.
What's it worth, she cried,
this land of Pilgrims' pride?
As much as love, I answered. More.
The globes spun.
I never won anything, I said,
I lost time and lovers, years,
but you, purple mountains,
you amber waves of grain, belong to me
as much as I do to you.
She sighed,
the band played,
the skin fell away from her bones.
Then the room went black
and I woke.
I want my life back,
the days of too much clarity,
the nights smelling of rage,
but it's gone.
If I could shift my body
that is too weak now,
I'd lie face down on this hospital bed,
this icy water called Ohio River.

I'd float past all the sad towns,
past all the dreamers onshore
with their hands out.
I'd hold on, I'd hold,
till the weight,
till the awful heaviness
tore from me,
sank to bottom and stayed.
Then I'd stand up
like Lazarus
and walk home across the water.

THE ÉMIGRÉ

I stare down from the terrace
at the firemen in their slickers,
black mice in black hats,
close my hand around some smoke,
then open it and that smoke is gone
like the Russia of my childhood.
When I was a girl,
my father worked for the Cheka.
One morning, he forced my mother outside
in her torn nightgown.
The apartment was filled with her scent —
ink, paper, fresh bread.
I was warm, full of potato latkes and milk.
I sang the song of the world revolution,
but that revolution betrayed my mother.
It's quiet now, as the fire trucks
pull out onto the asphalt sea
like tiny crimson arks,
as quiet as the apartment
when I stopped singing,
when my father said, *Come,
your mother's safe.*
I followed him down the steps,
but near bottom, I stopped.
He turned around

and held out his arms,
then I jumped.

I sit down at the word processor.
On the screen, a page
from the memoir I am writing.
Even now, I hear my father's voice
as he shouts at my mother.
She jerks her head toward me,
then raises her skirt and wipes her face.
I erase one word, another,
till the whole page is gone,
but I cannot erase that scene.
My mother is locked forever
in the Lubyanka inside me,
her dirty, bruised face
streaked with tears,
the handbills she'd printed
in that beautiful script of hers
torn and scattered about her on the floor
like mutilated black and yellow butterflies.

Now as I lean over the keys
with my eyes closed,
her face rises inside me,
a fat harvest moon
in a sky of India ink,
a face whose features are so clear,
so like my own
that I cannot deny them;
yet, I do deny them.
My life is mine. She's dead,
she died, she dies each time I write.
But no, she's alive.
She condemns me for leaving,
for bearing witness only in the dark.

I begin once more.
A scene fades in, out,
there are shouts from outside,

a door is flung back.
Mother *and* Father are taken from the room.
Father who worked for the Cheka,
murdered by the Cheka,
Mother who opposed it also murdered.
I go back to the window,
look up at the gray tarpaulin of sky
and see Father riding a red star
down from proletariat heaven
and farther out, Mother,
straddling her own renegade star,
gesturing and waving to me.
They want to teach me
to die for what I believe,
but I say disown the world, don't save it,
don't try. Live for what you believe.
Survive, survive another night.

But here they are, pressing their bloody faces
against the glass.
I slide the bolt back.
It's then our eyes meet,
my two brown, speckled marbles
and their sockets,
filled with the black, blinding light
of the universe.

THE MAN WITH THE SAXOPHONE

New York. Five A.M.
The sidewalks empty.
Only the steam
pouring from the manhole covers seems alive,
as I amble from shop window to shop window,
sometimes stopping to stare, sometimes not.
Last week's snow is brittle now
and unrecognizable as the soft, white hair
that bearded the face of the city.
I head farther down Fifth Avenue

toward the thirties,
my mind empty
like the Buddhists tell you is possible
if only you don't try.
If only I could
turn myself into a bird
like the shaman I was meant to be,
but I can't,
I'm earthbound
and solitude is my companion,
the only one you can count on.
Don't, don't try to tell me otherwise.
I've had it all and lost it
and I never want it back,
only give me this morning to keep,
the city asleep
and there on the corner of Thirty-fourth and Fifth,
the man with the saxophone,
his fingerless gloves caked with grime,
his face also,
the layers of clothes welded to his skin.
I set down my case,
he steps backward
to let me know I'm welcome,
and we stand a few minutes
in the silence so complete
I think I must be somewhere else, not here,
not in this city, this heartland of pure noise.
Then he puts the sax to his lips again
and I raise mine.
I suck the air up from my diaphragm
and bend over into the cold, golden reed,
waiting for the notes to come,
and when they do,
for that one moment,
I'm the unencumbered bird of my imagination,
rising only to fall back
toward concrete,
each note a black flower,
opening, mercifully opening
into the unforgiving new day.

THE GOOD SHEPHERD: ATLANTA, 1981

I lift the boy's body
from the trunk,
set it down,
then push it over the embankment
with my foot.
I watch it roll
down into the river
and feel I'm rolling with it,
feel the first cold slap of the water,
wheeze and fall down on one knee.
So tired, so cold.
Lord, I need a new coat,
not polyester, but wool,
new and pure
like the little lamb
I killed tonight.
With my right hand,
that same hand that hits
with such force,
I push myself up gently.
I know what I'd like —
some hot cocoa by the heater.

Once home, I stand at the kitchen sink,
letting the water run
till it overflows the pot,
then I remember the blood
in the bathroom
and so upstairs.
I take cleanser,
begin to scrub
the tub, tiles, the toilet bowl,
then the bathroom.
Mop, vacuum, and dust rag.
Work, work for the joy of it,
for the black boys
who know too much,
but not enough to stay away,

and sometimes a girl, the girls too.
How their hands
grab at my ankles, my knees.
And don't I lead them
like a good shepherd?
I stand at the sink,
where the water is still
overflowing the pot,
turn off the faucet,
then heat the water and sit down.
After the last sweet mouthful of chocolate
burns its way down my throat,
I open the library book,
the one on mythology,
and begin to read.
Saturn, it says, devours his children.
Yes, it's true, I know it.
An ordinary man, though, a man like me
eats and is full.
Only God is never satisfied.

SALOME

I scissor the stem of the red carnation
and set it in a bowl of water.
It floats the way your head would,
if I cut it off.
But what if I tore you apart
for those afternoons
when I was fifteen
and so like a bird of paradise
slaughtered for its feathers.
Even my name suggested wings,
wicker cages, flight.
Come, sit on my lap, you said.
I felt as if I had flown there;
I was weightless.
You were forty and married.
That she was my mother never mattered.

She was a door that opened onto me.
The three of us blended into a kind of somnolence
and musk, the musk of Sundays. Sweat and sweetness.
That dried plum and licorice taste
always back of my tongue
and your tongue against my teeth,
then touching mine. How many times? —
I counted, but could never remember.
And when I thought we'd go on forever,
that nothing could stop us
as we fell endlessly from consciousness,
orders came: War in the north.
Your sword, the gold epaulets,
the uniform so brightly colored,
so unlike war, I thought.
And your horse; how you rode out the gate.
No, how that horse danced beneath you
toward the sound of cannon fire.
I could hear it, so many leagues away.
I could see you fall, your face scarlet,
the horse dancing on without you.
And at the same moment,
Mother sighed and turned clumsily in the hammock,
the Madeira in the thin-stemmed glass
spilled into the grass,
and I felt myself hardening to a brandy-colored wood
my skin, a thousand strings drawn so taut
that when I walked to the house
I could hear music
tumbling like a waterfall of China silk
behind me.
I took your letter from my bodice.
Salome, I heard your voice,
little bird, fly. But I did not.
I untied the lilac ribbon at my breasts
and lay down on your bed.
After a while, I heard Mother's footsteps,
watched her walk to the window.
I closed my eyes
and when I opened them

the shadow of a sword passed through my throat
and Mother, dressed like a grenadier,
bent and kissed me on the lips.

THE MOTHER'S TALE

Once when I was young, Juanito,
there was a ballroom in Lima
where Hernán, your father,
danced with another woman
and I cut him across the cheek
with a pocketknife.
Oh, the pitch of the music sometimes,
the smoke and rustle of crinoline.
But what things to remember now
on your wedding day.
I pour a kettle of hot water
into the wooden tub where you are sitting.
I was young, free.
But Juanito, how free is a woman? —
born with Eve's sin between her legs,
and inside her,
Lucifer sits on a throne of abalone shells,
his staff with the head of John the Baptist
skewered on it.
And in judgment, son, in judgment he says
that women will bear the fruit of the tree
we wished so much to eat
and that fruit will devour us
generation by generation,
so my son,
you must beat Rosita often.
She must know the weight of a man's hand,
the bruises that are like the wounds of Christ.
Her blood that is black at the heart
must flow until it is as red and pure as His.
And she must be pregnant always
if not with child

then with the knowledge
that she is alive because of you.
That you can take her life
more easily than she creates it,
that suffering is her inheritance from you
and through you, from Christ,
who walked on his mother's body
to be the King of Heaven.

SAINT ANNE'S REEL, 1870

That morning, the preacher
held the Bible up to the window,
the sun shone through it,
and the word walked upright
on the other side —
you, a man in a blue wool suit,
with a woman's long hair
and girl's hands,
a pint bottle in your back pocket.
I stood beside my father
in my calico wedding dress
and thought
how I used to have pride in myself,
how I used to do things alone —
I raised the adobe wall
north side of this house,
I rubbed salve on my father's groin,
because he needed it
and I was unashamed.

After the wedding,
you made yourself a mother to me.
You sewed, cooked,
you hung the wash on Saturdays,
you danced between the bluish sheets
with clothespins in your mouth,
holding me by the waist, the hands,

then only with your grace.
No man could move like you,
and sometimes, I hid my face
against your shoulder,
as we reeled through ten years
to the hired man in our bed this morning,
me beside him.
Your tears.
And your forgiveness.
But I didn't want any of it.
I packed the buckboard
and loaded the boy, the girls,
the broken plates and skillet.
I drove the horses into the road.
You stood on the porch,
wearing the patched wool jacket,
a bottle to your lips,
your feet beginning to move easily
to the fiddle music in your head.
That music held us,
somehow still holds me,
but Jesse, nobody,
nobody can live between forgiveness
and a dance.

THE DEATH OF FRANCISCO PIZARRO

Tonight Atahualpa's ghost
crowned me with cocoa leaves
and called me his little monkey.
But I knew who I was: Francisco Pizarro.
And when I died hours later,
I sailed away
down the green slide of Amazon to Galilee,
where Jesus was standing in a boat,
His brown hair like copper coins
strung on invisible wire.
Lord, I cried in my desolation,
to take a man like me —

and showed Him my hands,
hands that had held a continent,
and He plucked my head off my shoulders.
How small it looked as He turned it
'round and 'round in His surgeon's fingers.
I am thy Lord and thy God, He said,
with your last words, such bitter nuts
between my teeth.
Then He put my head in His mouth
and bit down hard.
My skull cracked like parchment
and my blood spilled from His mouth
onto His blue mantle.
See how you stain me, He said,
but I did not answer.
And He turned to the hard, rude men in the boat,
the ordinary men of all the ages of mankind,
who moaned and cried out in terror
and He said, *The kingdom of God is in you,*
but you must fight to keep it.
Even Pizarro has fallen in the battle.
And He opened His hands —
white feathers fell from them
and bones, so many bones
I could not count them all,
and He said,
Come, my lambs, come.
Who else can save you?

THE PRIEST'S CONFESSION

1

I didn't say mass this morning.
I stood in the bell tower
and watched Rosamund, the orphan,
chase butterflies, her laughter
rising, slamming into me,
while the almond scent of her body

wrapped around my neck like a noose.
Let me go, I told her once,
you'll have to let me go,
but she held on.
She was twelve.
She annoyed me,
lying in her little bed —
Tell me a story, Father.
Father, I can't sleep. I miss my mother.
Can I sleep with you?
I carried her into my room —
the crucifix, the bare white walls.
While she slept,
she threw the covers back.
Her cotton gown was wedged above her thighs.
I nearly touched her.
I prayed for deliverance, but none came.
Later, I broke my rosary.
The huge, black wooden beads
clattered to the floor
like ovoid marbles,
and I in my black robe,
a bead on God's own broken rosary,
also rolled there on the floor
in a kind of ecstasy.
I remembered how when I was six
Lizabeta, the witch, blessed me,
rocking in her ladder-back chair,
while I drank pig's blood
and ate it smeared across a slice of bread.
She said, *Eat, Emilio, eat.*
Hell is only as far as your next breath
and heaven unimaginably distant.
Gate after gate stands between you and God,
so why not meet the devil instead?
He at least has time for people.
When she died, the villagers
burned her house.

I lay my hand on the bell.
Sometimes when I ring this,

I feel I'll fragment,
then reassemble
and I'll be some other thing —
a club to beat,
a stick to heave at something:
between the act and the actor
there can be no separateness.
That is Gnostic. Heresy.
Lord, I crave things,
Rosamund's bird's nest of hair
barely covered by her drawers.
I want to know that you love me,
that the screams of men,
as loud as any trumpet,
have brought down the gates of stone
between us.

2

The next four years,
Rosamund's breasts grew
and grew in secret
like two evil thoughts.
I made her confess to me
and one night, she swooned,
she fell against me
and I laid her down.
I bent her legs this way and that.
I pressed my face between them
to smell "Our Lady's Roses"
and finally, I wanted to eat them.
I bit down, her hair was like thorns,
my mouth bled, but I didn't stop.
She was so quiet,
then suddenly she cried out
and sat up;
her face, a hazy flame,
moved closer and closer to mine,
until our lips touched.
I called her woman then
because I knew what it meant.

But I call you God, the Father,
and you're a stranger to me.

3

I pull the thick rope
from the rafter
and roll it up.
I thought I'd use this today,
that I'd kick off the needlepoint footstool
and swing out over the churchyard
as if it were the blue and weary Earth,
that as I flew out into space,
I'd lose my skin, my bones
to the sound of one bell
ringing in the empty sky.
Your voice, Lord.
Instead, I hear Rosamund's laughter,
sometimes her screams,
and behind them, my name,
calling from the roots of trees,
flowers, plants,
from the navel of Lucifer
from which all that is living
grows and ascends toward you,
a journey not home,
not back to the source of things,
but away from it,
toward a harsh, purifying light
that keeps nothing whole —
while my sweet, dark Kyries
became the wine of water
and I drank you.
I married you,
not with my imperfect body,
but with my perfect soul.
Yet, I know I'd have climbed
and climbed through the seven heavens
and found each empty.

I lean from the bell tower.
It's twilight;
smoke is beginning to gray the sky.
Rosamund has gone inside
to wait for me.
She's loosened her hair
and unbuttoned her blouse
the way I like,
set table,
and prayed,
as I do —
one more night.
Lamb stew, salty butter.
I'm the hard, black bread on the water.
Lord, come walk with me.

KRISTALLNACHT

1

I used to think
that dying is endless
like a fall from a high window.
But now that I am seventy,
I know it's more like a child
who is dying,
as I was in 1922,
a child who when he closes his eyes
sees ocean, miles of it,
a shore. And on that shore
dead children
all looking back over their shoulders.
And what those children see —
a child on a small rope bed,
his skin becoming
the electric blue of crushed lapis lazuli,
his head twisted back over a shoulder
death has whittled thin and sharp.

And angels on either side of the bed,
their wings not white, but gold,
their faces violet,
their hair iridescent —
speaking to the boy
or to anyone,
fluttery girlish voices
he can't make out.
What? What did you say? —
but the children on the shore understand.
They stretch out their hands to him.
The angels disappear
into a deep, deep pink
that must be smoke
and the boy falls back on the goose-down pillow,
thinking he'll fly into everlasting regret.

That's what dying is, I say,
and swing my thin legs
over the side of the bed
and sit up.
Or what I thought it was —
something too ugly
or too beautiful
to be kept secret.
I put out my cigarette.
Here I am, alive
in spite of myself
and not that boy
lying alone in a room
full of incense
and his own grating breath.
The nuns who cared for him,
having commended him
into the hands of Jesus Christ, our Lord,
having freed themselves
from one more mortal
and terrifying soul.
Someone who ascended a ladder of air
to an unearthly music,

his flesh vibrating and loosening
until he felt something grab him
around the waist and pull him back
toward the rope bed and candle light
to Sister Dominique
lifting the sheet to cover his face.
His breath coming suddenly, a divine wind,
and the sheet a sail,
carrying him across a river of stars.
Stars in his hair, his eyes, his mouth
and the nun's fingers to his lips,
as his lips pursed to kiss them,
but his teeth doing something else,
biting, biting till blood came
and everything so quiet:
Paul Mornais,
waking again in the world.

2

I was born in Cologne.
That word again: *Cologne.*
I let my mouth fill with it
as my mother did
when the pains began
and that word was black currant jam
on her tongue.
The sweetness filled her,
as the iron bed painted gold gleamed,
as the cottage began to spin,
as she herself spun
on the sharp end of nothingness,
until even her dark brown hair
had become blonde
and she became her own memory.
I wake beside the wicker basket
I slept in years ago.
Did it happen,
or did I dream it all, Mother? — you,
my German father,

killed before I was born,
the dove flying into my forehead
the moment I woke,
and pain as the beak broke through skin,
and then the smell of roses.
And petals falling to the floor
from the wound in my head,
as I bent to touch them
as they disappeared
into petals and late snow
beside your grave, Mother,
when I was twenty.
I was an orphan.
Why couldn't I accept that?
Didn't I have everything? —
that freedom from past
people had died for.

I stand back from my desk
and stare out the window.
I put my hands against the glass.
Cold. Snow. Winter in another country.
I blow on the glass and watch it fog up,
then I draw a cross on it
and circle it with my finger. The world.
One red line intersected by one black line.
Two roads,
and where they meet, a grave
and in that grave
bones wrapped in a coverlet of rose-red light —
you, Mother.
Just bones and a name and words:
Eulalie Mornais, who loved to dance.
Born 1882, died 1913.
God carry her to paradise
and dance there with her immortal soul.

3

The room was half in shadow,
half in light

and one white mum
arced toward me
from the turquoise enamel vase,
thirty-five years ago
in Paris in 1943
when a woman left me.
She was a woman like you,
fragile and thirty.
But I'm your psychiatrist.
I never touch you with my hands,
only with my voice, a pin,
I stick inside you
when you are drifting away
with your crayons and chocolate.
Tell me about your life, you say.
I look at my watch. Sunday at ten?
You stand and almost glide out the door.
What could I tell you? —
that in 1943, I was thirty,
a collaborator,
that Paris was mine
and I didn't want it.
That you make me feel as I did then —
frightened, mortal, and free.
I lift the phone and dial.
How are you? I say.
And you tell me you're afraid,
you feel like crying,
and I tell you
to color more diligently
and say good-by.
But what I wanted to say —
what was it really?
I close the curtains.
My wife knocks on the door. Lunch?
I remember lunch in Paris —
bread, Château Margaux, cheese, olives,
those nice full black ones
and machine guns across the street.
What did we French have to fear? —
sudden death, rape, torture,

or merely the passage of an ordinary day,
as I feared it
in my small room,
which the concierge kept so clean for me,
as she was sure my mother would.
If only I could have killed her cat;
it slept with me and I hated it —
the sexual clawing at the bedspread
when I was almost asleep,
that clawing like your presence day after day.
I walk to the door and open it
and suddenly I am back in Paris in 1943.
I see my friend Klaus
dragging a young woman up the stairs.
He shoves her toward me.
For you, Paul, he says.
Untouched. For you.

4

The Jewess stood behind
the millinery shop window
and cursed us
and it seemed like the great wind
of the Bible was there with her
among the felt, the straw and feathers.
Her tongue was a snake.
Medusa, I thought,
and knew I'd turn to stone.
I had to stop her.
My voice and the voices
of the other good citizens of Berlin
that night in 1938
was a black wave filled with stars
that would wash over the Jews
and suspend them in atonement and broken glass.
I threw one rock and another
and realized I was alone —
glass was everywhere,
even in my hair,

and the Jewess lay at my feet,
her blood on my pants, my shirt.
I turned my face up
and glass fell in my eyes
and it felt like water, only water.
Paul, someone calls me, *it's raining.*
Come inside.

I walk back through the window
where the Jewess is still standing
and past her,
where a woman is bending
over the white wicker basket.
She looks up
and at that moment, I recognize you
and then you're gone, Mother,
and I'm standing alone,
beside the pond in the old convent yard,
where you are buried.
A woman is there on the water.
She lifts her arms
and the waves rise higher and higher,
but she does not drown.
I stretch out my hands.
Mother, strangle me.
Pretend I did not escape the rope bed,
but that you arrived as planned
in your velvet cloak the color of claret
and wrapped a silk cord around my neck
and pulled it tight.
Pretend I died for nothing
instead of living for it.

IMMORTALITY

I dreamed I was digging a grave
that kept filling with water.
The next day, you died.
I dressed you in a wool skirt

and jacket,
because you were always cold
and I had promised to do that much for you.
Then I took a potato to eat, went outside,
and started to dig.

I thought of the Great War;
the day we met.
You, thin as a spade handle,
wearing cotton in deep winter.
The sunset, a clot of dull red
floating in a bowl of cobalt blue,
as we lay on our backs in the mud,
my hand on your mons
and yours pushing at it,
pushing it away,
just like that.
And just like that, we parted.
Then one day you found me hoeing potatoes.
Let me help, you said,
and handed me a child
with bright red hair like yours.
I married you. We fought.
Blood sanctifies and blesses;
it binds.
Anna, where are you now? —
waltzing down a long mirrored corridor,
wrapped in glory that is red, bitter.

I toss a shovelful of dirt on your coffin.
It isn't that I hate you for giving it all up
with your poison.
But I wanted to do it —
to finally ease this hunger
to be holy in my devotion to you
and have you acknowledge it
the moment before I brought
the mallet down and set you free.
Life to you was yellow
like the vicar's daughter's braids,

it was morning-glories,
All Hallows' Eve,
your dead sister's baby teeth
for good luck.
But I wanted us to go on
day and night, without terror or hope.
I can't forgive your going.
I take the potato from my pocket.
One bite, then another,
if only this were all it took
to live forever.

ELEGY

For my cousin John, 1946–1967

Hundreds of flies
rise from my face
and I feel as if I'm flying.
But it's only a daydream.
I'm seventy-five,
in the veterans' hospital
and this isn't 1917.
On TV, Saigon is splitting apart
like a cheap Moroccan leather suitcase
and we are leaving it all behind;
our dirty, dirty laundry.
Maybe it's the right thing to do.
Maybe soldiers are reborn infinitely
to do each century's killing and mopping up.
We stand at attention in full dress.
A general rides by in an open car
and we cheer. How I cheered.
Here's to the trenches, the mud,
the bullet-riddled days and nights,
that one night in November 1917,
when I thought I was dead,
when I felt myself rising
straight for the moon's green, cheesy heart.
But I wasn't dead,

I was on a troop ship in the English Channel
twenty-seven years later
and nothing had changed.
Last night, I dreamed about my mother.
She was pregnant with me
and I was also there with her
as a young man.
I wanted to end it inside her womb
with my bayonet.
And somehow, I cut my way to the child.
I took him by the feet
and flung him high
over a smoky black rainbow.

2

Suddenly, my body jerks forward, then back
and just as suddenly,
the TV screen darkens
and the voices of the journalists fade,
then hang in the air like whispers,
as the orderly takes hold of my wheelchair.
When we move down the hallway,
small, almond-eyed people
cheer as I roll by.
I recognize them all:
that one was with me in the trenches,
that one in the concentration camp,
and that vapor there from Nagasaki.
The orderly lifts me into bed
and folds the mended blanket across my chest.
Imagining things, I say to him.
Well, what if I am? —
just lower the coffin.
Let those clods of earth come down
like a hundred blows.
You say never you, never,
but when it's your turn,
you'll pack your sweet dreams
in your old kit bag and go.

And on that true last day,
you and I will rise toward heaven
like two great brass notes
from Gabriel's horn.
We'll shout, *Hallelujah,*
the war is over.
We'll shout the gates
of heaven down.

THEY SHALL NOT PASS

Above me, the sky is all Atlantic
and I taste vinegar, salt,
and those hot yellow peppers
Natividad used to eat
with tamales and beer.
And the sweat above her lip —
I can taste that too.
And I have to remind myself
why I left Mexico,
why I'm dying here in Madrid
when I should be standing,
thumbs hooked in my belt loops,
a Lucky Strike caught in the corner of my mouth.

I was a Wobbly like my father
and like him, I always bought two drinks:
one for myself and one for the ghost
of universal brotherhood,
with his tattered suitcase, checkered tie,
and a thirst for handshakes and hammers,
always leaning at the bar when I'd arrive,
with his *Joe, buy me a drink, just one more.*
He was in Vera Cruz the night I left,
he stood on the deck with me before I sailed,
squinting at the dock, pointing out the ones
who were his,
while I stood there, empty of everything
but what I believed:

that your brother was your brother
and you had to spare a dime,
that when you went down,
the next man would stand up,
hand in his pocket,
that there were angels
who walked among the honored dead
carrying red sickles,
that Joe Stalin sat like Ole King Cole
top of the world
and I'd sit next to him someday
with the back pay of a thousand years
in my own hands.
I had a heart like a goddamn sponge.
You could fill me
with slogans, with songs and marches,
with dead men —
like Sunshine.

He was next to me
when he split up the middle,
out of luck, out of dimes;
when there was terror no one told me existed:
betrayers, idealists — hysterical and uneven fighters.

Only this: They shall not pass.
I said it over and over to myself
as we defended the University of Madrid,
even as I took this slow glide down,
my blood like thick bolts of cloth,
hitting the ground as I fell,
while the layers of ice and ash
floated down from kingdom come.

A chrome ship slides across the sky's smooth surface
and Franco himself lifts the Stars and Stripes sail.
My whole face is numb.
I wanted to hit the coast of Spain
like a fist ramming an old man's belly,
but instead found what's-his-name

in the first bar I stepped into,
wearing a Saint Patrick's Day smile:
Cold sober, Joe, he said, and he spat on the sawdust floor.
I'm my own man, first time in years.
You should try it.
Then he told me
a man can kill without hate,
that that's how it's done,
that Jesus Christ is the bullet
that makes everything right.
But it doesn't matter
now that the glorious perfumed air
is filled with butterflies
which have men's faces, men's feet,
now that the cocoon of flesh
that held me splits apart
and I step left, right, left,
and what's-his-name swaggers head of the line
and his voice floats over us
like the Holy Ghost:
Victory, friends, brothers;
as we march
all in a row
into the motionless sea.

THE TESTIMONY OF J. ROBERT OPPENHEIMER
A Fiction

When I attained enlightenment,
I threw off the night like an old skin.
My eyes filled with light
and I fell to the ground.
I lay in Los Alamos,
while at the same time,
I fell
toward Hiroshima,
faster and faster,
till the earth,
till the morning

slipped away beneath me.
Some say when I hit
there was an explosion,
a searing wind that swept the dead before it,
but there was only silence,
only the soothing baby-blue morning
rocking me in its cradle of cumulus cloud,
only rest.
There beyond the blur of mortality,
the roots of the trees of Life and Death,
the trees William Blake called Art and Science,
joined in a kind of Gordian knot
even Alexander couldn't cut.
To me, the ideological high wire
is for fools to balance on with their illusions.
It is better to leap into the void.
Isn't that what we all want anyway? —
to eliminate all pretense
till like the oppressed who in the end
identifies with the oppressor,
we accept the worst in ourselves
and are set free.

In high school, they told me
all scientists
start from the hypothesis "what if"
and it's true.
What we as a brotherhood lack in imagination
we make up for with curiosity.
I was always motivated
by a ferocious need to know.
Can you tell me, gentlemen,
that you don't want it too? —
the public collapse,
the big fall smooth as honey down a throat.
Anything that gets you closer
to what you are.
Oh, to be born again and again
from that dark, metal womb,
the sweet, intoxicating smell of decay

the imminent dead give off
rising to embrace me.

But I could say anything, couldn't I?
Like a bed we make and unmake at whim,
the truth is always changing,
always shaped by the latest
collective urge to destroy.
So I sit here,
gnawed down by the teeth
of my nightmares.
My soul, a wound that will not heal.
All I know is that urge,
the pure, sibylline intensity of it.
Now, here at parade's end
all that matters:
our military in readiness,
our private citizens
in a constant frenzy of patriotism
and jingoistic pride,
our enemies endless,
our need to defend infinite.
Good soldiers,
we do not regret or mourn,
but pick up the guns of our fallen.

Like characters in the funny papers,
under the heading
"Further Adventures of the Lost Tribe,"
we march past the third eye of History,
as it rocks back and forth
in its hammock of stars.
We strip away the tattered fabric
of the universe
to the juicy, dark meat,
the nothing beyond time.
We tear ourselves down atom by atom,
till electron and positron,
we become our own transcendent annihilation.

THE DETECTIVE

I lie on my daughter's body
to hold her in the earth,
but she won't stay;
she rises, lifting me with her,
as if she were air
and not some remnant
of failed reeducation
in a Cambodian mass grave.
We rise, till I wake.
I sit up, turn on the lamp,
and stare at the photo of the girl
who died yesterday,
at her Vietnamese mother
and her American father.
Jewel van duc Thompson,
murdered in Springfield, Ohio,
in her eighteenth year,
gone the day she was born
like in the cartoons,
when somebody rolls up the road
that stretches into the horizon
and the TV screen goes black . . .

Go home, Captain,
the cop said yesterday,
as he gripped my hand
and hauled himself
up from the ditch
where they'd found her
like Persephone
climbing from the underworld
one more time,
his eyes bright,
the hunger for life
and a good time
riding his back like a jockey.
Death is a vacation, I answered.
Then my hand was free

and I could see
how she was thrown
from the highway
down the embankment.
Where were Art and Rationality
when it counted? I thought —
always around the corner
from somebody else's street.
Even the ice cream man
never, ever made your block,
though you could hear the bells,
though you could feel the chill
like a shock
those hot days
when your company beat the bushes,
when you bit into death's chocolate-covered center
and froze . . .

I turn off the lamp
and lie still in the dark.
Somewhere in time, it is 1968.
I am bending over a wounded man
with my knife.
My company calls me the Angel of Mercy.
I don't remember yesterday
and there is no tomorrow.
There is only the moment
the knife descends
from the equatorial dark.
Only a step
across the Cambodian border
from Vietnam
to search and destroy the enemy,
but it is just a short time
till the enemy discovers me
and I would die,
but for the woman
who takes me to the border,
who crosses with me from the underworld
back to the underworld.

I open the curtain.
Outside, the early morning
is spinning, gathering speed,
and moving down the street
like a whirlwind.
I pull the curtain shut again
and switch on my tape
of the murderer's confession,
hear the faint, raspy voice
playing and replaying itself.
It was Saturday night.
She stood alone at the bus stop.
When she took the first step
toward my car,
I dropped the key once, twice.
She smiled, she picked it up.
I lie back on the bed,
while the voice
wears itself out.
Yes, I think,
you live for a while.
You get tired.
You walk the road into the interior
and never come back.
You disappear
the way the woman
and your child disappear
into Cambodia
in the pink light of dawn,
early April 1975.
You say you'll go back,
but you never do.
Springfield, Phnom Penh.
So many thousands of miles
between a lie and the truth.
No, just a step.
The murderer's voice rises,
becomes shrill.
Man, he says, *is it wrong*

to do what is necessary?
I switch off the tape.
Each time I sit down,
I think I won't get up again;
I sink through the bed, the floor,
and out the other side of the Earth.
There my daughter denounces me.
She turns me back
at the muddy border of forgiveness.
I get up, dress quickly,
then open the curtain wide.

At the door,
I put my hand on the knob, hesitate,
then step out into sunlight.
I get into the car,
lift the key to the ignition,
drop it.
My hand is shaking.
I look into the back seat.
The Twentieth Century is there,
wearing a necklace of grenades
that glitters against its black skin.
I stare, see the pins
have all been pulled.
Drive, says the voice.
I turn to the wheel,
imagine the explosions,
house after house
disintegrating in flames,
but all is silent.
People go on with their lives
on this day that is one hundred years long,
on this sad red balloon of a planet,
the air escaping from it
like the hot, sour breath of a child.

THE JOURNALIST

1

In the old photograph,
I'm holding my nose
and my friend Stutz
has a finger down his throat.
We're sixteen, in Cedar Falls.
It's all still a joke.
In my mind, I'm back there.
The woman who used me
like a dirty rag is gone
in a red convertible.
The top is down.
She sits beside the Greek
from out of town,
his hair slicked down
with bergamot.
I don't care, I do care
that she cruises the streets
of Little America without me.
I take a last drag off my Lucky,
pull my cap low,
and take the old road to the fairground.
I'm sixteen. What do I know
about love and passion, I think,
as I watch the circus set up,
watch as the elephants pitch and sway,
heads and trunks swinging wildly.
When the yellow leaves stir
and spin around me,
I walk back to the river
and skim stones
across the clear, gold water
of early evening,
till the 7:18 whistle blows.
Then as if on command,
I start running from childhood,
from the hometown

that keeps me a boy
when I want to be a man.
Manhood, a dream, an illusion, I think,
as I lay down the photograph
and stand still in the anemic glow
of the darkroom lights,
my body giving off the formaldehyde smell
of the unknown.

2

In Vietnam in 1966,
I stood among the gathering crowd,
as the Buddhist nun
doused her robe with gasoline.
As an American, I couldn't understand
and as I stood there,
I imagined myself
moving through the crowd
to stop her, but I didn't.
I held my camera in position.
Then it happened so quickly —
her assistant stepped forward
with a match.
Flames rose up the nun's robe
and covered her face,
then her charred body
slowly fell to the ground.
That year in Vietnam,
I threw my life in the air
like a silver baton.
I could catch it with my eyes closed.
Till one night,
it sailed into black space like a wish
and disappeared.
Or was it me who vanished,
sucking the hard rock candy
of the future,
sure that a man's life is art,
that mine had to be?

But tonight, I'm fifty-three.
I've drunk my way to the bottom
of that river of my youth
and I'm lying there
like a fat carp,
belly-down in the muck.
And nothing, not the blonde,
the red car,
or the smell of new money,
can get me up again.

I lay out the photographs of the nun.
I remember how her assistant
spoke to the crowd,
how no one acknowledged her,
how we stood another two or three minutes,
till I put my hand in my pocket,
brought out the matchbook,
and threw it to the nun's side.
I stare at the last photograph —
the nun's heart that would not burn,
the assistant, her hand stretched toward me
with the matchbook in it.
What is left out? —
a man, me, stepping forward,
tearing off a match, striking it
and touching it to the heart.
I throw the photographs
in the metal wastebasket,
then take the nun's heart
from the glass container of formaldehyde.
I light a match.
Still the heart won't burn.
I put the fire out,
close my eyes
and see myself running,
holding a lump
wrapped in a handkerchief.
I think someone will stop me
or try to, but no one does.

I open my eyes,
take the heart,
and hold it against my own.
When I was sixteen,
I was the dutiful son.
I washed my hands,
helped my mother set the table,
got my hair cut, my shoes shined.
I tipped the black man
I called "boy" a dime.
I didn't excel,
but I knew I could be heroic
if I had to.
I'd set the sharp end
of the compass
down on blank paper
and with the pencil end
I was drawing the circle
that would contain me —
everything I wanted,
everything I'd settle for.
Life and all its imitations.
That day in Hue,
I had the chance to step
from the circle
and I took it.
But when I turned back,
everything inside it was burning.
My past was gone. I was gone.
But the boy was still there.
He watched the flames take the nun.
He took her heart. He was running.
I was bound, he said to himself, *I'm free.*
But it was a lie.

I put the heart back in the container,
hear the heavy footsteps
of my wife, the blonde,
who is gray now,
who is clumping up the stairs

in her rubber boots
like some female Santa Claus.
In the heavy canvas bag
slung over her shoulder —
all the smashed toys of my life.
Wait, I say, as I stand
with my shoulder against the door.
Wait. You haven't heard
the best part yet —
A boy is running away from home.
He's lost his cap.
He's wearing the icy wind
like an overcoat.
He can't go back. He won't go back.
He never left.

Fate

GO

For Mary Jo Kopechne and Edward Kennedy

Once upon a Massachusetts midnight,
under a sky smoothed of light,
as if wiped by flannel,
a car sailed off a bridge
but did not float.
Then the water, the dark gray water,
opened its mouth
and I slid down its throat.
But when it tried to swallow
the man they call my lover *and* my killer,
it choked and spat him back into your faces.
He carried no traces of me on his body
or in his heart,
but the part I played in his destruction
made me worthy of all of Shakespeare's villains
Yet why doesn't somebody
tear me from the bit player's cold embrace
and let me set the stage on fire,
dressed up in revisionists' flesh?
Why doesn't someone write the monologue
that will finally explain this melodrama
and let me claim it?
Let me perform my own exorcism
as I performed the music of my dying
to someone else's rhythm.
Give 'em a show, Mary Jo Kopechne,
the one they really paid to see.
Bring down the house of Kennedy for good,
or, like Jehovah, re-create it in its soiled image.
I don't know. I don't know.
What scene is this, what act?
How did I miss the part where I enter to applause,
where the prince of make-believe
is waiting beside the hearse,
all its doors thrown open?
But right here in the script
somebody's written *Enter* beside the word *Exit*

and under that *You Choose.*
But when I do,
a human wall closes round me
and I can't get to you, Teddy,
behind your friends,
their arms raised to fend off blows,
even my own parents, with chests bared
to take for you any condemnation
aimed like a bullet.
If I shove those dominoes, will they fall
while I go marching in,
some Satchmo who'll blow the walls
of this Jericho of lies down?
But this aside's too complicated,
too weighed by metaphors and similes.

All right, I'll say it plainly.
Jack or Bobby would have died with me.
Think of publicity, the headlines —
you'd have been a hero.
Instead you caught your media resurrection
in your teeth and let it go.

You dove and dove
for that woman
so often reduced by the press
to just breasts and Mound of Venus,
but I broke free of all that.
I found another kind of ecstasy.
I'd always thought my only calling
would be acquiescent mate,
but goodness doesn't count
among self-made nobility,
especially the Irish Catholic ones.
What does is the pose of sacrifice,
so I swam deeper and deeper down,
hoping you'd understand and follow,
but each time you rose for air,
you sucked it like a child at breast.
It should have been mine,

full of death's sweet buttermilk,
but yes, you broke the skin of water
one last time,
you climbed onto Dyke Bridge
alive, but dead to the world.
If only you'd realized it.

How ironic that from your stained integrity
came the conscience of what's left
of the Democratic party,
brought to its knobby knees by Mistress Fortune.
You have earned that,
you who've grown fat and jowly
at the table where no feast is ever served,
just sparkling water with a twist of lime,
where once a glass of gin and tonic stood,
a good son's hands about to raise it in a toast
in praise of brothers.
Sometimes, stunned, you ask the dark
beyond the footlights
what happened to that life.
Other times, you slowly strip
to a Bessie Smith blues song,
you know the one about dues
and jelly, always jellyroll,
or you play the old magic trick —
a member of the audience holds up
an object from your past
and you identify it with charades.
But if you'd only ask me,
I'd erase those lines you've drawn on air
and deconstruct my own unfinished masterpiece,
a family portrait
of one man
and one true wife,
who, though the race was lost long ago,
stands behind him
with a starting gun
as he forever runs and runs in place.

LYNDON LIBRE

They'll chew you up
and spit you out, said Mother,
Mother said, but she was dead
before she saw the first red marks,
where the teeth bit deepest.
Praise God she never knew
that it would become patriotic
for quixotic Americans
to turn against their comet of a man
until, like wolves in dove's clothing,
they ran him down
on the steps of a white house,
the front door like that plywood door
of Reata Ranch in *Giant,*
opening on nothing,
though you all call it president.
In ancient times, a pharaoh
might sacrifice himself,
might through the shedding of his blood
save his subjects from drought,
disease, and other forms of tragedy,
until the ritual became
simply strapping on a panther's tail,
a symbol of renewal,
so when my falling came,
I pulled on my handlasted boots,
my spurs, Stetson,
chaps, and six-gun
and with a thunderclap
chose to ride the range
where only thorny, yellow roses grow
upon the once and future fruited plain.
Historians say that toward the end
I disengaged, even staged
my own tumble from the precipice called Vietnam.
I called her name in my sleep,
the black-haired bitch
who kept her knees together.

Whether I cursed, cried, or begged
she denied me,
and even when tied down and spread-legged,
she gave me no pleasure.
Defeat was the only treasure buried there.
Three days, I lay in Gallup's cave,
until the stonehearted populace rolled back
and I was saved by a cowboy all in black.
He gave me tobacco, hardtack,
two packhorses, and a map
and said, retrace your life,
and everywhere I set my feet,
my own face looked up at me
without a trace of recognition,
and only when I camped on the banks of this Mekong
of the mind did I find
I had not been erased.
Now I sit before the fire.
I swap tales with myself and sing
of herding human cattle endlessly
across the borders wars can always penetrate
but never quite make disappear,
while those who suffer fear, poverty,
race and class hate
are still outside barbed wire fences, iron gates,
anyplace but beside us at the table,
eating off our spotless plates.
I tried to change that
but could not break the locks
that kept me in the magic circle
known as the sovereign state.
My Great Society cavalry arrived too late
to deliver me from the calvary I had created
and only one man waited
at the foot of my rugged cross.
As I climbed down,
Bobby caught the dice I threw him,
blew on them twice,
tossed them, and said, "Luck o' the Irish."

Before they hit the ground, his heart exploded
and showered silver coins instead of blood,
yet cost me all a second time,
for martyrs never lose.
Blame my gradual disintegration
on intellectuals too,
ungrateful Negroes and the poor,
all beating at the door, until I bade them enter,
then found myself at epicenter of an earthquake
that still shakes the foundations of this country,
because in my wake came Nixon's Watergate
and later the final betrayal of FDR's New Deal,
the ideology which now and then
Republicans steal
to accommodate the latest twists and turns
of their crooked highways.
But I know you'll cry
who am I to condemn,
who am I to say what price should be paid
to win and not.
If somehow the ends got mixed up with the means,
well, that's not communism, that's democracy,
that's the thin red line
between the white and blue.
I hope to God that will save you
from the politician's stew
of promises impossible to keep,
but me, I'm having barbecued spareribs
this Fourth of July, 1989,
pinto beans, corn on the cob.
At last I want to celebrate the brief time
inside the walls of Camelot
when I was king of comedy,
before I abdicated.

JIMMY HOFFA'S ODYSSEY

I remember summers
when the ice man used to come,

a hunk of winter
caught between his iron tongs,
and in the kitchen, my ma with a rag,
wiping the floor when he'd gone;
sweet song of the vegetable man
like the music
a million silver dollars make,
as they jingle, jangle
in that big pocket of your dreams.
Dreams. Yes, and lies.
When I was a boy, I hauled ashes
in a wagon,
pulled by a bony horse
not even good enough for soap,
so later, when they called me
stocky little dockworker
with my slicked-back black hair,
my two-tone shoes, cheap suits,
and fat, smelly cigars,
I didn't care.
I had my compensation.
Bobby Kennedy didn't want to understand,
but to the teamsters back in '58 . . .
I had 'em all in my pocket then,
statesmen, lawyers, movie stars,
Joe Louis, for God's sake.
For a time, I won spin after spin
on the tin wheel of fate,
but in the end, like those glory boys
Jack and Bobby,
I was only icing on the sucker cake.

I know the alibis, the lies,
stacked up like bodies
on a gurney going nowhere,
but Hoffa went, he went
walking in a parking lot one day,
while he waited for a so-called
friend, a peacemaker, ha.
See him there, bored and sweating.

See the car roll toward him
as he does a little dance, a polka step or two,
when the doors open
and the glare of sunlight off a windshield
becomes so bright
that he is blinded by it.
Later, I come to,
while a blue broccoli-looking creature
is taking tubes from my arms and legs.
Then he walks me round and round
till I can stand on my own.
He talks to me through some machine,
tells me I'm on a spaceship,
tells me he's lonely,
then he sits me down at the controls,
he talks to me about his life in some galaxy
whose name I can't pronounce.
I become a confidant of sorts, a friend,
until one day outside Roswell, New Mexico,
his skin begins to rot,
so I start collecting specimens for him:
rocks, bugs, plants,
my walks taking me farther and farther
till I find this abandoned gas station,
and when he dies,
I put up signs along the highway,
the ones that say, "10 miles, 5, 1 mile
to see THE THING!"
And fifty cents for kids, a dollar for adults,
buys a glimpse of a spaceman
in an airtight case
and Hoffa on the other side of the glass,
Hoffa who chooses to let everybody think
he was pulverized in some New Jersey nightmare.
I drink an Orange Crush, prop my feet up,
and watch the sun go down,
the moon come up. A year goes by like this,
two, when suddenly it's not enough.
In a rage, I smash the case
and burn down the shack

with the spaceman inside.
I hitch a ride to town and take a job
at McDonald's,
and when I raise enough cash,
take a Greyhound to Detroit,
but in the station,
as if commanded by a force outside myself,
buy a ticket back.
In the desert once again, I board the spaceship
and take off,
and one night,
kidnap two hunters in Maine,
later, a family in Texas,
a telephone lineman in upstate New York.
I want to tell them who I am,
but all I do is mumble, stare, and touch them,
as if I'd never been a man among men,
when the dollar sign was a benediction.
Instead of words what comes are images
of Hoffa smacked in the head
so hard he hurls himself forward,
then slams back in the seat,
and later, shot through each eye, each ear,
his mouth,
his body heaved in a trash compactor
and to its whir, whine, and moan,
crushed beyond anger.
Again and again, I play memory games
in the casino of the past.
Yes, half a chance,
I'd do it all the same,
so aim that pistol, wise guy,
and fire and keep on firing.
Let me go, let me go,
but give the bosses of the world,
the brass-assed monkeys
who haven't paid the price in blood,
this warning:
sometime when they are least expecting,
I am coming back

to take my place on the picket line,
because, like any other union man,
I earned it.

BOYS AND GIRLS, LENNY BRUCE,
OR BACK FROM THE DEAD

For Willem Dafoe, Ron Vawter, and the Wooster Group

1

So how's it going, folks? —
broke, exhausted,
shtuped and duped again.
You can take it.
Hell, the meaning of life
is taking it,
in the mouth, the ass, the —
o-o-o-h
it feels so good.
All together now, stand up, bend over,
and say *a-a-a-h*.
Now sit down, relax, enjoy the show
that asks the magic question,
with such a stink,
can shit be far behind?
But no, what you smell is an odor
of another kind,
fear, disgust, plus all the things
you don't want to hear,
the things that drive you
from the club,
a body, a name, and nothing more.
Alone, on stage, I take
what you have left behind
and wear it like a wide, gaudy tie,
a sight gag
for the next show,
when I'll pick at some other scab
until it bleeds,

until that blood turns to wine
and we get drunk
on the incomprehensible
raison d'être of our lives.

2

I address myself
most often to guys,
because guys are least
able to express themselves.
You women know that.
You've read it in *Ms.* and *Cosmo.*
I am not a woman hater;
I'm a woman baiter, I like
to argue, I like confrontation
as long as I win,
but you women make it hard,
you don't play by rules
but by emotions.
One minute you're devoted,
the next you've placed
an ad in *New York Magazine*
that says we're impotent.
Know what I'm saying?
You women tell each other things
a guy does not want told.
You hold these secret sessions
over coffee and croissants.
We disappear in your complaints,
and in our places, those things
you've created.
So guys, I advise let 'em know
you won't be violated,
you won't be changed
into their tormentor.
You women out there,
all I'm trying to say,
in the end,
we're only bad impersonations

of our fantasies.
Just let the accusation waltz be ended,
not the dance.

3

I tried to reach
that state of grace
when performer and audience fuse,
but each show left a hunger
even sex couldn't satisfy.
The closest thing —
heroin. No,
like the Velvet Underground sang it —
her-row-in.
Shot, snorted, smoked,
even laced with sugar
and spread on cereal for breakfast.
But I was cool, it was cool,
until one night I thought
to hell with this moderation shit.
I took one needle too many
in that last uncollapsed vein,
that trail up the cold Himalayas.
I climbed and climbed
and finally it was just me
and the abominable snowman,
starring in my own *Lost Horizon*.
I had *arrived*
to Miles playing background trumpet.
Ice encased me from the neck down;
the snowman never moved,
never made a sound,
maybe he wasn't even there,
maybe he was the pure air of imagination.
That's o-x-y-g-e-n.
I breathed faster
and faster, then slow
and let it all come down,

but that was just before
the floor, the Hollywood
night and smog,
the quick trip to the morgue
to identify
someone I used to know.
He looked like me, he was
me,
but in some other form
or incarnation,
my rib cage cut open, my guts
bluish gray and shriveled,
liver going black,
heart too,
my dick sucked back inside,
as if through a straw or tube.
I lay like that for days
while they hunted me for drugs,
as if prospecting gold
and that gold was my disgrace,
but now I'm back
to claim my share of whatever's
left out there among the ruins.
And on stage,
under the white-hot spotlights,
give it all I've got.
So greetings from the reclamation zone.
Like Christmas, it was bound to come,
and like some hostage savior,
I'm here to stay
till everybody's sanctified
in laughter.
That's right, it's not your balls, your pussy,
or your money
that I'm after; it's your soul.

GENERAL GEORGE ARMSTRONG CUSTER: MY LIFE IN THE THEATER

After the blood wedding
at Little Big Horn,
I rose from death,
a bride loved past desire
yet unsatisfied,
and walked among the mutilated corpses.
Skin stripped from them,
they were as white as marble,
their raw scalps like red bathing caps.
Sometimes I bent to stroke the dying horses
as dew bathed my feet.
When I tore the arrows from my genitals,
I heard again the sound of the squaws.
The trills on their tongues thrilled me.
Those sounds were victory
and I was victory's slave
and she was a better lover than my wife
or the colored laundress
I took under a wagon one night
when I was hot with my invincibility.
Why, eventually even Sitting Bull
joined a Wild West show.
He rode a dancing pony
and sold his autograph to anyone who'd pay
and I might have become president,
my buckskin suit, white hat,
two guns, and rifle
flung in some closet
while I wore silk shirts
and trousers made of cotton
milled on my own shores
and took my manly pleasures
with more accomplished whores.
Instead I dress in lies and contradictions
and no one recognizes me.
All they see is the tall, skinny mercenary
with yellow hair

and blue, vacant eyes that stare,
so while I chew the tips of my mustache,
the cameras pass over me.
The journalists interview that guy or that one
and I want to shoot them down,
but that's been done before
by some back-door assassin or other
who kills publicly for sport,
but I kill for
the spectacle, the operatic pitch
of the little civil wars
that decimate from inside,
as in Belfast, Beirut, or Los Angeles,
where people know how it feels to be
somebody's personal Indian,
a few arrows, a few bullets short of home,
then left behind to roam this afterlife.
Once I knelt on one knee,
firing from my circle of self-deceit,
no thought but to extinguish thought,
until I brought down each brave,
but it was his red hand that wounded me,
no matter how many times I shot,
clubbed, clawed, or bit him,
my mouth overflowing with blood,
the rubbery flesh I chewed
that left no evidence of my savagery.
When I raised the gun to my own head,
I recalled the fields and fields of yellow flowers
that lit my way as I rode to battle.
How beautiful they were,
how often I stopped to pick them.
I twined them in my horse's mane
and in my hair,
but they were useless amulets
that could not stop my bullet
as it sizzled through flesh, then bone.
Now misfortune's soldier,
black armband on sleeve and hand on heart,
I pledge no fear

as chance propels me
into another breach
from which there is no deliverance,
only the tragicomedy of defeat acted out
in the belly of the cosmic whale,
where I swim against the dark, relentless tide.

INTERVIEW WITH A POLICEMAN

You say you want this story
in my own words,
but you won't tell it my way.
Reporters never do.
If everybody's racist,
that means you too.
I grab your finger
as you jab it at my chest.
So what, the minicam caught that?
You want to know all about it, right? —
the liquor store, the black kid
who pulled his gun
at the wrong time.
You saw the dollars he fell on and bloodied.
Remember how cold it was that night,
but I was sweating.
I'd worked hard, I was through
for twenty-four hours,
and I wanted some brew.
When I heard a shout,
I turned and saw the clerk
with his hands in the air,
saw the kid drop his gun
as I yelled and ran from the back.
I only fired when he bent down,
picked up his gun, and again dropped it.
I saw he was terrified,
saw his shoulder and head jerk to the side
as the next bullet hit.
When I dove down, he got his gun once more

and fired wildly.
Liquor poured onto the counter, the floor
onto which he fell back finally,
still firing now toward the door,
when his arm flung itself behind him.
As I crawled toward him,
I could hear dance music
over the sound of liquor spilling and spilling,
and when I balanced on my hands
and stared at him, a cough or spasm
sent a stream of blood out of his mouth
that hit me in the face.

Later, I felt as if I'd left part of myself
stranded on that other side,
where anyplace you turn is down,
is out for money, for drugs,
or just for something new like shoes
or sunglasses,
where your own rage
destroys everything in its wake,
including you.
Especially you.
Go on, set your pad and pencil down,
turn off the camera, the tape.
The ape in the gilded cage
looks too familiar, doesn't he,
and underneath it all,
like me, you just want to forget him.
Tonight, though, for a while you'll lie awake.
You'll hear the sound of gunshots
in someone else's neighborhood,
then, comforted, turn over in your bed
and close your eyes,
but the boy like a shark redeemed at last
yet unrepentant
will reenter your life
by the unlocked door of sleep
to take everything but his fury back.

JAMES DEAN

Night after night,
I danced on dynamite,
as light of foot as Fred Astaire,
until I drove the road
like the back of a black panther,
speckled with the gold
of the cold and distant stars
and the slam, bang, bam
of metal jammed against metal.
My head nearly tore from my neck,
my bones broke in fragments
like half-remembered sentences,
and my body,
as if it had been beaten
by a thousand fists,
bruised dark blue;
yet a breath entered my wide-open mouth
and the odor of sweet grass
filled my nose. I died,
but the cameras kept filming
some guy named James,
kept me stranded among the so-called living,
though if anybody'd let me,
I'd have proved
that I was made of nothing
but one long, sweet kiss
before I wasn't there.

Still, I wear
my red jacket, blue jeans.
Sometimes I'm an empty space in line
at some Broadway cattle call,
or a shadow on a movie screen;
sometimes I caress a woman in her dreams,
kiss, undress her anyplace,
and make love to her
until she cries.
I cry out

as she squeezes me tight
between her thighs,
but when she grabs my hair,
my head comes off in her hands
and I take the grave again.
Maybe I never wanted a woman
as much as that anyway,
or even the spice of man on man
that I encountered once or twice,
the hole where I shoved myself,
framed by an aureole of coarse hair.
By that twilight in '55,
I had devised a way
of living in between
the rules that other people make.
The bongos, the dance classes with Eartha Kitt,
and finally racing cars,
I loved the incongruity of it.
They used to say that I was always on
and couldn't separate myself
from the characters I played,
and if I hadn't died,
I'd have burned out anyway,
but I didn't give Quaker's shit, man,
I gave performances.
I even peed on the set of *Giant* —
that's right —
and turned around
and did a scene with Liz Taylor.
I didn't wash my hands first.
All the same, I didn't need an audience.
That's the difference
between an actor
and some sly pretender
who manipulates himself
up on the tarnished silver screen.
I didn't *do* method; I did James Dean.
Since then, the posters, photographs, biographies
keep me unbetrayed by age or fashion,
and as many shows a night as it's requested,

I reenact my passion play
for anyone who's interested,
and when my Porsche
slams into that Ford,
I'm doing one hundred eighty-six thousand
miles a second,
but I never leave the stage.

THE RESURRECTION OF ELVIS PRESLEY

Once upon a time, I practiced moves in a mirror —
half spastic, half Nijinsky,
with a dash of belly dancer
to make the little girls burn.
I dyed my dark blond hair black
and coated it with Royal Crown pomade,
that stuff the Negroes used,
till it shone
with a porcelainlike glaze.
Some nights I'd wake in a sweat.
I'd have to take off my p.j.'s.
I'd imagine I was Tony Curtis
and I'd get a hard-on,
then, ashamed, get up
and stare at myself in the mirror by nightlight
and, shaking as if I had a fever,
step, cross step, pump my belly,
grind my hips, and jump back
and fling one arm above my head,
the other toward the floor,
fingers spread wide
to indicate true feeling.
But where was he
when I bit the hook
and got reeled in
and at the bitter end of the rod
found not God but Papa Hemingway,
banished too to this island
in the stream of unconsciousness,

to await the Apocalypse of Revelations
or just another big fish?

2

I don't know how it happened,
but I became all appetite.
I took another pill, another woman,
or built another room
to store the gifts I got from fans
till neither preachers, priests,
nor Yogananda's autobiography
could help me.
The Colonel tied a string around my neck
and led me anywhere he wanted.
I was his teddy bear
and yours and yours and yours.
But did I whine, did I complain about it?
Like a greased pig,
I slid through everybody's hands
till I got caught between the undertaker's sheets.
And now I wait
to be raised up like some *Titanic*
from the Rock 'n' Roll Atlantic.
Now as I cast my line,
tongues of flame
lick the air above my head,
announcing some Pentecost,
or transcendental storm,
but Papa tells me it's only death who's coming
and he's just a mutated brother
who skims the dark floor
of all our troubled waters
and rises now and then to eat the bait.
But once he wrestled me
like Jacob's angel
and I let him win
because he promised resurrection
in some sweeter by-and-by,
and when he comes to me again

I'll pin him down
until he claims me
from the walleye of this hurricane
and takes me
I don't care how,
as long as he just takes me.
But Papa says forget him
and catch what I can,
even if it's just sweet time,
because it's better than nothing,
better even than waiting
in the heavenly deep-freeze,
then he tells me don't move,
don't talk,
and for Chrissakes don't sing,
and I do what he wants,
me, the king of noise,
but in my memories
this country boy *is* singing,
he's dancing in the dark
and always will.

LAST SEEN

For Alfred Hitchcock

Good evening. I know you thought
you'd seen and heard
the last of me,
martini in hand
and vitriolic monologue upon the tongue,
not at all surprised to find myself
locked out of Paradise.
Why not? Consummation never lives
up to its promise.
Liver and onions with bacon
crumbled on the top
can serve you just as well,
whether you eat it

and/or hit your lover
with the skillet it was cooked in.
If the thirst for love
is not the thirst for death, what is it? —
a minute or two of heaving over the crapper,
a wipe, a flush,
a reverent hush before a scream
covers your body like a shroud.
Here lies Alfred Hitchcock,
a bloody nuisance
when he wasn't just a bloody bore.
He made films about unpleasant things and people.
He sold his name to magazines and television,
and some of you were patrons to his whores.
You cried, *Auteur, auteur,*
but all that ever mattered to him was the next scene:
a dark, deserted street, a large foreign car,
the camera far off, but moving nearer, nearer,
until the car's back end lifts slightly,
settles and shakes,
until I hear the muffled sobs,
the crack of a slap,
and a man snarling, *Bloody bitch. Bitch.*
Then silence as the camera moves back unsteadily
but suddenly goes forward again
to come to rest against the glass,
through which at last
by the unexpected flash of a match
I see his face,
suspended like a pasty moon
over the body of a woman
he continues to choke with one hand,
the sweat oozing off his rolls of fat,
as he wheezes and jerks
and with a groan ejaculates onto the corpse.
No, I'll not cut that bit from "sweat" down.
It's time somebody showed that side
of what is loosely called creation.
Wait. Wait. What if

a scant five minutes before,
we shot another window, perhaps catty-corner,
a convent window,
where a novice gazes down on the night
and its detritus,
on a blonde alone under a lamp,
beside a car
from which a puffy hand is extended
like a father's hand to a child.
She wants to *be* the blonde,
who's free to choose and discard
the rotten fruit of her desire
and in turmoil retires
to pray all night without solace,
while the other leans into the wide-open door.
Now fast forward
to the fat man on his knees, beside the body
he has just shoved onto the sidewalk,
grief and joy drawing him
down to the wide-open mouth, the purple tongue . . .
Cut! I cry
as I rise from my bed
and enter the other scene
that is shimmering before me.
Though the cameras keep rolling,
I wash off my leading lady's make-up,
unpin her hair.
She's wearing her seductive smile,
pearls, black taffeta, and Shalimar.
I run my hands over her breasts
and down her stomach
into the V where the hair must be almost white,
then I turn her over, lift her dress,
and start to slide toward nothingness.
I keep my hand over her mouth
until I feel her body slacken,
and when I take my hand away,
a growl foams up her throat,
then I'm slamming against the door
she kept locked so long

until it cracks and caves in.
But she's gone.
On the vanity, a tube of Love That Red,
a cake of pale pink powder,
and scribbled across the mirror

No regrets

G

As always, she abandons me
at the scene of a crime of passion,
but this time
I fit the chalk outline on the floor perfectly,
and it's my blood
gushing from a neck wound,
my blood, not hers, splashed over the set,
as if some imitation Jackson Pollock
had flung it against the cardboard walls
and called it art.
How it spills into the pristine
aisles of the theater,
only to coagulate at the feet of the murderer,
who's seated in the first row,
throwing candy wrappers and popcorn.
He wears the bow tie of clean conscience,
the wingtips of respectability,
the frayed charm of an aging boy
so well nobody suspects him,
not the mayor,
or the ladies in floral print dresses,
leaning forward in their seats
like wilted bouquets.
Finally, our exchange of identities is complete,
but now he doesn't want it.
He wants his silent witness back
and suddenly leaps up
and runs into the screen.
With a kiss, he resurrects me.
My double, my failed indemnity

against the starved, merciless self, I say
as I raise my hands to his neck
and squeeze.

EVE'S STORY

One Sunday morning Mama-cat
gave birth to a kitten
with no front legs.
Daddy was just a mouthful of Alabama dust,
but he had strength enough
to twist the kitten's head clean off.
The body was still soft and spongy
when I buried it.
I was sixteen. I left behind my cat,
my sister, and a ragdoll
when I ran down the empty road,
and I didn't stop
until I came to a tent set up in a cotton field.
When the evangelist looked up from the pulpit,
I saw his eyes were the size of blue glass dimes.
That night I joined his pitiful crusade.
I want you to understand
I made my sacrifices willingly,
because no matter what you think,
he didn't believe any less in Jesus
with a whore's titties in his hands,
with her hands pulling and jerking him,
until he shot his seed in a white handkerchief.
Afterwards, we'd pray together, the three of us,
before a painting of the Crucifixion.
Then he'd drive her to some corner
or motel, come back,
and rest his head on my bosom
and call me sweet sister, sweet,
until he met that "decent" girl in Galveston.
When finally he could not stop himself,
I taped her mouth, I held her less,
while he shuddered inside her.

Later, he was so terrified by what he'd done,
I even had to zip his pants.
Then I watched as he apologized to her
on his knees.
"Please," he begged, drawing out the *ease,*
"honey, please."
I said he couldn't help it,
it was my cross
and I bore it out of love.
After all, he'd taught me how to read and write.
She believed it. She was the type —
a white-faced cow
underneath the make-up and Neiman Marcus cloth.
When we packed up, she followed us.
I'd go out and get his whores for him
and she'd join them
while I drank Scotch on the rocks
and read *TV Guide* or did crosswords.
Then I'd drive the whores
back into their ratholes
while the reverend and his press secretary
squabbled about his image. We had gone video,
but I wasn't in them.
I did not fit his image anymore.
Cheryl did, with her blue contacts, blonde hair,
and silicone implants.
I don't remember when I decided.
It wasn't jealousy, nor wanting to do right,
though I pretend it was.
That's too simple.
If they had known about the film I'd make
that one night,
would it have mattered?
When the first call came,
he didn't believe it,
and it was too late when he did.
Everyone began to desert him
while he stayed in his room,
watching the video over and over.
At last, even Cheryl told all on a talk show.

She got an agent, a book contract,
a condo in Beverly Hills,
where celebrities go to party
and complain
about how "rough the public is on us."
We lost everything, of course;
I mean, he did.
I'd saved up for my old age,
so now we live like any other
retired couple in Sarasota,
but we don't socialize.
Cheryl keeps in touch,
and now and then when she's down this way,
we meet for lunch
and don't know what to say to each other,
like sisters who once
had so much in common
but now have nothing but blood between them.
Before our meetings end,
she always takes my hand
and says, "You are a saint,"
then she rises and goes teetering off
on her spike heels,
though today, she does not take her hand away,
but holds mine down on the tablecloth
between the breadsticks and rolls.
We laugh, touching knees under the table,
then she hands me a packet of photographs —
first shot, the reverend, grinning,
as he jacks off into the camera's eye
and me overseeing it all
from my director's chair.
"If you hadn't," she says.
Of a sudden, I realize
this is how Eve must have done it.
The snake and God were only props
she discarded when she left Adam
writhing on the ground.
Once the scent of burning flesh and hair
pressed down upon her like a lover's body.

but now the smell of apple blossoms
hovered in the air,
promising sweet fruit,
promising everything we ever wanted.

REUNIONS WITH A GHOST

For Jim

The first night God created was too weak;
it fell down on its back,
a woman in a cobalt blue dress.
I was that woman and I didn't die.
I lived for you,
but you don't care. You're drunk again,
turned inward as always.
Nobody has trouble like I do, you tell me,
unzipping your pants
to show me the scar on your thigh,
where the train sliced into you
when you were ten.
You talk about it with wonder and self-contempt,
because you didn't die
and you think you deserved to.
When I kneel to touch it,
you just stand there
with your eyes closed,
your pants and underwear bunched at your ankles.
I slide my hand up your thigh
to the scar and you shiver
and grab me by the hair.
We kiss, we sink to the floor,
but we never touch it,
we just go on and on tumbling through space
like two bits of stardust that shed no light,
until it's finished,
our descent, our falling in place.
We sit up. Nothing's different, nothing.
Is it love, is it friendship
that pins us down,

until we give in,
then rise defeated once more
to reenter the sanctuary of our separate lives?
Sober now, you dress,
then sit watching me
go through the motions of reconstruction —
reddening cheeks, eyeshadowing eyelids,
sticking bobby pins here and there.
We kiss outside
and you walk off, arm in arm with your demon.
So I've come through the ordeal of loving once again,
sane, whole, wise, I think as I watch you,
and when you turn back, I see in your eyes
acceptance, resignation,
certainty that we must collide from time to time.
Yes. Yes, I meant goodbye when I said it.

CAPTURE

And that's how I found him,
hoeing weeds
in his garden.
He was shirtless,
his pants rolled below his navel.
I stopped and watched
as he swung the hoe down
to cut the head from a dark red flower.
He looked up then and smiled
and said, "It's like that with men."
He was not handsome;
his face was too flawed for that,
but somehow that made him beautiful,
with his thin hawk's nose over full lips
and the deep lines
that sliced his forehead.
His eyes gleamed
like two pale green chips of ice.
I said, "I'm a stranger here."
"You haven't seen our lake then,

shall I take you there?" he asked.
"When?"
"Now," he said, dropping the hoe.
He began to walk faster and faster
and I had to run to catch up to him.
There was no trail,
but he strode on through bushes that pricked me
and past low-hanging branches
that caught my skirt. Tore my skirt.
Then we were there.
"*Lake,* lake," I cried, then laughed,
threw my head back
the way laborers and drunks do,
and roared, or tried to.
"It's a pond for children to wade in.
At home, at home *we* have a lake
you can swim in;
it takes a whole day to cross it."
He stood with his back to me;
he was oily with sweat
and he shone like some living metal.
He turned to me. "Swim.
Swim?" he said with a question mark.
"I haven't got a suit."
"Ha!" he said. "Ha,"
and rolled his pants up to his waist,
daring me,
then lowered them all the way down.
I covered my eyes, and when I looked
he was walking into the water.
"Modesty, that's your name," he said
over his shoulder.
"And yours?" I asked.
"I don't need a name.
I am what you see."
He laughed and slapped the water
with his long, thin hands.
Then he swam from one side to the other;
he floated on his back
and I watched him, of course I did,

and when he was done,
he lay in the sun,
surrendered to the sun and my eyes.
"Do I pass now?" he asked
as he came to stand in front of me.
Then he said, "Seen one lately?
It's a fine one," he went on,
taking his cock in his hands.
"Touch it."
I shook my head.
"Get you," he said and began to walk off,
but I grabbed his hard, smooth calves
and kissed them,
and with my tongue
licked my way down to his feet
and kissed each toe.
He sank down beside me,
took my face in his hands,
and lifted my head back.
Then he kissed me;
our tongues battered our teeth. Touched.
He raised my skirt with one hand,
pressed me back
and held me to the earth
with the weight of his body.
I bit his shoulder
as he pushed into me again. Again.
I kept my eyes open. He did too.
He stared and stared until he knew.
"You tricked me," he gasped
as he poured himself into my glass
and I drank him like *grappa*
made from grapes
I'd picked with my own hands.

FATE

Sin must be cleansed by more and more blood,
as when the smooth, flat rock

the thin, pinched-faced antiabortionist
is hurling spins for a moment in midair
before it descends like Christ
into the body of a woman,
who cannot defend herself
against the judgment of men and God,
for we have always been the receivers
of what is given without love or permission
or whatever it is
that sends me to the well
as a Roman soldier gallops past,
dragging the body of a zealot
on a rope tied to his horse.
A swirl of dust rises skyward,
then a gust of wind blows it into my eyes.
First, a stinging that becomes an itch,
which radiates outward from my irises
like light from a star,
then Gabriel stepping from a golden cloud
to hold my head in his lap
and tell me how I must have the child,
that this shivering,
this heat and wetness
I feel between my thighs, is not real,
that he never lay beside me,
his robe open,
his man-thing covered by downy hair,
that I never pressed my mouth there
or felt him swell, or sat on him
and lifted myself up and down,
that this morning
as I plucked the Sabbath chicken,
the feathery touch below my navel
was just the spirit growing in me
and that the cry as I fell
with the jug of water was of joy,
the same joy I'll feel
when the head of the son who'll never be mine
rends my pelvis in two.

Now, who comes to me for advice,
who strikes her breasts thrice
to the ringing of bells,
as the smell of frankincense
wafts through motherhood's cathedral.
So many times, I've climbed
from my pedestal to stand among the protesters,
while the cameras beam another tableau of rage
onto television screens
like any other night's entertainment.
If I pushed them aside
to kneel beside the woman, who'd recognize me?
Who'd believe I'd forgive her,
for that is the province of men,
who condemn what they cannot abide.
It is true there are women who cast stones too,
but what if the price of their collusion
were infanticide?
What path would they choose then,
whose child abandoned
on some woman's Via Dolorosa
would they take into themselves
to swim the Fallopian tubes
to fuse to them and grow?
Are some children born to suffer,
because we say so?
If I hadn't let go my own son,
had held on to him only in the abstract,
not the fact,
maybe I'd have spared us all the decision
to have, or not.
I'd have stretched out by the table
laid with speculum, tenaculum, dilators, forceps,
the abortionist's humble tools,
to have my womb vacuumed as clean
as a vacated room.
Instead I lay down
in the blue abyss of His sacrifice
out of love and fear too,

the elemental kind that terrifies children
and those who send Hail Marys up
with the smoke of lit candles,
but Father nails them and their prayers to a stake
through their mother's heart
and departs to the sound of tambourines
and choirs singing,
ringing bells
and the crowd screaming *Baby killer*,
as I finally take my place beside the woman
and say my last Station of the Cross
to lost virginity,
the two of us a same-sex pietà of flesh and blood;
yet once we undressed by the failed light
of God and man's desire
and felt no shame
when He came inside us
with a ferocity that claimed everything we are
and remain.

EVIDENCE: FROM A REPORTER'S NOTEBOOK

1

The city tosses and turns on the third rail
as the intern slams the clipboard on the desk.
He says, "We aren't finished with her yet."
"But Doc," I say, "maybe she's finished with you."
Schmoozing with an edge is what I call this.
He doesn't want the bruise of the six o'clock news
to blue-blacken his name by association.
He just wants someday to escape to a clinic
attached to a golf course
and drive his balls out
into the green bay it overlooks,
while back here, we all cook
in the same old grease
gone rancid from ceaseless poverty and crime.

"If I had a dime," he says, "if I had a dime . . ."
Then his voice trails off
and he stands and tries to swim
through the forty-foot waves
of three whole days and nights without sleep,
but each time, he's thrown back
on the hospital beach,
along with the dirty syringes, gauze,
and those who've drowned
in the contaminated water of their lives.
I say, "You know the hymn that goes,
'Some poor drowning, dying seaman
you may rescue, you may save'?"
"No," he shrugs, "it's more Charles Ives to me,
discord and disharmony
to go with all the inhumanity
that welcomes me each night
with open jaws and glistening teeth.
The victim, if she is one, is down the hall
and on the right. And this time, Maggie,
try to leave the way you came.
Don't make promises, or false claims of justice.
Let the lame stay lame,
don't set them dancing across the floor
in their own blood before they realize it."
"And what?" I say. "Go too far? But Doctor,
they're already there,
along with you and me, we need them,
they feed our superiority complexes.
You don't do Temple, I don't do Church,
but we've got faith, we're missionaries,
in search of some religion, some congregation
to place us in context,
even if it's someone else's.
And she *will* dance, as you and I will
and the TV viewers too,
to the fascinatin' rhythm of vaginal rape
and sodomization with a foreign object.
Hand me my tap shoes. I can't wait."

2

"You some reporter, right?" she says.
"It was a white man did this.
Said it is to show you niggers
who climbed from back of bus
to sit with us.
You nigger bitch, you get what you deserve,
and then he twist my arm behind me.
See the scratches, the splotches.
He drags me through some bushes and I got cuts.
You see 'em. You do.
He bit me too."
She tears at her skirt
and raises her knee, so I can see
high up her inner thigh,
too high, almost to knotted hair where underwear
of shiny fabric, nylon, I guess, begins.
"And when he finished with me," she says,
"he spit between my legs and rub it in."
I have learned not to wince
when such details are given;
still, I feel a slight
tightening of stomach muscles
before I make myself unclench
and do the true reporter thing,
which is to be the victim,
to relive with her again, again,
until it is my own night of degradation,
my own graduation from the shit to shit.
"Go on," she says, "write it down or somethin',
tape it, film it.
We got to hit him hard, hurt him. OK?"
"We will," I say, my smile in place now
like my hair, my friendship a brand-new dress
I wear until I wear it out or down,
but even as I take her hand extended to me,
so that we are banded together
in her stormy weather,
both without raincoats, umbrellas,

I flash on the report just read —
questionable rape, no tears, no bleeding there
or in the other place,
and bites that could be self-inflicted.
"Dirty sonofabitch," I say,
"is this United States of Revenge, or what?
We've got everything we need, got television,
and I have got your story
before the competition."

3

Six straight days, she's front-page news.
She makes guest appearances by dozens.
Everybody's cousin wants their piece
of tender meat,
but I've already eaten there
and I'm still hungry.
I'm suffocating too and I need air,
I need a long vacation from myself
and from my protégée
in all the ways manipulation pays,
when you play off the outrage
and the sympathy of others.
And she's a natural, she was born to do it,
should have her own byline in *New York Times,*
and I should have a Watergate,
should get my chance for Pulitzer glory,
but even Woodward faded like a paper rose
once he got his story.
I mean, you've got to know when to let it ride
and let it go, or else you wind up
some side show in Hackensack, or Tupelo.

You see, I couldn't prove that she was lying
and I couldn't prove she wasn't,
but that doesn't mean I abandoned her.
I swear the story led me somewhere else,
to the truth,
whatever that is, an excuse, I know, but valid.

172

Reality is a fruit salad anyway.
You take one bite, another, all those flavors,
which one is right?
She chose the role of victim
and for a while, I went along,
until tonight, when I look out
my window over Central Park
and think of other women whimpering
and bleeding in the darkness,
an infinity of suffering and abuse
to choose my next big winner from.
What I do, I take my own advice.
I whip my horse across the finish line
before I shoot it.
I step over her body
while the black sun rises behind me,
smoking like an old pistol.
The unofficial rules of this game
are that once found out,
you aim your tear-stained face into the camera.
You make your disgrace, your shame, work for you.
They don't burn bitches anymore,
they greet them at the back door with corsages
and slide them out the front into a reed basket
to float down the Nile, repentance,
into the arms of all us Little Egypts.
Welcome back.

4

My latest eyewitness news report,
focused on false accusations,
took as a prime example
my own delectable sample of the sport.
Even Warhol would have been proud,
would have remained in awe
long enough to list her name in his diaries,
might have understood her appetite,
have gained insight into her need,
though even her staunchest supporters

cannot explain away all contradictions,
all claims of violation that don't add up.
But really, if they only knew, in spite of that,
the lens through which we view the truth
is often cracked and filthy with the facts.
It could have happened. That is the bridge
that links the world of Kafka to us still,
the black pearl in pig's mouth
that won't be blasted out no matter what we do,
that finds us both on Oprah
or on Donahue, facing the packed pews
of the damned and the saved,
to send our innocence,
our guilt, across the crowded airwaves
to be filtered through
the ultimate democracy of TV,
which equalizes everything it sees
and freezes us to the screen between commercials
for movies of the week and shaving cream,
each show a rehearsal for the afternoon
when with a cry
she spreads her chocolate thighs
while I kneel down to look,
but still I find no evidence
of racist's or even boyfriend's semen.
I press my fingers hard against her,
then hold them up before the audience,
wet only with the thick spit of my betrayal.

THE SHADOWBOXER

You know what hunger is, Father,
it's the soothing half-dark
of the library men's room
and the reference librarian,
his head pressed against my thigh
as tears run down his pudgy face.
Sometimes I unzip for him
and let him look,

but never touch, never taste.
After all, I'm here to try to reconcile
the classics
with the Batman-comics philosophy of life,
and this pathetic masquerade,
this can't be life in caps or even lower case.
This is 1955, and all I know is boredom and desire,
so when I leave, I cruise down Main Street
for girls and a quick feel.
They call it the ugliest street in America,
but I don't know yet
that it's just another in a lifetime of streets
that end kissing somebody's feet or ass.
I just tell myself to drive and keep on driving,
but like always, I swerve into our yard.
You're still at Henrahan's,
drunk and daring anyone to hit you,
because you're a man goddamnit.

I climb the stairs to my room
and lie down under your boxing gloves,
hung above my bed
since your last fight in Havana.
When I can't sleep,
I take them down, put them on,
and shadowbox, until I swing,
lose my balance, and fall,
and on the count of six
you rise off the canvas,
only to be knocked backward into the ropes,
sure that half your face
flew out of the ring,
but it was only blood flung
like so much rum from a glass
into all the screaming faces,
into one woman's face
as she stands
and leans into the next spray of blood.
Do it, she cries
as she raises her fists, *do it.*

Bathed, stitched, and taped together,
you manage to dress
and get halfway to the street door
before you feel her
behind you in the darkness primeval,
but when you call, nobody answers
and you're twelfth floor up
Hotel Delirious
with Billie Holiday on the hi-fi.
Don't explain, she sings,
and the rum on the night table,
for the sweet dreams
it never really does bring, sings back, *Do,*
as you perform your latest attempt
to escape you, Father,
and what happened one night
when I stopped believing
even in the power of money to absolve.
Remember?
The first time I had a woman,
I even called your name. You didn't answer,
but you do answer the three short knocks,
and my mother, Rose,
still wearing her blood-spattered clothes,
crosses the threshold.
Turn back before it's too late, I tell her,
as she peels the tape off your face,
licks and kisses your wounds,
then mounts you
and plunges you deeper each time,
crying, *Show me what a good man can do,*
and you, Father, you,
rocking with her
until you must slow her; must ease her off
and stanch the blood above your eye.
Can you feel me, Father, breaking into a run
down conception road,
nothing but nasty business on my mind,
just two steps ahead
of all the bloody noses,

the broken bones
and blackened eyes you'll give me?
Nobody believes the lies you tell,
but they want to
and that's enough.
It's tough without a mother,
but fatherless is tougher on a boy, they say.
Nobody sees how twisted up I am
or how squeezed dry of anything resembling love.
I loved my mother,
but she left us to our few feet of deep space
for the hard chest and thighs of a comer,
the postcards she sent now and then from Venezuela,
Australia, even Paris,
reminding you of what you want to forget,
and when your good eye lingers on your son,
all you see is one more reason to hit him.

Then one night, you stagger to my room.
I don't resist when you slap and kick me.
Faggot, you scream
as you tear my T-shirt and shorts off me,
I heard about the library.
Then, then, you rape me.
You're snoring when I pack my gym bag
and take the boxing gloves
and stuff them in with my underwear
and Old Spice soap-on-a-rope.
I don't know where I'm going,
I just go as far as I can,
which in the end is Bellevue Detox,
is suddenly the smell of Gleason's gym —
men's sweat,
men's armpits, crotches,
men's wins and losses,
all that's left of Rosy Jack, Jack Rose,
middleweight loser
and sometime trainer of other losers mostly
or movie stars
and novelists who think the fights are glamorous,

who want to get in touch with themselves
by hitting someone else,
or for a "serious" role,
but I tell them
it's really all about a boy
finally beaten to submission.
Although he's crying *More*,
because he's been taught to think
he deserves to be punished,
he doesn't hear himself
as he locks the door
to keep his father in the wretched past
where he belongs,
but the past is now,
is you, Father, in this corner
and me in mine, stripped
to your level at last,
as the bell sounds
and the crowd bites down
on its collective tongue,
when the first punch stuns me
and the second knocks me all the way
to kingdom come and gone.

THE COCKFIGHTER'S DAUGHTER

I found my father,
face down, in his homemade chili
and had to hit the bowl
with a hammer to get it off,
then scrape the pinto beans
and chunks of ground beef
off his face with a knife.
Once he was clean
I called the police,
described the dirt road
that snaked from the highway
to his trailer beside the river.
The rooster was in the bedroom,

tied to a table leg.
Nearby stood a tin of cloudy water
and a few seeds scattered on a piece of wax paper,
the cheap green carpet
stained by gobs of darker green shit.
I was careful not to get too close,
because, though his beak was tied shut,
he could still jump for me and claw me
as he had my father.
The scars ran down his arms to a hole
where the rooster had torn the flesh
and run with it,
finally spitting it out.

When the old man stopped the bleeding,
the rooster was waiting on top of the pickup,
his red eyes like Pentecostal flames.
That's when Father named him Preacher.
He lured him down with a hen
he kept penned in a coop,
fortified with the kind of grille
you find in those New York taxicabs.
It had slots for food and water
and a trap door on top,
so he could reach in and pull her out by the neck.
One morning he found her stiff and glassy-eyed
and stood watching
as the rooster attacked her carcass
until she was ripped
to bits of bloody flesh and feathers.
I cursed and screamed, but he told me to shut up,
stay inside, what did a girl know about it?
Then he looked at me with desire and disdain.
Later, he loaded the truck and left.
I was sixteen and I had a mean streak,
carried a knife
and wore such tight jeans I could hardly walk.
They all talked about me in town,
but I didn't care.
My hair was stringy and greasy and I was easy

for the truckers and the bar clowns
that hung around night after night,
fighting sometimes
just for the sheer pleasure of it.
I'd quit high school, but I could write my name
and add two plus two without a calculator.
And this time, I got to thinking,
I got to planning, and one morning
I hitched a ride
on a semi that was headed for California
in the blaze of a west Texas sunrise.
I remember how he'd sit reading
his schedules of bouts and planning his routes
to the heart of a country
he thought he could conquer with only one soldier,
the $1000 cockfight always further down the pike,
or balanced on the knife edge,
but he wanted to deny me even that,
wanted me silent and finally wife
to some other unfinished businessman,
but tonight, it's just me and this old rooster,
and when I'm ready, I untie him
and he runs through the trailer,
flapping his wings and crowing
like it's daybreak
and maybe it is.

Maybe we've both come our separate ways
to reconciliation,
or to placating the patron saint
of roosters and lost children,
and when I go outside, he strolls after me
until I kneel down and we stare at each other
from the cages we were born to,
both knowing what it's like
to fly at an enemy's face
and take him down for the final count.
Preacher, I say, I got my GED,
a AA degree in computer science,
a husband, and a son named Gerald, who's three.

I've been to L.A., Chicago,
and New York City on a dare, and know what? —
it's shitty everywhere, but at least it's not home.

After the coroner's gone, I clean up the trailer,
and later, smoke one of Father's
hand-rolled cigarettes
as I walk by the river,
a quivering way down in my guts,
while Preacher huddles in his cage.
A fat frog catches the lit cigarette
and swallows it.
I go back and look at the picture
of my husband and son,
reread the only letter I ever sent
and which he did not answer,
then tear it all to shreds.
I hitch the pickup to the trailer
and put Preacher's cage on the seat,
then I aim my car for the river, start it,
and jump out just before it hits.
I start the pickup and sit
bent over the steering wheel,
shaking and crying, until I hear Preacher
clawing at the wire,
my path clear,
my fear drained from me like blood from a cut
that's still not deep enough
to kill you off, Father,
to spill you out of me for good.
What was it that made us kin,
that sends daughters crawling after fathers
who abandon them at the womb's door?
What a great and liberating crowing
comes from your rooster
as another sunrise breaks the night apart
with bare hands
and the engine roars
as I press the pedal to the floor
and we shoot forward onto the road.

Your schedule of fights,
clipped above the dashboard,
flutters in the breeze.
Barstow, El Centro, then swing back
to Truth or Consequences, New Mexico,
and a twenty-minute soak in the hot springs
where Geronimo once bathed,
before we wind back again into Arizona,
then all the way to Idaho by way of Colorado,
the climb, then the slow, inevitable descent
toward the unknown
mine now. Mine.

Greed

RIOT ACT, APRIL 29, 1992

I'm going out and get something.
I don't know what.
I don't care.
Whatever's out there, I'm going to get it.
Look in those shop windows at boxes
and boxes of Reeboks and Nikes
to make me fly through the air
like Michael Jordan
like Magic.
While I'm up there, I see Spike Lee.
Looks like he's flying too
straight through the glass
that separates me
from the virtual reality
I watch everyday on TV.
I know the difference between
what it is and what it isn't.
Just because I can't touch it
doesn't mean it isn't real.
All I have to do is smash the screen,
reach in and take what I want.
Break out of prison.
South Central homey's newly risen
from the night of living dead,
but this time he lives,
he gets to give the zombies
a taste of their own medicine.
Open wide and let me in,
or else I'll set your world on fire,
but you pretend that you don't hear.
You haven't heard the word is coming down
like the hammer of the gun
of this black son, locked out of the big house,
while massa looks out the window and sees only smoke.
Massa doesn't see anything else,
not because he can't,
but because he won't.
He'd rather hear me talking about mo' money,

mo' honeys and gold chains
and see me carrying my favorite things
from looted stores
than admit that underneath my Raiders' cap,
the aftermath is staring back
unblinking through the camera's lens,
courtesy of CNN,
my arms loaded with boxes of shoes
that I will sell at the swap meet
to make a few cents on the declining dollar.
And if I destroy myself
and my neighborhood
"ain't nobody's business, if I do,"
but the police are knocking hard
at my door
and before I can open it,
they break it down
and drag me in the yard.
They take me in to be processed and charged,
to await trial,
while Americans forget
the day the wealth finally trickled down
to the rest of us.

SELF DEFENSE

For Marion Barry

Y'all listen to me.
Why can't I get a witness?
Why can't I testify?
You heard the bitch. You heard her say
I can't even caress her breast.
Unless I smoke for sex,
I get next to nothing.
I get set up for spread thighs.
I am the mayor of Washington, D.C.
and I can be as nasty as I wanta.
You think you can chew me up
and spit me down in the gutter,

but I am there already.
I have no other choice.
I am a victim of the white press,
but I have the antidote for all your poison.
The rock of this age is crack
and like the primal urge to procreate,
desire for it surges through you,
until you praise its name
in the same breath as you do Jesus.
The need seizes addicts and lifts them to heaven
by the scruff of the neck,
then hurls them back,
drops in my lap a slut
who wouldn't even squeeze my nuts
for old times' sake,
but made me puff that substitute,
until you FBI came bursting in.
Now I'm sure you think you should have shot me,
should have pretended I pulled a gun
and to defend yourselves, you had to do it.
You could have been through with it.
I could have been just another statistic.
I *am* realistic.
I am a man condemned for his weakness.
Had I been white,
I would have been the object of sympathy, not ridicule.
Trick me? Convict me?
Now, now you know
I'm not a man you can control.
The good ole days of slaves out pickin' cotton
ain't coming back no more. No,
with one drag, I took my stand against injustice.
Must a man give up his vices
because he is the mayor?
You made me a scapegoat,
one black man against the mistah massa race.
You thought I would cave in
and take my whuppin',
take my place
back of the endless soupline of the nineteen nineties,

as if it were still the fine and white fifties,
where y'all drink tea in the palour
and the colored maids don't get no farther
than the next paycheck,
the next hand-me-downs from Mrs. so and so.
Po' ole mammies, po' ole black Joes,
working for low wages.
You don't need to quote my rights to me.
Don't they stick in your throat? Don't they?
All that marching and riding,
even torching Watts and Cleveland
gave us the right to vote,
but reading rights won't make a difference
if the verdict is already in.
You can't depend on nothing.
You got to toughen yourself.
I paid for my slice of American pie,
but you lie and say I stole it.
That is how you hold the nigger down
and beat him to death with his own freedom.

ENDANGERED SPECIES

The color of violence is black.
Those are the facts, spread-eagled
against a white background,
where policemen have cornered the enemy,
where he shouldn't be, which is seen.
Of course, they can't always believe their eyes,
so they have to rely on instinct,
which tells them I am incapable
of civilized behavior,
therefore, I am guilty
of driving through my own neighborhood
and must take my punishment
must relax and enjoy
like a good boy.
If not, they are prepared to purge me
of my illusions of justice, of truth,

which is indeed elusive,
much like Sasquatch,
whose footprints and shit
are only the physical evidence
of what cannot be proved to exist,
much like me,
the "distinguished" professor of lit,
pulled from my car,
because I look suspicious.
My briefcase, filled with today's assignment,
could contain drugs,
instead of essays arranged
according to quality of content,
not my students' color of skin,
but then who am I to say
that doesn't require a beating too?—
a solution that leaves no confusion
as to who can do whatever he wants to whom,
because there is a line directly
from slave to perpetrator,
to my face staring out of newspapers and TV,
or described over and over as a black male.
I am deprived of my separate identity
and must always be a race instead of a man
going to work in the land of opportunity,
because slavery didn't really disappear.
It simply put on a new mask
and now it feeds off fear
that is mostly justified,
because the suicides of the ghetto
have chosen to take somebody with them
and it may as well be you
passing through fire,
as I'm being taught
that injustice is merely another way
of looking at the truth.
At some point, we will meet
at the tip of the bullet,
the blade, or the whip
as it draws blood,

but only one of us will change,
only one of us will slip
past the captain and crew of this ship
and the other submit to the chains
of a nation
that delivered rhetoric
in exchange for its promises.

HOOVER, EDGAR J.

1

I'm the man behind the man
behind the man
and I have got my hands
in everybody's pockets.
I know who's been sticking his plug
in Marilyn Monroe's socket.
The shock it would give,
if everybody knew what King Arthur Jack
won't do to keep his rocket fueled.
I have files on everyone who counts,
yet they would amount to nothing,
if I did not have the will to use them.
Citizens must know their place,
but so must the President,
who simply decided one day
to hock his family jewels to the Mob.
They call me a cruel sonofabitch
just to aggravate me,
but my strength is truth.
I have the proof
of every kind of infidelity
and that makes me the one free man
in a country of prisoners
of lust, greed, hatred, need
greater than the fear of reprisal,
all the recognized sins
and all those unrecognizable,

except to me and God. Maybe God.
Sometimes my whole body aches
and I lie down on the floor,
just staring at the ceiling,
until I am feeling in control again,
my old confidence surging back
through me like electricity
and I get up, Frankenstein, revived
by the weakness of others
and as unstoppable as a handful of pills
that might kill you on a night like this,
like the night when Marilyn kissed it all goodbye.
It only came up roses after her show closed.
Too bad she had to row, row her boat
in lava lake.
They said they would make her a star.
Now far out in space,
her face big as a planet,
she looks down
on the whole pathetic, human race, wasting time,
as it shivers and shakes
down the conga line
behind Jack, Bobby, and me too.
When the voice on the phone
cried *"We're through"* and hung up,
she took an overdose,
trusting someone to save her,
but now she whispers,
"Honey, don't trust anybody
and never, ever fuck the head of state."

2

I had a head bald
as a licked clean plate
and a face . . .
Nobody ever said grace at my table,
yet, the god of judgment hovered over my head.
He led me down
dark halls to motel rooms,

where a locked door
and heavy perfume
could neither conceal, nor contain
the fumes of love that proclaimed
another fallen angel by his name.
Martin Luther King, Jr. preaches freedom,
but it means slavery for the white man.
It hands our keys to the robbers
and says, please, don't take anything.
Look at him on his knees
before pussy's altar.
Tomorrow with his wife beside him
he won't falter, as he shouts
from the pulpit about equality.
His words are a disease sweeping
through the colored people.
I can stop it if I choose.
I can release the tapes, the photographs
and end the so-called peaceful revolution,
but my solution is to sabotage discreetly,
to let someone else take the blame,
the Klan, or even another smoke,
who's younger and not broken in by privilege.
Someone like that Malcolm X,
that showstopping nigger,
who respects no boundaries
and hates the white man,
because he understands him.
He doesn't want to vote,
he doesn't want to tote that bail
in the name of integration.
He wants to sail back into blackness
and I say let him.
There is no such thing as freedom
and there never will be,
even for the white man.
The X-man knows it is eat, or be eaten
and Grandpa Hoover
has the biggest teeth.

3

They all wanted me
to take the A train to anonymity,
those who would seduce their own mothers,
after an audience with the Pope.
The Holy joke I call him.
I'd like to get a tape, or two,
of that crew in Rome.
A two-way mirror
somewhere in the Vatican, the camera rolling,
while some Cardinal is jerking off
over a silver bowl,
until his Vesuvius erupts again and again.
But I digress.
Now Lyndon Johnson and a negress,
that *is* delicious,
something best served on a platter.
Save it until after the elections
when it really matters.
I'm so scattered lately.
I feel like shattering all my Waterford crystal.
Ask me anything you want, but don't touch me.
I keep my pistol loaded.
Don't say I told you. Do.
I want the lowdown sonsofbitches
who betray me to know
I'm on to them like a fly on shit.
I will not rest,
until I spit in their mouths
and piss on their faces. The fools.
J. Edgar Hoover runs this country.
J. Edgar Hoover rules.

HOOVER TRISMEGISTUS

I rode the tail of a comet into the world.
Whether I were Edgar, or Mary
meant nothing to me.

I could be both, couldn't I?
That part was easy,
but what I couldn't tolerate
was the face in the bathroom mirror.
Was I a throwback to some buck
who sat hunched over in the hull
of a ship,
while the whip lashed his back?
"Do I look colored to you?" I ask Clyde,
who always, always turns aside my question,
as if he already knows the truth,
as if I have the proof in my possession
like a passport to destruction,
but a man who has fear on his side
can do anything.
Any dictator knows that.
You think Castro doesn't know it, or Chairman Mao?
There's a man I secretly admired.
We could have used a cultural revolution here.
Hell, we nearly had one.
The House un-American activities were a start,
but we didn't go far enough.
When they called Joe McCarthy's bluff,
he grabbed his nuts and ran
and the others banned together
to save their asses
anyway they could,
except for good old Roy Cohn,
a man after my own heart,
because he has none.
"Mary," he always tells me,
"what a red dress and high heels won't do
to lift a gal's spirits."
He's right.
When I have another one of my nightmares
of walking through high cotton
to a tree, where the boy swinging
at the end of a rope
opens his mouth and speaks to me,
saying, "One more nigger to go,"

I tell Roy to book that suite at the Plaza.
I know that Mississippi
is a state of mind we all carry in us
like a virus that activates
just when we think we're safe,
so of course, it isn't long
before I find my darker side
at a party up in Harlem.
He comes to me only once,
the love that twice dares not
speak its name.
See my divine black boy, fumbling with his zipper
while I wait impatiently,
hoping someone will see
that I am being had against my will
that I will deny the darkie inside me by killing him.
Still, he rises when he's done with me,
the gunshot wound through his heart
still bleeding profusely,
the knife still protruding from his back.
In other words, he is my destiny.
Afterward, Roy arranges transportation for him,
plus a few dollars.
He tells him to chalk it up
to experience and let it be,
because there is no future in loving me.
I like *that.*
"You hear me, boy?" Roy asks him.
"Yes," he whispers.
"Yes, what?" asks Roy.
"Yes, sir!"
He may as well say, yes, master.
"Ask her," the boy says, meaning me,
"whether or not she is satisfied."
"Please," says Roy, "leave while you still can."
After that, my experiments in degradation
begin in earnest.
How many nights do I fight my desire
by giving in to it
and dreaming about him?

How many times do I pull down his pants
as he now swings from that rope,
only to find bloody holes,
where his genitals should be
and foiled again,
descend into the ship of myself,
where the slaves are jammed in so tightly,
all I can see is a mass of darkness,
not people,
though I can smell them,
though it is nothing compared
to the smell of my own fear,
because it's here I belong,
here on the endless crossing
into whiteness.

JACK RUBY ON ICE

"Shit, I heard they [Ruby and Oswald] were queer for each other."
—*Double Cross*, SAM AND CHUCK GIANCANA

A man needs ammunition,
because a bullet at the right time
accomplishes the ultimate divorce
and simplifies business.
I, myself, believe that force
allows the resolution of conflict.
I also believe in the right to bear arms
and the God-given right to settle scores,
but I did not measure my courage
by the size of my dick,
which I shook always after I peed,
so I would not stain my jockeys,
though people claim I was careless
with my appearance
and kept a dirty apartment—
rolls of toilet paper strewn on the carpet,
along with cigar butts, wads of money
condoms (so what?),

and other stuff too useless to name.
On that same floor, I lay with whores
without touching once,
if they were not clean,
if they had not washed
with hot water and Dial soap
that would not float like Ivory,
but was better for germs.
Imagine. A man stands trial among gentiles,
who regard him as the enemy,
a Jew they think will steal the pennies
off a dead man's eyes:
therefore, no one comes to his rescue.
Promises are broken.
I am not a man made in the image of my protectors,
so what do I get?—zilch.
Yet, I pay my debts, because I am a stand-up guy.
Even so, they song and dance me.
They light a powder keg under my feet,
which I must tell you always gave me trouble—
calluses, corns, bunions, toenails ingrown.
The chiropodist's office was my home away.
I spent a fortune just to be able
to walk without pain.
Still I could handle whatever came my way
and I can say that without a trace of shame.
A man can brag, if a man's aim is good enough.
But where was my glory,
where was my flag for wrapping in
when shots were fired
and the hired man collapsed
before the other hired man,
who once handed him cold cash
for services rendered
after Lee surrendered cherry like a bride?
Dream lover, he says, you are so mean.
I hit him, sure, not hard,
but just enough to make it rough and make him ready.
I am no fucking queer,
but a man, who enjoys the respect of other men.

I bend him over the couch, take out my strap
and whack his ass, then *him* I allow in my bed.
Afterward, I bathe him with these hands.
I lather him and wash him
the way a mother would a child.
My Lee was an adventurous boy.
One night, he even shows up with an MP,
the kind who calls you kike
and expects you to lick his spit-shined boots
and like it. I am as mad as hell at Lee.
He hits me back. First time.
The smile on his face like the day I shot him.
Next weekend, Ferrie the fairy arrives
and I have to put up with *his* craziness.
He brings a rat in a cage, gets drunk,
lets it out, sobers up. No rat.
He claims he's lost the cure for cancer.
I go out and buy another rat
and pretend I've found the other.
He cannot tell the difference.
Peace restored.
We turn to more pressing problems.
"People with an interest are asking
what we do about Lee," he says,
fixing me with what he thinks is a theatening stare.
"In competition, you know, sports, someone wins
and someone is eliminated."
I nod, no more.
"The door," he asks, "is closed on this then?"
"With a bang," I tell him.
When he's gone, I do some calculating.
I have troubles with the IRS.
There are threats to be met with action.
I am a man without regrets, yet, I know this thing
with Lee will not be easy to forget.
By now, he is like a son to me
and I am Abraham with no reprieve,
because unlike God,
men do not have the luxury of mercy.
So Lee becomes the patsy

and we dishonorable men
obey the first rule of self-preservation,
which is to find a fool to take the blame.
When it's him, or me
who needs a complicated explanation?
Another lone gunman has a plan,
but sometimes plans go awry.
He doesn't realize he, too, is a sacrifice,
until he smells his own flesh burning.

A President is taken by surprise
under the wide-open skies of Texas.
The kings of hearts cry,
"Off with Jack O'lantern's head,"
and two long days later,
I fill the chamber of my snub-nosed .38
with a silver bullet.
I am so patient, standing in the basement,
wearing a new shirt, tie, and suit,
old shoes, my favorite hat.
News is what I am going to make.
I will hand out interviews
as if they are doubloons
and replace Kennedy's and Oswald's faces.
When the elevator doors open,
I stride forward like a businessman
going to make the deal of a lifetime,
but all I do is seal my fate in concrete.
I do not even feel the trigger.
I am as numb as Lee is stunned by my betrayal.
The trap sprung at last, he passes into oblivion
and I pass gas from another bad meal
of pastrami and green onions
and the fact that my ass is now
on the griddle being done.
I am afraid my mask will slip
and I will tip the scales of justice
in the direction of the other assassins,
behind the rose-colored glass,
where Oswald and Ruby take the fall

and all the evidence is made to fit the crime,
at least until I've been abandoned by my friends.
Only then, I say, Chief Justice, I am in danger.
I will tell all if you arrange safe passage to D.C.,
but I receive a strange answer.
Can it be the Chief is a master of deception too?
The Chief says, "You do what's best."
My request for sanctuary is denied.
Now I am nothing but cancer cells.
Even my wife, Sheba, wouldn't recognize me.
So she is a dachshund?
She is the only woman good enough for me.
If only we could be together,
but I walk alone down a tunnel of white light,
then come out in a field of sunflowers,
their heads nodding hello, goodbye.
Some old acquaintances
whose names I can't remember
slap my back, then wander off
and I settle into an endless afternoon
without punishment, or reward
until a dark angel
in the guise of an evangelist
from Los Angeles appears
with the sword of justice in one hand
and a video camera in the other.
He offers me the chance to dance
on the graves of the slaves to the official story,
but why bother?
I bow my head over the edge of the precipice,
where the life I lead
lies dead in its own arms,
while the other victims of the resurrection
are stumbling toward an open car.
They are doomed to repeat the past,
but who can prove the truth
really isn't what you make it,
when it's so easy to fake?
Yet, his argument is so convincing that I waver.
I'll cooperate for one small favor, I tell him,

so we negotiate a detour on the road
to reopened files.
Now, on a city street,
paved with fool's gold,
I testify about the abuse of firearms
and the absolute power of lies,
then I take the few glistening coins from my hat
and throw them in the air.
They rise and rise, then fall back
on the eyes of America,
D-O-A inside a cardboard box.

OSWALD INCOGNITO & ASTRAL TRAVELS

I've seen that face before,
staring at me
from the sixth floor
of the School Book Depository.
Is it déjà vu,
or is it the old story
of finally seeing yourself
in someone else's eyes?
Fake eyes, like the one
Sammy Davis Jr. wore
and used to slip into a stranger's glass of booze.
Once it got caught in somebody's throat.
They had to cut him open.
After Sammy washed it in boiling water,
he popped it back in.
He winked at himself in the mirror,
then he disappeared in a flash of gunfire
left over from the last hour of the assassin,
when three shots either narrowed, or widened, a plot,
depending on how you look at it,
not how it happened.
It wasn't easy being two places the same time,
but I managed the rarest of all magic tricks
with the flick of an eyelid,
I split down the middle,

I ran two directions,
but the lesson in this is
I ran in a circle,
came back where I started.
In my palm, a coin
was gleaming like twilight.
I dropped it down the slot
and got a Coke for my trouble.
The bubbles went up my nose.
I closed my eyes,
but that was no defense
against the magnificence of murder.
I admit to losing my perspective.
I couldn't see not only
that I had become ineffective,
but expendable,
so it was natural that the prime directive
would be to eliminate me.
Who could have predicted
that the shooter would be the man,
who kept boys as, uh, roommates,
who carried rolls of toilet paper
wherever he went as a talisman against disaster
sent straight to the bowels
and expelled with a howl of pleasure.
I'm only here to give voice
to what you've been thinking,
but were afraid to say in front of witnesses,
because they, too, could be the enemy
sent to do you in on TV,
which is itself a form of not being seen.
From the time I was a kid, I hid,
you know, in the back of my mind,
where it's cluttered with boxes of old comics,
whose heroes seduce children
into believing that evil and good
can be recognized by a kiss on the lips,
but my Judas pissed in his coffee,
before offering a sip.
It tasted like it always had,

slightly bitter, then sweet.
I knew what it meant
when Jack stepped from the shadows,
yet, I wanted to believe he was rescuing me.
I would take the gun
and in the best cowboy tradition,
go down in a hail of bullets,
In a split second, I imagined my hand
gripping the weapon,
but as I lay in the ambulance,
I understood the significance
of my death by deception.
Since I had only assumed the identity of myself,
it was somebody else who died,
who'd been saved by his unwitting defection from life.
Termination is, after all, a kind
of natural selection for spies.
It implies survival by escape
from the mass suicides of the pack.
Clowns like Jack Ruby move
through a crowd undetected,
but I am unprotected,
even my pubic hair isn't safe from scrutiny.
I'm not there either.
If I'm anywhere, I'm still trapped
in the palace of lies,
where I'm clothed in illusion
and fed confusion with a spoon.
I take the steps downstairs two-at-a-time.
I flip a penny to see if I should go.
Heads! I stay, but in a moment of panic,
I write my name on the wall
beside the Coke machine. OSWALD
in capital letters.
I erase it with spit and my shirttail,
but it keeps reappearing,
each time the letters get larger,
until the "O" is a hole
I can walk through
and when I finally do, it closes around me

like a mouth around the mouth of a rifle.
The question, though,
isn't what's in a name,
but what's in the barrel.
The answer is nothing,
but when I follow the arrow,
I find it pointing straight at me,
huddled beside a window,
as the President rides by unsuspecting,
only his eyes reflecting surprise
at the moment of impact.
Only one of his eyes breaks free of the socket
and is launched like a rocket,
while a man, shining shoes stops to listen,
as "Birth of the Blues" wafts down the alley,
from a club where Sammy is playing
to standing ovations.
"I need a vacation," Sammy thinks,
when a patron drinks the martini,
where the glass eye is hidden
among the olives and pearl onions
like a gunman on a grassy knoll.
Later, with my shoes buffed to a high sheen,
I stroll into the club,
when Sammy gets booed off the stage,
because of a joke he played that backfired.
"Show's over," the manager tells
the assortment of losers and swells,
so Sammy sits down at the bar.
I offer him a Cuban cigar,
then I light up another.
We smoke in silence,
broken only by the shush
of cars through the slush
of November, turning to winter.
"Ain't it a bitch," Sammy says, at last,
pitching ash in his whiskey,
which he drinks anyway.
"They killed the President
and it's like nothing happened."

I nod, I tug at my threadbare shirt,
as if it can protect me
from the infinite cold.
"One more for the road, babe?" he asks.
I say, no, one last toast
to the President, before I go,
then I raise my glass,
open my mouth wide and swallow.

PARTY LINE

The phone rang this morning,
which is strange,
because our phones rarely work.
No, not even mine.
I stood beside it, my hand
suspended above the receiver.
Finally, I told my aide to answer it,
but the ringing stopped when he picked it up.
As soon as he set it back, however,
it began to ring again.
I started counting backward
5, 4, 3, 2. On 1, I said
Esta es una mala noticia?
The voice repeated my question in English.
Is this bad news?
When I didn't respond, he said, *Fidel?*
There was something familiar about his voice
that came out of the past
the way Kirk Douglas comes for Robert Mitchum
in that movie of the same name.
What comes is back pay, I mean payback.
That's how the Americans say it, no?
But what did I owe this voice
and what did I have left to give,
except my life—the truth, maybe,
but what good would it do me, or you, Jack? I said,
because at last I realized who had phoned me
from his private zone of twilight.

Can I speak to Che,
or is this line restricted to former heads of state?
Only silence greeted my laughter,
then he said, *Why don't you let go too*
like the Russians? You might save your ass and space
on the last plane out, after the coup.
Take the advice of someone who knows
how easily a head explodes
when shot at close range.
I fought a war, remember?
The revolution that broke the stranglehold
you corrupt capitalists had around our balls.
We were even starting to grow breasts.
Yes, I saw with my own eyes,
but instead of destroying our resolve,
it gave us the strength to go on.
Can you say the same?
What did your death inspire? What fierce battles
raged in your memory?
Who paid for your death, aside from that,
what did he call himself, patsy,
who wasn't even guilty?
OK, I said it.
I wrote the book on conspiracies.
Wasn't I the victim of dynamite,
jammed in exhaust pipes, poison pills,
the infamous cigars
and a live grenade in a bar of soap?

I turn everything into a question,
because it keeps the curious at bay.
I disarm that way.
Only Celia knew the true Fidel.
The rest is a ruse.
I'll tell you a joke.
You know how to diffuse a bomb?—
you throw yourself on top of it.
Yes, I know you landed on that blond bomb
of a different kind, though just as lethal.

She shared your secrets. She had keys
to doors that should not be opened.
My friend, it is the nature of whores
to seek to reform themselves by using honesty
the way they once used sex.
It too becomes a commodity.
It is the sweetest revenge.
The sinned against use it
to defend their tarnished honor,
even if it destroys them.
Marilyn Monroe saw you and Bobby
for what you were then,
young men propelled
into a dangerous liaison by their appetites,
but you fooled her. You were not controlled by them.
You were merely compromised,
but she was dead. What a price she paid.
Instead of wedding bells,
she got a lonely immortality.
Eventually, you found your own way there.
Perhaps she got what she wanted after all,
but we did not.
I have lived to see a state of anarchy
descend on my allies
because of a lack of faith.
The Soviets call it dissolution,
as if it were an Alka Seltzer tablet,
dropped in a glass of water.
All that waste, all that haste to get a crumb
off the rapidly emptying table
of the United States.
If this is the answer to our problems,
it has come too late.
In 1963, assassins' guns
severed the one tie I had with anyone
I respected in that government of imperialists,
cut down the only man of vision.
You were a man like me.
I kicked the Mafia out of Cuba, United Fruit,

eliminated prostitution, gambling,
raised the literacy rate.
So I clamped down on intellectuals, created strawberries
which had no taste,
bred cows that gave neither milk, nor meat,
had to import enough to eat, and fuel.
A cruel, unenlightened leader would have killed.
I merely imprisoned those who had defied me
and denied the revolution its due.
A true leader can admit he made mistakes
for the greater good.
Fidel is Cuba; Cuba is Fidel.
I will not lie about my ties to the Medellin Cartel.
Selling drugs is not my business,
no matter what they say,
but the CIA knows all about such things.
I needn't tell you that.
Just follow the trail of disinformation back
to the assassination.
A man in my situation
has to be prepared to slow dance with his enemies.
Everything is permissible
in the struggle for liberation, or for domination.
Therefore, black is white is gray.
Today, I may condemn the man who shot my friend,
tomorrow embrace him.
Statesmanship demands the pistol, the whip,
the kiss of betrayal
and the slipperiness of eels.
I became a master of concealment,
because I knew the game was played for ideology.
Even you were only skin,
stretched over the crumbling page of history.
When you understand you are expendable,
you begin to control your destiny,
while other men become its victims.
I admit misgivings.
I may have outlived my usefulness.
Perhaps I should retire to a ranch
and raise llamas and ostriches,

creatures as exotic as I am now.
The thought torments me.
Has the pried-open fist of thirty-odd years
suddenly revealed socialism as another bankrupt ideal,
sealed in the blood of martyrs to the cause?
No, I cannot believe it. No, even to you
from whom out of respect, I hide nothing,
I still say, save socialism.
Socialism, or death.

MIRACLE IN MANILA

A man could never do
as much for Imelda
as a pair of shoes.
I always knew if she had to choose,
it would be pumps instead of passion.
Although her Ferdinand was handy
with his tongue and his fingers,
she preferred to linger
over coffee and a stack of magazines
rather than to have him between her legs.
I could only get the flower
of the Philippines in bed,
when I was dressed in a red jock strap
and tap shoes.
Even then, she might fade
into another rambling monologue,
or nap fitfully,
until I tap-danced and sang, "Feelings,"
a song I hated,
but marriage is a compromise
and many times, I had to sing two choruses,
before she woke and sang along
and with the last ounce of my energy,
I would take off those goddamn shoes
and do my duty as a man.
A woman like Imelda
must be wooed again and again,

because she is controlled by her moods,
which are dark and greedy,
and every day, they chew her up
and spit her out,
less a few clothes and jewels
and more of the slum she came from.
Now she's too old to play the ingenue.
The loyal few won't admit
that she no longer matters.
They grovel at her feet,
while she holds court
in a hotel suite.
Otherwise, she's mostly ignored,
so isolated and bored with herself,
she takes to her beloved stores.
She gives away her shopping bags of evening clothes
to the poor maids,
who have no more use for them than I do,
lying in my refrigerated coffin.
Finally, she has a meeting with Mother B,
who has been crucified every Good Friday
for the last five years.
Between sips of diet soda and tears,
Imelda decides the time is right
for her own brief sojourn on the cross,
so she goes to San Fernando with her entourage.
She wears a simple shift designed in Paris,
and handmade flats.
She even holds the special nails,
soaked in alcohol for a year,
to her nose, and inhales,
before she lets the attendants
drive them into her hands and feet,
just missing bones and blood vessels.
Only a few heartbeats and she is down,
waving to the crowd,
who shout her name,
as if she really is the President.
It's then she starts to bleed
from her palms.

Somebody screams, then they all do.
It seems like hours
before they rush toward her,
tearing at her clothes, her hair,
pleading for cures, for food,
for everything they've ever needed.
Only gunfire drives them back
and she flees, both horrified and pleased
that the trick worked.
Once the fake blood's washed off,
she stares at her hands,
almost wishing she really had stigmata.
She doesn't even make the news.
I mean, they get her confused with Mother B,
who seizes credit for the "miracle."
Imelda lets it go.
She settles for self-mockery
and sings "Memories,"
while her guests dine on Kentucky Fried Chicken,
flown in by Federal Express.
When she's alone, she gets undressed
and lies down,
not even bothering to get beneath the covers.

Next morning, they find her
drained of her blood,
but her heart's still beating
and she suddenly sits up,
repeating my name.
She says in a vision,
I gave her a pair of magic slippers,
that allow her to walk on water.
She's lying, but I'm past caring
and I'm done with shoes.
Anyway, she doesn't need me,
because she's got her illusions.
After a transfusion, a facial,
and a manicure,
she's campaigning again, although it's useless
and I'm back tap-dancing by her side,

while she proclaims herself
the only candidate
who can rise from the dead.

KNOCKOUT

For Desiree Washington and Mike Tyson

So Miss Desiree Washington was a feast
for the sweet beast.
Well, I ain't no good Christian girl.
Ain't nobody gonna give up they seat
on the bus for me.
I don't even get nothing to eat
before they have me up against the wall,
or down on the floor.
Y'all think it's all the same
that we just poor black crackwhores
lay on our asses all day,
then come out at night like vampires
to suck up all your money.
Y'all think we spread our legs
and AIDS comes flying out.
Say we get paid to do it.
Got no right to fight
if y'all men get it into y'all heads
to make us fuck a whole housefulaniggers for free,
then kick us in the teeth,
'cause we gave it up easy,
but y'all folks look at her a different way.
Y'all say she respectable, educated.
Say Tyson shoulda waited
'til he found himself a squeezer like me.
Y'all say nothing shaking there 'cept her hair,
but this where I disagree, see,
'cause it's a fine line
between rape and a good time.
You find that out real fast
when you got an uninvited dick up your ass.
It ain't that far from "Star Search"

to leaning in car windows
asking for more money than you ever gonna get,
even if you shit gold.
This one bitch know what she talking about.
I ain't gonna shut up.
This is my mouth. You ain't paying my rent.
I ain't got no pimp.
I don't need no sonofabitch taking my money.
I let them bill collectors do that.
I got two kids living with my mama.
She trying to take 'em
like she gonna be able to raise 'em by herself.
She says I'm irresponsible,
a whore and a drug addict.
It's just talk. She take my money, don't she?
Then she walk over to the store,
get her some wine and a pack of cigarettes
before she buy them kids a thing to eat.
I seen her do it. But they clean, though.
They got a place to sleep.
I can't say that.
I got evicted last week.
Come home, found all my shit in the street.
Niggers picking through it like it was trash.
Had to almost fight to get my own shit back.
One of my friends out there.
He said, "Rhonda, what you doing back so early?"
And what she doing out with a man
that time of morning,
if she so goody-goody?
I'll tell you what.
She think 'cause she special,
she gonna be safe.
Hell, ain't nobody safe no more.
She walk into the lion's cage,
but she ain't Daniel.
She just another black girl
in a man's world
and she on the bottom getting fucked
just like I am.

FINISHED

You force me to touch
the black, rubber flaps
of the garbage disposal
that is open like a mouth saying, ah.
You tell me it's the last thing I'll feel
before I go numb.
Is it my screaming that finally stops you,
or is it the fear
that even you are too near the edge
of this Niagara to come back from?
You jerk my hand out
and give me just enough room
to stagger around you.
I lean against the refrigerator,
not looking at you, or anything,
just staring at a space which you no longer inhabit,
that you've abandoned completely now
to footsteps receding
to the next feeding station,
where a woman will be eaten alive
after cocktails at five.
The flowers and chocolates, the kisses,
the swings and near misses of new love
will confuse her,
until you start to abuse her,
verbally at first.
As if trying to quench a thirst,
you'll drink her
in small outbursts of rage
then you'll whip out your semiautomatic,
make her undress, or to listen to hours
of radio static as torture
for being amazed that the man of her dreams
is a nightmare, who only seems happy
when he's making her suffer.

The first time you hit me,
I left you, remember?

It was December. An icy rain was falling
and it froze on the roads,
so that driving was unsafe, but not as unsafe
as staying with you.
I ran outside in my nightgown,
while you yelled at me to come back.
When you came after me,
I was locked in the car.
You smashed the window with a crowbar,
but I drove off anyway.
I was back the next day
and we were on the bare mattress,
because you'd ripped up the sheets,
saying you'd teach me a lesson.
You wouldn't speak except
to tell me I needed discipline,
needed training in the fine art
of remaining still
when your fist slammed into my jaw.
You taught me how ropes could be tied
so I'd strangle myself,
how pressure could be applied to old wounds
until I cried for mercy,
until tonight, when those years
of our double exposure end
with shot after shot.

How strange it is to be unafraid.
When the police come,
I'm sitting at the table,
the cup of coffee
that I am unable to drink
as cold as your body.
I shot him, I say, he beat me.
I do not tell them how the emancipation from pain
leaves nothing in its place.

RESPECT, 1967

The porch light isn't even on,
when I come home, ready to fight.
My wife hopes I'll trip on the steps,
crack my head open and bleed to death,
so that when she gets up,
all she has to do is phone the police,
the ambulance, and my mother,
who will agree with her that I had it coming,
coming home all hours, slamming doors,
all the while godamning women and children,
who stand in the way of a man's good time.
You bitches, I yell, as I go
from empty room to occupied,
I decide how much is too much noise,
so get ready, because I'm putting on Aretha Franklin.
She knows what I need,
although what I've got is marriage,
is babies and bills,
instead of chills up the spine
and wine chilled on ice
by a nice piece of ass,
who doesn't talk back.
You sluts are going to take what I'm giving,
whether it's beatings, or dick.
A man is not kneeling for whores.
Open your doors, or I'll kick them in,
or I'll send a whole legion of men,
armed with their rage
against the paycheck that must be saved for diapers
and milk, Tampax
and all the messy stuff that is female,
when us males want silk underwear
to tear off strange women, who don't care
if we're late, if we're impotent, or make requests
for sex, sex, and sex
and let us go spinning like the asteroids we are,
broken off from one planet of responsibility
to ram ourselves into another,

or to burn up in the atmosphere
of the fear that is manhood.

FAMILY PORTRAIT, 1960

"Sutton," my wife says,
"the girls won't wash between their legs."
What am I supposed to do about it? I think,
having just come in
from buying round steak
that I will try to tenderize with a mallet,
then salt and pepper, dredge in flour
and fry
and serve with green peas, biscuits, gravy.
But Stella (Peggy to her friends),
yells from her bed,
"Girls, go in the bathroom
and take off your clothes."
She leans back on her pillow,
a box of Melba toast,
cradled in one arm
like a cardboard teddybear,
a barrier against the poverty and disappointment
which have put her there. Colitis, doctor says.
And where is this?—
one of those apartments
with a courtyard in Los Angeles,
where waitressing in cafe once
she served the guy from TV,
Route 66, that is, coffee,
but now I bring her coffee, bring her cigarettes
and pretend to sympathize,
but now my daughters stand before me,
wearing only shower caps:
Roslynn, seven years,
thin and unpredictable,
and Florence, eleven,
also thin and obedient to a fault.
I hand them washcloths, soap,

and shoo them in the shower.
They stand in the water
and wait for my commands.
"Go on," I say, "you know how to start."
Necks and shoulders, chests, backs and bellies.
Down they go and in between the smooth,
hairless entrances into themselves.
"You call that washing?" I say,
and lean forward on my toes,
bend my knees and spread them.
"See," I say
and use my hand between my own legs,
"like this, get in there,
scrub your little pussies."

After dinner,
Florence washes dishes, Roslynn dries.
Stella watches television,
while I doze
and chaos kept at bay,
lies down to sleep with us
until daylight.

LIFE STORY

For Father Ritter and other priests accused of sexual abuse.

Nuns are the brides of Christ,
but priests are His sons,
sons denied the sexual release
of giving themselves up to the spirit.
Christ is not raped, until he hails Caesar,
no, not Him,
but isn't it logical,
can't we imagine it going that far?
For examined in that context,
the rest snaps into place.
To rape is to erase the other's identity
and replace it with your own,
so why not ram it home, eh,

the Roman way (copied from the Greeks, of course).
Strip Him, whip Him, bend Him over and . . .
Suddenly, I imagine the blond hustler
with the black Georgia O'Keefe crosses
tattooed on his butt cheeks.
Ah, let me count the ways.
But most days, I conduct myself
in a conventional fashion.
I perform my desperate acts only in my thoughts.
I talk to God from one side of my mouth.
I say Mass, pass out the host
and most of the time,
I only drink wine for consolation,
but once in a while,
I raise the black flag of moral surrender
and I get out my visual aids.
My hand trembles, as I turn each page,
where men and boys are displayed like offerings,
their cocks to be seized and squeezed,
until I drown in jizzum,
until I leave my prison
to walk the tightrope
to the next broken boy,
the next indiscretion that could destroy me.
This one's what they used to call consumptive.
"Do you need a place to stay?" I ask.
In bed, he says, he's afraid of the dark,
so I leave the light on.
Toward daylight, I strike.
He says, "Daddy, don't,"
but daddy do and do
and when I'm through,
I give him a few dollars
and a card that says
Need Help? Call 1 (800) 4-Refuge.
But what about my own help line to salvation?
The voice always says,
I'm not in right now, leave a message,
so at the sound of sizzling flesh,
I repeat my request for rescue.

What is it I want to escape?
Are the boys merely substitutes
to save me from some greater abomination?
In my dreams, the centurion has my face,
holds Christ by the waist
and kisses his navel,
sticks his tongue there,
surprised to find the taste
of honey filling his mouth.
The sound of bees also fill his ears,
as he spreads his cloak on the floor
and shoves Christ down on it.
When he feels stinging in his groin,
he finds his pubic hair alive with bees.
His cock swells to an enormous size,
turns black and he dies,
staring into Christ's eyes.
Still He had not spoken,
had seemed to open and open Himself
to the centurion,
only to take His revenge
at the moment of consummation.
Am I going somewhere with this,
or am I only trying to discover who is who
in the locked room of sexual abuse?
One is the picture
and the other is the frame around it.
I found it!—the photograph
of Father Harrigan and me when I am five.
He holds me in his lap.
I'm tired, though I've had my nap.
It's June, I mean he said he had a june bug,
to come to his room to see.
Did I say he is my uncle?
By the time I'm thirteen,
we have so many secrets between us—
my tiny hand, a penis
that I stroke
the way he taught me,
he who bought me my first missal

and who later welcomes me into the seminary.
He teaches me how to capture little boys
with promises of toys,
until a free meal
becomes the lure
with which the fish
are hooked, then filleted
and cooked.
I remember how he shook me,
when I wouldn't touch.
"Do not tease me, boy. Please me," he said,
"or, or . . ."
He shuddered, he jerked away from me
and that was that, until next time.
Finally, I'm at his grave.
When I fall on my knees, father pulls me up.
"I know everything," he whispers, "I know.
When we get home, you pack. You leave."
When he has his final heart attack,
I sit with his body for hours.
I think some power to change
may drain from him to me,
but I feel nothing
brushing against my soul,
except the old urge.

After the funeral,
mother and I find letters from my uncle
in a tattered, old suitcase.
Before I can stop her, she opens them.
She smothers a cry
when she comes to the photograph of me
in the buff, a dust broom
stuck up my anus.
I stare at it, amazed I had forgotten it happened.
Uncle begs forgiveness, in each letter,
but father never forgives.
The last, dated the year before he died
is five pages (the shortest).
Again he describes how he robbed me of my innocence,

but says I can at least do good as a priest.
Twice mother tries to speak.
At last, she says, "You were always such a sweet boy."
She rips the letters up
and throws them in the trash.
"And give me that," she cries.
Finally, the photograph in shreds, she opens her hands
in a gesture of helplessness,
then says, "I'll fix you supper."

Later, we embrace and I go outside.
I spread my arms around the ancient oak,
where uncle tied me once,
until I took him inside my mouth.
I thought my throat would close,
but instead it froze open,
while snow and semen
spilled down into me.
I was ten and I was praying to die,
praying I would choke,
while he commanded me to open wider.
Finally, I couldn't breathe.
I passed out and when I came 'round,
my mouth tasted of soap.
Uncle spoke, "Lie on your side."
I felt him poking me with something,
then I felt myself pried apart,
as I began to lose consciousness again.

"Still friends?" he asked next time.
"What are you drawing?"
It was a flying man, his head
severed from his body
and falling to earth,
but I said, "It's the Holy Ghost."
"No," he said, "this is your uncle,
this is the end of hope."
He hung himself with rope.
We priests did our best to hide it,
pretended not to know the truth,

though the proof was in his room.
One filthy magazine after another
and nude photos, scattered on the bed and floor
were there for unavoidable discovery.
They delegated me the burning
of the evidence,
the lies about the whys of his closed casket.
We found a way around it all,
got him into hallowed ground.
An accident, a fall, we told everyone.
Hit his head, bled profusely,
found dead hours later . . .
I slammed his head against the radiator,
then notified the police.
We came to an agreement
for the good of the Church.
They would not release the report.
We could sort it out ourselves, couldn't we?

I throw my duffle in the car
and back out of the drive.
When the hustler I pick up
moves across the seat,
I feel no beast rising beneath his hand.
"Go on, get out," I say
"and stay away from creeps like me."
"I'll see you again," he says, because he knows.
I know he will too, unless I lose my head some afternoon
and like a June bride, marry groom death.
At the next intersection,
I head west, instead of south.
Along the way, I shed my priesthood
like a skin.
I work my way from one end
of decline to another.
Sometimes I drink for days,
then take any job that pays enough
for sandwiches.
After two thousand miles, I sell the car
and tend bar in Wickenburg,

until a memory disturbs my false serenity.
Twin boys, who lived on our street,
forced to eat off the floor,
while uncle bored into them
with a vibrator.
Later, he showed a video of Peter Pan,
which was written by a man
not too different from me,
for as I understand it,
Captain Hook may be taken
as the unexpressed desire
to molest a child, to threaten him with harm,
then ultimately to defile him.
Now when people stare at the stub
where my hand was, I smile and rub it,
as if a genie will appear
and grant three wishes.
I am that which I fear.
Is that why you cleared out, uncle dear,
though here you are in a puff of smoke,
the scar of your life healed over now.
How much farther must I go?
Why is my destination so uncertain?
What is the difference between nothing and zero?
Cackling, you fade to black
and I'm staring through the bars
at LA County, where I am incarcerated
for another sex-related incident
that escalated into violence.
He participated willingly I told them,
as the boy was hustled off
to join the war against the saints,
who aren't just the good ones, no,
but also the ones who struggle again and again
against the flow of raw sewage,
only to drown in its undertow.

THE ICE CREAM MAN
National Ice Cream Day, 1991

You know what I've got
in my white van besides popsicles,
Eskimo pies, and ice cream sandwiches?
Little girl, I've got video cameras, props,
cans of whipped cream for hot fudge sundaes
that are not for eating, but for teasing
the camera and the man behind it.
Come on in, Sherry.
Suck a pop-up for Jerry.
Get it way down your throat. You won't choke.
Old Jerry won't let you. Let me get you another.
Your mother won't mind.
How 'bout if I give you this shiny new dime?
Abracadabra! See? It's yours,
if you give me something too.
Fair's fair, right?
And if the boogie man comes tonight,
you can give it to him to leave you alone,
or better yet, tomorrow,
when mommy and daddy aren't home,
call old Jer' on the phone. No, better not.
OK, honey, now how 'bout we play
the mommy and daddy game? Let's see.
What's Jerry got in his dress-up box? Whoa.
A feather boa, green to go
with those green eyes,
bright red lipstick for my piggy wiggy.
Surprise! Look what I found,
a gown just like mommy wears
on nights when daddy's head's down
where it shouldn't be.
Oh, I see them all right.
My mommy and Stan, my brand-new daddy,
who puts his hand down my pants,
when mommy isn't there.
He wears a torn tee shirt and no undies

and neither does mommy,
as they roll on the floor
and I can't get away before she sees me
and he does
and she says, "Come here, Gerald dear,"
but I won't go near. I'm afraid.
I start to cry, but she gets up
and squeezes me against her.
She's so smelly and sticky and I can't breathe.
It's so icky.
Then she says, "Kiss me
and give Daddy Stan a kiss, too,"
and what's he doing to my wee-wee?
Sherry, Sher, open your legs for Jer.
That's right. Smile for the camera and Jerry
and for mommy and Stan on his knees
with his mouth open
and his sharp yellow teeth that bite
until I bleed.
Smile for me, honey,
or better yet, just say, "freeze."

ARCHANGEL

For Chet Baker

You stepped through
the Van Gogh blue curtain
into my dream.
That day in Paris,
we sat at the outdoor café for hours.
I had high breasts
and my dress was cut low.
You leaned close to me, so close;
yet, did not touch.
"I don't need to," you said, "it's the dope,
it's the rush
so much better than lust.
Hush, take a deep breath

and you'll just go to sleep like I did."
I knew you were hustling me,
that underneath the hipster philosophy
lay the same old Chet out to score.
Still, I lent you money, still I followed you
to the pissoir,
where Lucien gave you "le fix."
Shaking his head, he pocketed the money and said,
"I heard you were dead,"
and you answered, "I am."
You said when you slammed into the pavement,
Amsterdam shook, then settled back into apathy,
the way we all do, when we are through
with the foolishness of living.
You ended up sharing your works with a whore
who waited outside the pissoir door,
your generosity as pathetic
as it was predictable.
You wanted sainthood like everybody else.
Instead, you earned the wings
that were too late to save you,
but not too late to raise you
up to junkie heaven.
Later, we stood on the steps of Notre Dame.
You were calm, as you pointed to the bell tower.
You said you saw Quasimodo up there,
holding Esmeralda over the edge
by her hair,
but all I saw staring down were the gargoyles
who'd found peace,
because it meant nothing to them.
"I see," I lied, to please you,
but you knew and you blew me a kiss.
You wished me "bonne chance,"
then you eased into flight,
as the cool, jazzy, starry night
opened its arms to retrieve you.

LUST, LOVE, AND LOSS

1 ZERO VELOCITY, I

Leave your porkpie hat on, lover,
the one you bought in that vintage clothing store.
Do it for mother, do it for your little whore.
What poor excuses for passion we use
to get the juices going
now that we've been together four years.
You say, "Please don't do it,"
but you know it will arouse me,
because begging is all that's left to unfreeze me.
I tear your black tee shirt off you.
I try to bite through your underwear too,
but you stop me when my teeth
get caught in your pubic hair,
tangled and damp, reddish brown and wiry,
so different from the hair on your head,
which is fine and straight.
You make me wait as you slip the black bikinis
below your hips
and I take the tip of your cock in my mouth,
then let it slip out as you back up and move forward
making your own rhythm,
taking me the way you always do.
When you yell and jerk against my mouth,
come splashes my chest
and you rub it into my skin,
as if marking me somehow,
but it's too late,
though once we were in whatever this is together.
"You shouldn't ever have to defend yourself
for loving," you say,
but every time we fuck, you ask too much of me.
You want ecstasy
when all there is is apology.
"I came too fast," you say, "forgive me."
Forgive you? I ask. Forgive you?
I take the side by the window, you by the door.

You begin to snore and mumble in your sleep.
I keep telling myself that suffering just for love,
or want of it
only counts in literature,
until you slide your hand between my thighs.
Your eyes are closed, but you are awake.
Your rough as a cat's tongue rakes my nipples.
O baby, you murmur,
are you ready for your popsicle?
Everything seems wet; even the walls are sweating,
as we grind and groan down the road
we've been traveling
since the afternoon when I picked you up hitchhiking.
Heading east? I asked.
"Anyplace but here," you said.
I told you that was the title of a novel
and you said you didn't read,
you watched TV and peed outside when you could.
I knew we would fuck,
because you were so different from me
and I needed that then,
but I didn't expect the eternity of true lust
to keep holding on to me.
Let me go, I moan,
but you just go on, until the spasms subside
and I feel like I'm up above my body looking down,
as our breath slows, our hearts,
everything, until it starts all over
like the motor, when I turned the key
and we shot forward
at such high speed
no one could even see us.

2 ZERO VELOCITY, II

Whatever it is, you want it.
You want to buy
the tomato-red '55 Cadillac convertible
and just drive,
maybe with me beside you, maybe not.

You want to bite into my heart's green apple,
and more than that,
if you can get it and you can
from me, or any other woman.
You want to blow this town,
without goodbyes, regrets,
but when the car finally stops
at the edge, it's I, not you, who jump,
I, who leave you standing
in your cutoffs and GAP tee shirt,
my eyes closed, until the sound of spinning wheels,
until you fall through the air beside me,
just pass me and crash
and climb from the wreck
and ask whether it was as good for me
as it was for you?
But I don't answer, because I'm forty-two,
because I'm crashing into the cliché
you just erected between us.
Then I have my hands around your penis
and here among the glass and twisted metal,
the trash tossed out the window
of my last affair,
we try to scare ourselves into each other. We try.
We always say it's the other one's fault,
it's the memory of salt from some other wound
that burns us until we swoon
into the arms of a stranger,
the danger passed out like a drunk in a doorway,
until next time.
You pretend it doesn't matter and so do I,
though unlike you, I know it's only jaded innocence
that keeps me cruising passion's strip
for someone. "Anyone," I whisper,
as you lift my pelvis to your mouth,
your tongue, your pale skin one blur
against the blue blur of the sky.

3 APPOMATTOX

The bus was full the rainy afternoon
we sat across the aisle from one another
and unashamed, I stared at you.
You had a choirboy's face,
tempered by the promise of sin.
I thought you were a pretty man,
the kind who was too dangerous
for anything but friendship.
When I got off, I was surprised
to find you matching my stride
through the pools of standing water.
One block, two blocks,
upstairs to my apartment.
I still remember the slow, sweet time
before the foreplay ended.
We never spoke.
We kept our separate war and peace to ourselves,
until one day, you broke the spell.
"I'm James," you said,
and I told you the intimacy of names
was still too much to ask of me,
but you insisted,
and we lost the game of keeping things simple
and plain as a Shaker hatbox,
where we could store our past
poor failures at loving.
I don't want to see you anymore, I said, one day
as you were leaving,
but suddenly, I wanted to suck your fingertips
and twist those long strands of your hair
in my hands until you begged me
to make love to you again,
so I pulled you back inside.
I wish the floor had opened up and swallowed me,
but here we are five years from then,
locked in our wedded misery.
Sex without responsibility
could have saved us from disaster,

but now it's too late,
now love's a letter stamped "return to sender,"
stamped "surrender" on delivery.

4 DREAM LOVER

The blond man with high cheekbones
sent a shiver down my spine.
I knew he was mine
before we'd even spoken
and finally, when he broke through
the emptiness between us,
I sat above him and drove myself
down on his penis,
ground myself against him.
We kissed, until he bit my lip
and I accepted love in all its brutality and sweetness.
"My dove," I whispered, "my life to be,
to sleep beside and hold
against an eternity of loneliness."
But suddenly, I woke in the old brass bed.
My cats slept peacefully
curled against my legs and side.
I tasted blood,
as morning arrived, wearing its disguise of sunlight.

RECONCILIATION

1 BIRTH MOTHER

I wasn't wearing anything but my underwear
when the social worker opened the orphanage door.
I was only four months along
and I didn't show much.
I'd gone out the back
when your father'd come at me with a crowbar.
I'd been sitting on the bed,
painting my toenails the pearl pink he liked,
when he got too quiet.
It had doom in it, that quiet of his.

When he swung at me, I heard him say,
"Goddamn, I bit my tongue,"
but I was running so fast I got past him
and all he got was my slip,
when he grabbed at me.
I thought of staying, of taking the old knife
I used to slice hunks of roast beef
for him to eat Sunday dinner
and cutting him up
just like I'd do that meat for him,
before he'd even eat it
like he was a child, or something, not a man.
All he knew was giving pain and pleasure
and I knew I ought to leave,
but when I measured him against the others,
I only wanted him more.
Every time I swore I was through with him.
I was a blue and black bruise
without the will to choose another way of living,
until I knew that you were coming, son.
Born for no one and no one caring
whether you were dark haired and fair like your mother,
or had your father's olive skin,
brown hair, and hazel eyes.
You had nothing to lose,
so I left you at the orphanage,
when you were born.

After I went back to him,
he'd kid me about that night.
He called it the Friday night fight
and said they should have put it on TV,
then one day, he keeled over and died
in the middle of cursing me,
just like in a fantasy I'd had once. It was the best,
the sweetest revenge.
I packed up. I moved again.
The roads I traveled
with no end to them
and you were back there somewhere,

before it really fell apart for me,
before I couldn't go back,
even if I wanted to. But I did go back. At last,
and finally, I caught up with you
in some wild bar, among the white trash,
who were your kin, beneath your southern gentleman clothes.
Glasses of booze were lined up
on the bar in front of you
and your head was down in your hands
and when I came to stand beside you,
you raised your face and stared at me and turned away.
I knew those eyes
and I hated you. Inside my love was a hate
as fierce as it had ever been for him.
That's when I swung at you with my fist
and hit with all my strength
and didn't miss.

2 OEDIPUS, THE SON

When I was young,
I'd just pick up and go
when I got restless,
but now I know
all my runaways lead
to my adoptive mother,
to the backyard when I'm sixteen
and she slaps me hard,
when I tell her my drinking and dad's is her fault.
At the private schools
I'm always politely asked to leave,
everybody always says I only need another chance
and I always get it,
that is, until now at thirty-six,
when all I see glaring at me from the mirror
of my past is wasted time
and my mother's hand against my fly.
I'm too surprised to move, or even breathe,
until she squeezes me there.
I fall to my knees,

then onto my side, curled in a ball.
Even when the pain has eased,
I lie staring at the maple trees,
whose green leaves are turning gold.
Finally, I'm numb in a way that makes me whole,
makes me her son,
because she'd goaded me into it at last
and now that I am,
she wants to tear me to pieces
like those rags she uses
to wipe my dad's spilled drinks from the floor.

Later, while dad's passed out in the den,
I go into the bedroom.
The sheet only covers my mother's thighs.
The bra she wears is transparent
and her nipples are quarter-sized.
I walk to the bed,
she lifts her head, smiles and lies back,
when I sit down.
Soon, I find her mouth with mine.
At first, she's too tight to enter,
but eventually, she loosens for me
and when she cries, I press harder and deeper.
Afterward, we lie gasping and trembling,
until we sleep.
When I wake and dress,
I find my suitcase in the hall.
At the front door, she calls,
but I don't answer,
I walk outside
and turn down the walkway toward town.
I hear nothing but the sound of my own footsteps,
striking the pavement
and I imagine it is her flesh I am walking on
and that flesh collapsing into bone
under my weight.
At the crossroads, no sphinx greets me
with a riddle to link me to anything wrong
or out of the natural order of things.

One bird begins to sing, another,
the sky is lightening
and only now that I've come back again
to nurse her in my fashion,
now that she is old
and pretending to have forgotten everything,
I realize I did not violate the laws of the gods
which dictate our lives by destroying them
and by calling it fate,
but by taking my mother's body
not out of love, or even hate,
but merely out of self-defense.

3 MOTHERHOOD

When you caught me with my lover, son,
I wasn't ashamed.
I was glad to initiate you into my games of deception.
Though you were sixteen,
to me you were still the three-year-old
from the Irish Hill Orphanage,
crying as you held the dime
your birth mother'd left you out to me,
when I'd come to take you home.
You ought to know that love cannot be bought,
or sold, only taken,
when it's thrown at your feet
like a bone, the bit of meat still on it,
not enough to satisfy,
but just enough to make you hungrier,
to make you cry, until you've eaten
yourself alive, or dead.
That's all love is you know.
It's just a cry that goes unanswered,
a body on top of another body,
pretending to be something more.
Love is your mother
who slams the door in the face of her lover
at 4 PM on Saturdays
when your father is passed out again,

his latest bout of drinking dry martinis
over for the weekend.
His Sunday recovery, when he wakes
begins at noon
with steaks and new potatoes which he cannot eat,
but cooks for us,
as if performing some kind of penance
for the life sentence we call a family.
As always he breaks down, apologizes.
I stare at my plate, until he makes me look at him,
by yelling at me that it's my fault he drinks
and that you do,
then he screams go on, get out,
but we lift our forks, our knives.
We cut our meat,
until today when your seat is empty.
I find you in the yard,
the hard glare of the July sun
shining off the dime now hung
from the chain around your neck.
The table's set, come in, I say,
but you tell me I'm a whore
like your real mother. All women are.
I slap you across the mouth,
though what I want to do is inhale
the incense of whiskey I'll find there,
until I am drunk too
and free of myself like you and your father
pretend to be
just by swallowing your poison.
You think your will's as strong as mine,
but I'll take you to the edge and pull you back.
Only mother love can save you, son,
in a way that can't be measured, or understood.
It is a charm that only mothers possess,
even foster ones,
a spell that won't let go of you
until you give in, or are destroyed.
Men call it emasculation,
but women know it's simply a different kind

of penetration
much like our own when we are plowed and sown
by men who leave the waste
of their ejaculation inside us.
When I lay my hand against your fly
and squeeze you until it hurts,
I feel I can go on living.
I will not die forgiven for my sins
and later, when you sneak into my room,
we do not speak, but seek each other's emptiness,
as if we could ever fill ourselves.
Your lips, my tongue, we are one body.
While your father lies awake
in the next room,
we make our love out of our hatred,
then we sleep
and when we wake, I've packed your suitcase
and like your birth mother, one minute you are here,
then you are gone,
but that was all so long ago
and you've come back to nurse me
now that unlike Jocasta I know the only punishment
to fit my crime is forgetting it.
I'm going blind,
my eyes plucked out by time and not my fingers.
All our attempted suicides have failed forever.
We will never tear ourselves apart
from the afternoon that started this.
I *am* your mother, son
and it is awful. It is bliss.

4 FATHERHOOD

The smell of formaldehyde fills the car,
as your mother sleeps fitfully beside me.
In my mind, I rehearse our deceit.
The thing was better off, better gotten rid of,
so the deed was done
and everyone is safe from scandal:
You, son, me, your mother and her lover.

Although it wasn't mine, I paid for it to leave,
so it belongs to me
as surely as if it had spurted from me,
during one of your mother's and my rare couplings,
had clung to her uterine wall,
before being thrust out in a rush of air.
Now it's back there in the trunk,
a chunk of discarded meat,
floating in its sweet preservative.
Five hundred miles to Chicago to do it discreetly
and five hundred back.
At first, she lay cramped in the backseat,
but that was before we argued
about stopping at a motel.
She didn't want to,
she wanted only to go, go, until the trip was over
and she could slip back into her infidelities.
Once she'd healed, it would begin again.
I accepted that. Still I wanted some sign from her
to tell me that I mattered.
She sits on two pillows,
her head rolling this way and that,
sits as far apart from me as she can,
as the sky grows blacker and blacker.
They call this tornado weather.
I press my foot hard on the pedal,
then release it slowly,
because beneath it all I'm a coward.
I feel the bottle of bourbon, cradled between my legs,
its hard, cool, reassuring glass asking nothing of me,
only giving what I want and no more.
Your mother is not a whore, son,
nor any one of the poor names
that people call a woman of her kind.
It will serve, I guess, but if pressed, I'd have to choose
a less excusing word.
She uses men to do her bidding; therefore she is a queen
and her queendom is called
the art of seduction and control.
She holds men under her still waters,

until they start to drown in her rejection.
Those who revive always decide
she did not mean to do it.
That's how you get through it, son, you run
not away from her, but back into her arms,
crossed over her chest Egyptian style,
even when she lets you get close enough
to clean up her latest mess.
"Just an indiscretion," she said
two months after you left.
I pretended not to hear,
until my thirst for lies
made me look into her eyes,
red and swollen from crying
tears that meant nothing,
but I seized them anyway
like prizes won after a long struggle.
"I'm so glad I'm the one you turned to," I said,
"I'll help you through. You are my wife."
She said, "My life is ruined."
She never mentioned me, or you.
Until today, I didn't realize what I would do.
While she was with the doctor,
I gave his nurse two hundred dollars and in return
I got the proof of this last affair,
pickled in its juice like I am.

At home, I turn the covers down and carry her to bed.
After I'm sure she is asleep again,
I go to the garage and get a shovel
and in the backyard,
I pick a spot and start to dig.
The small, sealed jar could hold beets,
or even raspberry preserves
some grandmother stirred over a hot flame for hours
and not this nameless thing I'm burying
so deep in my heart no one but her can ever find it
and she will never try.
I pat the dirt down with my hands.
I'll leave her this time, I think. I will,

but when I stand up,
a tornado, shaped like a fetus,
smashes my resolve, before I can escape.

PENIS ENVY

My wife deserved to be shot.
I served time in the Gulf,
and I am telling you
when I came home and found her packed up and gone,
it wasn't long until I hatched a plan.
I located the man behind it all,
staked out his apartment and his job.
Then one afternoon, I dressed up in camouflage,
loaded my AK-47
and went to Hot Dog Heaven.
I found them in the parking lot,
sharing kisses over lunch.
I came up from behind, but changed my mind
and walked right in front,
and aimed through the windshield,
before they had a chance to see who it was.
I shouted my name, hoping she would hear as she died,
then I went to the passenger side
and fired at his head. A red mass
exploded like a sunburst.
At first, I couldn't believe I'd done it,
then I put the gun down
and looked at my hands, which were steady.
I pulled open the door,
before I knew what I was doing.
I just had to see what he was hiding in his pants.
It was pathetic, a sad, shriveled thing
there between his legs
and not the foot-long
she had said made her scream with pleasure.
I did hear screams, but they were coming
from my mouth, not hers.
Noise, I thought, as I fired at her body again.

Of course, I'd turned the gun on myself.
What else could I do to erase it all?—
the 911 calls, the sirens in the distance,
but the ordinariness of murder overwhelmed me,
possessed me like a spirit
and I thought how easy it would be
to take two or three more people with me.
Instead, I decided to give myself up,
plus I was out of ammunition.
I guess it is my destiny,
to be a living example for other men,
who are only bluffing when they threaten violence.
Now once a week, I write a column on relationships
for the prison publication.
I base my advice on actual situations.
For example, Clarence Thomas.
He had a dick fixation, just as I did.
For me, it was a torment and my downfall
and nearly his.
Ultimately, the question is always
how far are you willing to go?
I think within his perimeters,
Clarence went the distance.
As far as I'm concerned,
he's earned his place on the Supreme Court
and stands tall beside all the other men,
who haven't given in to a woman's scorn,
who are born again from the fire of their ridicule.
If you ask me, Anita Hill got off too easily.
I would have caught the bitch
some afternoon, while the cherry blossoms
were in bloom
and boom, solved all my problems.
Oops! I think I wobbled over the line
that separates fantasy from crime.
The counselors tell me all the time
I've got to get it straight
how the imagination sometimes
races on without us.
But I know Debby and Ed are off somewhere

eating wedding cake
and letting me take the fall for their betrayal.
Is it fair that on the other side of this wall
Clarence has it all
and I have nothing but a ball and chain?
That reminds me, I checked this Othello play
out of the library.
It's about a guy
who loses his reputation and his wife,
well, he kills her, but she made him.
I found some parallels to my own life and Clarence's.
Othello's black.
But the other subtler thing is how a man
must stand up to humiliation,
must retaliate, or lose himself,
who when he finds some pubic hair
in his can of Coke
must ask, regardless of the consequences,
who put it there?

GREED

I was named after my daddy, Vern,
but I was like my mama,
though I'd never admit it, until now.
Before she settled down,
she traveled from town to town
on the roller derby circuit
for the Texas Tornadoes.
Sometimes I went with her.
She always knew how to make me happy.
She'd take me to the nearest hot dog stand
and tell the man,
"Give Verna the works."
She was a big-boned farm girl with flame-red hair
and with the smallest, most delicate feet.
She had to have her skates made specially
and even then, she had to fill them in
with wads of cotton.

I looked like her, but I had daddy's feet,
wide, flat, and reliable.
I wore cowboy boots, a cowboy hat and jeans,
and I was high school rodeo queen of '75.
I learned to drive a tractor, brand cattle
and spit, after I took a bit of chaw.
The boys admired me and asked me out,
but I didn't trust them. They talked too much,
but Russ, the Viet Nam vet,
who drove the school bus was fine for me,
though all in all I'd have to say I wasn't half the girl
I could have been.
A wild mother sometimes makes a cautious child,
who takes the safest path to her destination.
In my case, it was a savings and loan bank,
where at nineteen, I sank
into the routine of being secretary
to Mr. Joe Bob Merriweather,
the president and decent, churchgoing family man.

My change of life began in '82,
when money started pouring in here
like heavy rain through a leaky roof.
All we had to do was set out buckets anyplace
and we would catch a mess of money.
I was polishing my nails lunch time one day,
when a man sailed in the door
and asked me for a date.
Just then, Joe Bob came out
and without a glance at me said, "Boy, she's taken."
After that, we were making love
at least three times a week,
sometimes across the desk
or in the backseat of his Pontiac.
He wasn't that good at it,
but he tried and I was grateful
just to be at his side,
when all his deals paid off.
Then he bought a Rolls.
He partied with politicians and whores,

until word got back to his wife
and she threatened to slit off a piece
of you know what.
After that, he thought he'd better quit it with me too,
so he bought me a sable coat from SAKS JANDEL.
He wished me well
and I sat at my desk, reading the *Wall Street Journal*.
I dabbled in real estate with my latest raise.
I was making one hundred thousand dollars a year,
plus monthly bonus,
and Joe Bob was clearing millions,
building condos, financed through his S & L,
his own contractors, and just plain old-fashioned kickbacks.
We were riding the crest of deregulations wave.
The S & L was like a building without foundation.
How could it stand
longer than a man's imagination?
We were drowning in the illusion of money.
We couldn't be saved.
But that was later.
For a while, I slaved for him,
but then I thought I'd work for my own benefit.
I told mama how he'd used me like I was a slut
he could tip when he got done.
All she said was, "You're just like me.
I could skate all right,
but I couldn't pick men worth a damn.
Your father's a fine example.
You have the brains, the looks.
What took you so long to get what you want?"
I told Joe Bob I'd tell his wife about us.
I said, "Pleading won't get you anywhere.
You're a betting man.
Take out the cards
and deal this hand."
When I went in my own office at last, I cried,
then poured a glass of champagne,
opened a box of Godiva chocolates,
and put my feet up on the desk.
The rest of the time, I learned the trade.

I stayed out of Joe Bob's way and he out of mine.
In time, I had my clients too, a few deals
that added up to two million dollars
in my personal account,
but you know, it didn't amount to much
without love,
which I didn't know was coming
in the form of Bubba Taylor.
Yes, love and hate were waiting in his arms.
He was a charming scoundrel,
who found a way to get my money
that was just setting like a laying hen on eggs.
When he got between my legs,
I was begging for destruction
and it came a mere six months to the day
after I met him.
He robbed me is what he did.
I admit I gave him access to my accounts.
He was my fiancé, wasn't he?
He disappeared just like he'd come
and I had to start over,
only now the government was cracking down
on what it once had ballyhooed
as the way to turn around the banking industry
and free it from the controls
it had enacted in the first place.
Ronald Reagan and his bunch threw out the rules,
but did not go down on the ship of fools,
when it foundered. We did
and we took a lot of people with us.
The unsold real estate piled up—
apartment buildings, condos, homes, and office towers.
Loans in default.
We ought to have known it couldn't last,
but we were past all reasoning.
We had to keep the money moving back and forth
to cover up the fact
that Santa Claus's sack was empty.

Joe Bob took off for parts unknown
and I went home to Abilene,
but not for long.
I was called back to Dallas to testify.
Joe Bob was tried and sentenced to twenty-five years
minimum security, reduced to three,
and when I finished my spiral down
the chain of lies,
I took up keeping books
at Clem's West Side Auto Supply.
They claim the S & L's are getting bailed out,
though it sounds like some of the same shenanigans
are going on at RTC.
They're moving money into other bottomless pockets,
behind the screen of fixing things.
The whole country's on the edge of insolvency,
but I am watching from the sidelines now
like a drunk who's pledged to stay off the bottle,
but the ledge where I'm standing is so narrow.
I could fall back in the fire,
where the money's burning like desire,
only with much more intensity.
Finally, mama and me moved to Vegas,
where I cocktail-waitress at the Sands
and each paycheck I tell the man
at the craps table,
let it ride, until it hurts.

.

Vice

RAPTURE
A Fiction

Memory is a highway,
where a car is speeding into the sunset.
The man inside that car has a gun.
He says he'll shoot himself
and be done with it, be dead,
but in the end, he doesn't do it.
If he had, the path to the truth
would have led straight from the gate
outside his ex-wife's house,
not end run around it,
leaving a trail of blood
the prosecution says is proof
that he used his power, his juice
to seduce death
by handing her two sacrifices,
but she promised what she would never deliver.
She left him a pair of loaded dice
and severed their connection
with one well-practiced slice.

Now in his cell,
he reads fan letters.
He doesn't dwell on the past.
If he did, he'd tell you to always go for broke,
because a man who can't go the distance is a joke,
is a failure.
"You can quote me on that," he says aloud,
then shocked by the sound of his own voice,
chokes back a cry.
When he looks himself in the eye,
he just sees a regular guy.
He sees a parade going by.
On the largest float,
the homecoming queen waves to the crowd.
She's a statuesque blond.
He's a football hero.
He's also a black man,

but that is no obstacle.
It's a license to do the impossible.
He waves back.
Maybe that isn't really what happened,
but it's close and he makes the most of it,
when he can see through the smoke
of his desire and his rage.
In a flash,
he feels the diamonds of hope,
cutting the smooth glass of his mind
into halfs and quarters,
as he runs backward in time,
a football tucked under his arm,
as he crosses the goal line,
only to find the stands are empty
and he is alone on the field.
Concealed in the ball is a bomb.
All he has to do to explode it is throw.
He listens to the silence inhaling,
then he lets go.
That's when the crowd appears
and over the loudspeaker
he hears his coach, saying, "Buddy, come on home,"
but home is the scene of the crime,
shown on TV so many times
that the murderer and victims cease to exist,
except in peripheral vision
and in the void between the goalposts,
thirty-two bits and pieces of his life
are all that survive the knife.

FALSE WITNESS
A Fiction

I did not buy you the tiara
with the fake jewels,
because your father said it made you look cheap,
although eventually, he confessed
that he was thrilled

to think of you wearing only tap shoes
and your crown of silver plate and paste,
but you took it out on me, you vixen.
That's when I swore to myself that you'd regret
making me get on my knees
and beg your forgiveness,
so you would play with Daddy
the way I taught you.
While I kneeled,
you told me I was a bad mommy
and made a face at me.
After I apologized,
I cut a crude tiara from cardboard
and set it on your head.
I said, "I'll buy you a real one tomorrow."
"But tomorrow's Christmas," you cried.
"The store will be open," I lied.
You knew it, but decided to taunt your father
instead of arguing with me.
You called him a mean old daddy
and pinched him hard,
then you played hide-and-seek
under the goose-down comforter,
until I said, "game."
Later, he told me he didn't know a six year old
could be such a cruel mistress
and I said, "Making men suffer is her destiny."
I was his enemy and you were my collaborator.
At first, I didn't even want you to be as debauched
as I had been, when my father first came to my bed,
but instead of suffering, you thrived
and so did your father,
or am I lying to myself to ease my guilt?
Lately, it lies back of my mind like silt
that I sift through
to try to find the woman
who became a mother
with no other thought than of revenge.
When you were five,
I tutored you in the art of seduction.

"Sit on Daddy's lap and rub your back against him," I said.
"Squirm too and don't be afraid of the bulge there.
It's made for girls like you."
And girls like me,
although sometimes I think that nothing happened
when my father said good night,
that he simply shut off the light
and closed the door
and I am an unreliable witness to my own life,
but if I'm not, I'm warning you
I won't be a victim twice.
You have too much power over your father now
and through him, over me.
Last evening, when I asked you to say grace,
you even stood up and showed me your panties
with the red hearts on them,
the ones I gave you after your first time.
Now you give your father a grudging kiss
that has no passion in it,
no tongue that tastes like a strawberry lollipop.
Although he pleads with you,
you keep your lips pressed together.
I tell him to let it go,
but he says the memory of that taste inflames him.
He says it's as though he's lying in a bowl
of strawberries and cream,
waiting to be devoured.
As I unbutton your pajama top,
he buries his face in the nest of your golden hair.
As usual, he starts to cry.
You are unmoved.
You sigh and reach for your favorite doll,
but I take her and throw her on the floor.
I think I see the glint of your father's tears
on your skin,
as I get the rope
and put it around your neck,
then I take the stick, insert it and twist.
"This is how to satisfy her," I tell him.
"Why do you make me suffer," he whimpers,

"because you know you can?"
Your mouth is half open,
as if you are about to speak.
I stare at you, looking for a sign
that you and I are kin,
but you are an imitation of the diamond that I am.
See what happens to naughty little girls?
They pay for their disobedience
in the arms of their fathers
at childhood's end.

SLEEPING BEAUTY
A Fiction

for the comatose patient raped by an aide

You steal into my room,
between darkness and noon
to doff the disguise as nurse's aide
and parade before me as you really are,
a man for whom time is deranged
and consists of your furtive visits to me,
while all the rest is just a gloomy reprieve
from your nothingness.
For me time is arranged without the past
or the future,
without tenses to suture me to my days and nights.
For me, there is only now,
when you are certain you won't be disturbed,
spread my legs apart
and break through the red door to my chamber.
After you've finished,
you use a clean, white towel
to wipe away the evidence
of how you mingled your life
with what is left of mine.
You think your crime won't be discovered
but the evidence survives
to dine on the flow of fluid
dripping into me,

as though I were merely a conduit
for the baby who knows me
only as its host
and never will as Mother
and you will never be Father,
baby never see,
you, who in a fever came to me.
I was "comma tose" as my mother calls it.
She hoped for a miracle,
but when it came, it was not the one she wanted,
when she prayed to Saint Jude,
patron saint of lost causes
and laid my photo on the altar
she'd erected in the living room,
beside a rose in a crystal vase.
My face almost glowed in the dark,
as if the spark of consciousness
leaped from me into the image
of what I was before I was swept away from myself,
only to return as someone else,
for whom language is silence,
language is thirst
that is not slaked.
Monster, you took all that was left of my body,
but could not break my body's vow
of renunciation of itself.
My eyes were open,
while you violated me.
All at once
you raised your hand and closed them,
but I could see
beyond the veil of your deceit.
At first, I thought you'd come to my rescue,
but instead of waking me with a kiss,
you pricked me with the thorn of violence
and I did not rise from my bed
to wed the handsome prince
as in the fairy tale
my mother once read to me,
when *forever* did not mean eternity.

CHARISMA
A Fiction

I didn't just read the Bible, I lived it.
I told my people, this is revolution.
I said, I interpret this attack
on my constitutional rights
with a gun and a guitar
to mean we are in trouble.
I held up a hand grenade, pulled the pin
and told them, "This one's for Jesus."
I prayed, "Lord, take me to heaven, take me today
and I won't falter on the way."
Did my people desert me,
did they say this man is crazy?
No, they didn't.
They prayed with me.
They lay facedown in Waco, Texas,
to await death and resurrection,
as it came from all directions, all in flames.
I never claimed to be the Jesus, who cured the sick
and caused the lame to walk.
I knew the sins of the flesh, I knew the shame
and I confessed my weakness.
I let my people be witness to it
and through it came my power
and the empty talk of changing sinful ways
that haunt a man,
until he betrays himself no longer
and gives in to the stronger urge
to fornicate and multiply dissolved.
I absolved myself between a woman's thighs
and I arose like Lazarus,
raised up from the dead
on the tip of his penis.
We had no life and death between us anymore,
we had rounds of ammunition
and all of you to listen to us burn
and in that burning learn
how to give your life for freedom

in Christian hunting season.
The AFT used child abuse as the excuse
to assault us in our home.
They had no proof
and if we had been left alone,
we might have shown the world
that God is like desire you cannot satisfy.
You must give in to Him, or die.
The Apocalypse cometh like a firestorm,
leaving some of us reborn,
others to smolder in the ruins
of New Jerusalem,
which will not come again,
until the war against the innocent is over.

THE ANTIHERO
A Fiction

for Police Officer Terry Yeakey, who committed suicide four days before he was to receive a medal of honor for rescuing people after the Oklahoma City bombing

I park my old maroon Ford in the field outside El Reno,
where wildflowers used to grow, when I was a kid,
but now only thorny memories push their heads
through the dirt like misplaced cacti.
At first, I just sit in the dark,
my heart racing,
then I take my Swiss Army Knife
and slit my wrists.
As blood runs down my hands, I feel exhilarated,
until I remember who I am—
a man with rat's eyes,
pink rimmed and sensitive to light.
When I was born,
the doctor pronounced me "albino."
I'm told my mother said,
"They run in the family,
but he's all right, he's my baby."
Six months later, I was adopted by another,

who loved me even though I wasn't an albino after all.
Much like a Siamese, who are born white,
parts of my body began to darken,
until I looked like any other boy.
When I was nine, Widow Dobbs, who lived next door,
brought home a Siamese.
She named him Buster Kitty.
He was a big, round-headed cat,
who hunted birds and tormented dogs,
when he wasn't sitting outside my window,
looking in at me,
as if I were a long-lost relative.
We respected each other,
but avoided too much contact.
When I went outside to play, he'd stroll away,
his tail lifted in the air, as if to say, "Take that."
One afternoon, he got run over by a moving van.
Widow Dobbs wasn't home and neither was my mother,
so I carried him to our backyard
and buried him in a hole I dug with a garden trowel.
I didn't tell anyone I'd done it.
After a week, the widow put up signs
offering a reward.
A few months later,
a stray dog dug up Buster's skeleton.
"I suppose you know nothing about it," said Mother.
"A truck hit him, he was dead, so I buried him," I confessed,
but Mother only said, "I found your water pistol."
Now Buster sits on my shoulder,
whispering that I'll get what I deserve.
I tell him I always do.
I used to see him two, or three times a day,
when I was a military policeman,
during the Persian Gulf War.
That's when I helped bury civilians in mass graves.
The corpses gave off the smell of chemicals and oil
and when I washed my hands,
a black film came off on my Handi Wipes.
There, as the smoke from the burning oil wells
blackened the light of each day,

I picked up the carcasses of birds
overcome by fumes,
having dropped from the air
after dying in midflight.
I buried them too,
as Buster scolded me about how I placed the bodies.
"No," he'd say, "don't drop them in like stones
down the well of death,"
and I didn't. I laid them down gently
like a mother, who has found her lost children.
After a while, he simply faded
into the scenery of that endless night
and when I went home to Oklahoma City,
he kept his distance.
It was enough to convince me that I was free of him,
until the day the Murrah building was bombed.
I was a policeman then too,
because I'd persuaded myself
it was the best way to help people.
That morning, I pulled three men and two women
from the rubble,
before I fell through a hole two floors
and lay helpless in the debris.
As body fluids dripped on me, Buster appeared,
but he didn't say anything,
only hovered in the air, until I passed out.
After I came home from the hospital,
my back hurt constantly
and I had nightmares about dead children.
I was afraid of what I might do,
without knowing what it was.
Waves of nausea often sent me to the bathroom,
where I kneeled in front of the toilet,
until a vile liquid bubbled up
from the pit of my stomach.
It tasted like green chilies
and burned the back of my throat.
I pissed blood and cursed Buster,
who truly knew me for what I was,
because I was to blame for his death

and hid my shame by covering it with dirt.
The day he died, I shot him with my water pistol.
That's when he darted in the path
of a Bekins truck.
That night, I made a promise to myself
that I would be of help to anyone who needed it.
Now as I listen to the drip, drip of my blood,
hitting the rubber floor mat and my shoes,
I realize I can't rescue the dead,
or erase the zero of my life
and make it count,
when all it amounts to is a few pints of blood,
turning to red mud,
as I stagger from the car to a gully nearby.
I kneel down and lay my Bible
and copy of *In Their Names* on the ground,
as Buster reappears to tell me it's all right,
I won't feel a thing,
but we both know he's lying
and when I raise my revolver to my head and fire,
a wave of desire washes over me
and I understand that what I always wanted
was release from my own pain,
but there's only the terrible surrender to it.

RWANDA

My neighbor used to come to our hut,
bringing melons so sweet
I thought I should not eat them,
because I would die
and haunt my family like a ghost
with hard, black seeds for eyes.
One day, he brought his uncle and two friends
and they asked my father to go outside with them.
I thought he had come to get permission to marry me
and I was glad because I loved him,
even though he wasn't a member of my tribe,
nor as educated as I was.

I wanted to stay,
but my mother gave me a basket of clothes
to wash at the river.
She said, "Don't come back,
until they are as clean as the Virgin Mary's soul."
"Mother," I said, "I'll never come back then."
"Shall I take my brother?" I asked,
as he ran to my father's side.
I was laughing, when she hissed, "Run,"
and I did because she frightened me.
As I rounded the hut,
I heard the *tat, tat, tat,* from guns
like the ones the soldiers carry.
I ran faster, still holding the basket.
It was frozen to my hands
and I still held it, even as I jumped in the river.
I thought I would die, so I closed my eyes.
When something bumped against me,
I opened them and saw my father's body.
As he floated past me,
his arm hooked around my neck,
almost taking me under
and I released the basket.
I reached for my father, as bullets hit the water
and I dove under him.
His body shielded me, until I couldn't breathe
and had to break the surface for air.
When I crawled onto the riverbank,
I hid in the grass behind the church.
Finally, when I was sure no one was around,
I beat on the rectory door,
until the priest opened it. "Hide me, Father," I begged.
Once inside, I was overjoyed to see my mother.
She told me when my neighbor shot at her,
she pretended to be dead
and while he dumped my father in the river,
she escaped and came here,
hoping I had survived.
She said we needed another place to hide,
but she could only find a small closet-size space

behind the altar, covered by a sheet of tin.
Only one of us could fit, so she made me go in
and covered the hole again.
When I heard screaming, I kicked the tin aside
and saw my mother was on fire.
I tried to help her, using only my hands,
but when she was completely covered in flames,
I broke a stained-glass window
with a statue of Saint Joseph and climbed out.
As I crawled back to the river,
a shiver of wind passed over me
through the grass and trees.
When I stopped to rest,
fear coiled around me like a snake,
but when I told myself I would not let them kill me,
it took the shape of a bird and flew away.
I crawled back to the church,
because I wanted to find my mother's ashes,
so I could bury them,
but my way was blocked by the rebels,
so I waited until dark.
Maybe I slept. I don't know.
When I heard my neighbor's voice,
it was as if I had awakened from a dream.
Relief flooded over me, until I sat up
and saw him standing above me, holding a machete.
"Sister," he said, "I won't hurt you."
I knew he was lying and I tried to get away,
but I was too weak
and he fell on top of me, tearing at my clothes.
When he was finished raping me,
I thought he would kill me,
but he only brought the machete close to my head,
then let it fall from his hands.
Dawn had come to the village
with more killing on its mind.
I heard screams and pleas for mercy,
then I realized those sounds were inside me.
They would never leave.
Now I am always talking to the dead.

Their bones are rattling around in my head.
Sometimes I can't hear anything else
and I go to the river with my son and cry.
When he was a few days old,
I took him there for the first time.
I stood looking at the water,
which was still the color of blood,
then I lifted him high above my head,
but my mother's bones said, "Killing is a sin,"
so I took him home
to raise him as if he really is my son
and not the issue of my neighbor,
who has returned to torment me
with skin that smells like burning flesh,
but in my heart I know
both his mother and father died long ago
and left this orphan to grow like a poisoned flower
beside the open grave that was my country.

STALKING MEMORY

Three months ago, I stabbed your cactus plant.
I thought that would be the end of it,
until I decided if I couldn't steal your heart,
I'd steal your peace of mind.
While you were gone today,
I broke into your house.
I rifled through your underwear drawer.
I held your panties to my nose
to inhale the scent of you,
but as I closed my eyes,
all I smelled was the odor of bleach.
One day soon,
when you've been seized by fear
as I have by love, my dear,
you'll be as bound as I am freed
from all restraints, except need.
I want to make you understand
how that need grew and grew,

until it consumed me.
I want to teach you what it's like
to live your life for someone else
with no regard for self.
Only you matter,
you whose throat I'd like to tear open
with my teeth, but I'm no werewolf,
I'm simply part of this ordinary night,
when you turn out the light and sleep,
unaware that I am sliding under the sheet
to lie beside you.
I'm so sorry I have to gag you and tie you up.
It isn't part of the plan,
but neither is my hand
inside the waistband of your pajama bottoms.
I only intend to beg you to kill me
and end my agony,
but suddenly, I see the past,
the present, and the future
all shouting at me like giant mouths
to "Do it, do it,"
and when you bite through the flimsy scarf
and try to scream,
I have to take extreme measures.
At first, I don't know how I'll live without you,
but after I get dressed, I'm sure I will.

Outside, the early morning air chills me
and I'm glad I brought a sweater.
Underneath your welcome mat,
I find my last letter to you.
I feel so much better now
that I don't have to wait for you to read it.
From now on, I resolve to be the kind of person
you would have wanted,
so I water all your plants, before I leave.
Once, I stood outside your bedroom window
barely breathing in the dark
and just two nights ago, parked my car
half a block away

and stayed awake by saying your name,
which after I shower, dress,
and go to work an hour early,
I'm afraid I can't remember.

THE PAPARAZZI

I'm on the ledge
outside your hotel bedroom,
when I glimpse your current lover,
as he bends over you on the bed
and deposits a cherry
he holds between his teeth
atop the mound of your very dark brown hair.
You're blonde to your adoring fans,
but I know where you're not.
For a second, I feel hot,
as I watch him, but I should be cold,
get the shot,
and go trespass on some other private property.
Come on baby, come.
I've got to pursue another asshole,
who thinks a TV role
makes him too good to be exposed warts and all
to those insatiable public coconspirators,
who want to know
all his dirty, little secrets,
or just his brand of soap.
The alcohol, miscarriages, divorces
marriages, face-lifts, coke binges,
homosexual, hetero and lesbian affairs.
I've been there through it all
and I am there for you,
a friend, not an enemy,
stalkerazzi, or a tabloid Nazi,
storm-trooping onto your yacht
to photograph you
in your latest embarrassing situation.
Think of me as a station of your cross

and the camera as your confessor,
who absolves you,
as you admit to lesser crimes
than I know you are guilty of.
You media whore, I didn't ask you for excuses,
I asked you for more
and I know you'll give it to me
before the public moves on
to the next shooting star,
but even then, occasionally I'll still
ambush you in rehab
and send the message
from the land of the fading career
that you are tumbling
through the stratosphere
just like you used to,
but now the only sound you hear
as you hit bottom once again
is the click of the shutter
and not applause and cheers.
I don't want the truth,
I want the lies,
so look this way,
say something nasty.
Don't be shy.

AFTERSCHOOL LESSONS FROM A HITMAN

What I do is
our secret.
Sh-h-h-h.
You gotta tell
I gotta bury it deep
deeper than that.
Everything is fine.
Everything is copacetic
as long as you keep
it all to yourself.
Don't let it—

Open your mouth.
Open it wider.

If you're gonna cry—

Your mother can't help.
Your father can't either.

A man is a man.
Sometimes he's neither.

You'll learn as you go.
You'll learn just like I did.

You know what you know.
You know kid?

That time in Jersey,
I put away my piece calmly
and eased past the customers,
looked straight ahead,
made it to the sidewalk,
got into the car
I left running.

You with me
so far?

U-m-m.

Now pull up your pants
and get outta my sight.

If I gotta dance,
I gotta dance solo
all right?

One more thing.
There's always a chance,
a chance that the hit might—

No, don't think about it.
Just go.

Wait. Take this calzone
my mother made
to your mother.

Hey, how's your brother?
Bring him next time.

You're never too young to
learn things.

I promise.
You'll know what I know.

I always say
it ain't a shame;
it's crime
and thank God somebody else
is paying.
This time.

CHANCE
written on learning of nuclear tests on unsuspecting
civilians by the U.S. Government

An ill wind with a Samsonite suitcase
was passing through White Sands, New Mexico,
in February, 1952,
when Mama, Daddy, my little sister and I
were en route to Tucson
from Fort Riley, Kansas.
We were on a vacation
no one knew would take Daddy to the cancer ward.
The hard facts can't be taken back,
or rearranged like Scrabble pieces
to form another word that is not terminal.
"Open the windows," said Daddy.

"Let in some fresh air. Don't tell me
you girls have to use the bathroom again.
We'll stop when we see a gas station
and please, Stella,
don't take any towels, or soap.
We don't want to look bad being Negroes.
It won't be good for the race."
"They'll just say we stole anyway," said Mama,
as we drove through the gray afternoon.
The sand was as white as the dress of a bride.
The sky was a groom, pressing down on her.
Their union was doomed to disaster, but who knew,
as we pulled to a stop and Mama got out
and scooped up some sand
she planned to store with the other souvenirs
she bore home in triumph?
I had on my red Roy Rogers cowboy hat,
my western shirt, cowboy boots, and Levi's
and I pulled my cap gun from its holster and fired
at the dim outline of the sun,
as the wind blew up the highway
to the next defenseless, unsuspecting town.

The other day, I found a mirror
Mama appropriated so long ago
and when I looked in it,
I saw us in our old Ford
with one door held closed by chicken wire.
Back then, Daddy had faith in Jesus and democracy.
He didn't fear what he couldn't see, taste, or feel,
as he laid his hands on the steering wheel
and drove into his own nuclear winter.

KNOCK, KNOCK

A Fiction

"Do you want a silver bullet?"
—RICHARD NIXON

Mother, help me. I feel as if I'm falling
from a great height,
as cold night sweats send me
shivering to the bathroom for fresh towels, more towels.
It feels as though it's ten below in here.
The heat is on,
but I'm cold and my footsteps
echo like a verdict,
spoken by an entire nation, "Guilty, guilty."
Now that Watergate's exploded like an atom bomb,
not even the Twenty-third Psalm can comfort me,
so I decide to drink another silver bullet.
When I turn on the air-conditioning,
because I want to hear the rumble of something
beside the artillery in my head,
when I lay it on the pillow
on the bed that might as well be a coffin,
I remember how comforting a fire is.
I take a few truly harmless scraps of paper
and add them to the wood in the fireplace
and I think, good, I am doing something practical.
Mother would be proud of me.
Mother, my cloud with the silver lining is a shroud
and I am dying without a shot being fired.
If Dick was going under, he wanted it to be
from a round of bullets,
because of some conspiracy he couldn't see coming,
when he was too busy running the country,
not because the men
who should have protected him let him down.
Isn't it pitiful that in the end,
all he had was slim chance, then none?
When other men could walk, I had to run.
I always had to be the one playing catch-up,

so I eavesdropped outside the doors of power
and before I stepped inside,
I knew the day, the hour and the score.
I am a sore loser, a sore winner
and what's more, I'm not ashamed of it.
The East Coast elite hate me,
because I'm poor.
They take me for an ass,
but I am a bull elephant,
rampaging through this cruel night,
before I take my final flight on *Air Force One*.
Mother, how come they all dislike Dick?
How come they spit, when he walks by
and when he looks them in the eyes, turn away?
Haven't I already paid a thousand times more
for my mistakes than any other president?
But if impeaching Dick is what it takes
to keep the country in the game,
then he says, "Go on, shake and bake him,
make him cry for mercy."
Mother, let's drink to new beginnings.
Let's celebrate my last night in office
with a toast to what is past,
then toss our glasses in the fireplace.
Stay with me. Please tell me what to do.
What's that, Mother?
You really think I should?
Yes, I agree, to go down in history
with a gesture says it best.
How about this one?
Of course, it's obscene.
Well, perhaps you're right.
It might offend somebody's mother.
Dick doesn't want that on his conscience.
"V" for victory then.
It's statesmanlike.
It's in good taste.
It's Dick.

BLOOD IN THE WATER
A Fiction
written after learning about a presidential affair

My granddaddy told me a man is nothing but appetite
sandwiched between his wife and mean lust.
I have a deep affection for my wife,
but also for the sweet, big-haired girls I'm partial to,
who never complain of tired jaws.
For a few stolen moments, I give them the deed to my heart,
signed and sealed with the only part of me
I've come to think is real.
At home, my wife telephones her friends
for advice about our marriage she never takes
and when I'm hot for her (not often)
makes me wait so long while she is in the bathroom
doing God knows what
I must take my own pleasure
and by the time she gets in bed,
I'm half asleep, my body depleted by the sheer effort
of keeping my desire for her alive.
We've been together well past the time
when couples find each other sexually attractive.
We have our child and our shared interests
which carry us forward each year,
without concern, or fear that one of us
will hear and heed the call of the wild
and seek permanent freedom in the arms of a warmer body.
No, there's comfort in a hot toddy
with an old friend beside the fire.
We're more like cousins,
who grew up together now
and when the feather of desire tickles us,
we smile and resume our separate lives
within the cocoon of malice, known as husband and wife,
having already experienced too much of kinship.
Doesn't everyone need to escape
from family business now and again?
Why then are my enemies and even some of my friends
beginning to shake their heads

and send me faxes about morality
and how the free love movement of the sixties
led to these public and humiliating revelations
of my supposed liaison with a young woman
I swear I do not know in the biblical sense,
although she presented herself to me
as if on a plate,
surrounded by French fries?
I saw in her eyes as she lay there
not submission to my will
but two hamburger patties sizzling on a grill.
They said, "Eat your fill,"
and God I wanted to, God, I willed myself
to refuse that generous offering
that now is being used
to justify the attempt by my rivals
to make me lose everything.
Now I stand as if naked on the evening news,
my chances of survival discussed
with no more care
than if I were dust,
beneath the heels of the righteous,
who are just as capable as I am
of falling from their high perches
into the muck that will suck them under
as it is doing me
once they are revealed to be human,
with human frailty.
My wife trusts me within the boundaries
we've set for each other;
yet the media and the other sharks,
who get off on seeing lives destroyed
won't accept that this is nothing
but another attempts to trap me in a lie.
Will a semen stain on a dress match my DNA?
Will I pay for my indiscretion? They ask,
as if it is a question that should be answered.
Damn them. Damn their eyes
and pass me the tortilla chips, salsa
and the latest polls,

so I can see what the public thinks of me.
They're not fooled.
They are forgiving
in spite of the jokes made at my expense
during monologues by TV hosts.
Although my rivals say if I'm not impeached
I'll lead the country into the twenty-first century
with my fly open, the electorate has spoken,
so subpoena me, subpoena everyone I know.
I am the captain of this ship of state
and I will sail us through the stormy seas of sleaze,
or we will all go down together
on our knees.

BACK IN THE WORLD

for Norman Fox

I took a shortcut through blood
to get back to you,
but the house where I left you is empty now.
You've packed up and moved on,
leaving this old photograph of the two of us,
taken before I left for Vietnam.
You've cut yourself out of it,
torn your half in pieces
and lain them on the mantle,
where your knickknacks used to be:
those godawful Hummels you'd been collecting for years
and a small glass vial you said
contained your grandmother's tears.
A thick film of dust comes off on my fingers,
when I rub them across the years
that came to separate us.

In a corner of the living room, facing a wall,
I find my last painting of you.
In it, you lie, naked, on the old iron bed,
your head hanging over the side,
your hair, flowing to the floor

like a wide, black river.
There, Max, the cat, is curled
in a gray, purring blur,
all fur and gooseberry green eyes that stare at me,
as if accusing me of some indiscretion
he doesn't dare mention.
Suddenly, he meows loudly
and rises as if he's been spooked,
runs through the house,
then swoops back to his place beside you,
and beside the night table,
on which I've painted a heart on a white plate,
and a knife and fork on a red-checkered napkin.
You hate the painting. You say I'm perverse
to paint you that way, and worse, an amateur.
"Do you want to tear out my heart and eat it
like the Aztecs used to do,
so you can prove you don't need me?" you ask.
"But I do need you," I say. "That's the point."
"I don't get it," you say,
as you dress for some party
you claim you are going to, but I'm on to your game.
It's your lover who's waiting for you.
"I know who he is," I say,
"but I don't know his name,"
then I run to the bathroom,
grab a handful of Trojans
and throw them at you,
as you slam the door on me,
before I can slam it on you.
You don't come back, until you get word
that I've enlisted in the army.
I'm packing, when you show up.
"You heard," I say
and you tell me that it's perverse of me too.
"Who are you kidding, you, a soldier?
And what's that?" you ask.
I give you the small canvas I've just finished.
"A sample of my new work," I say.
"There's nothing on it," you say.

"That's right," I tell you. "It's white like the plate,
after I ate your heart."
"Don't start," you say, "don't."
We part with a brief kiss like two strangers
who miss the act of pressing one mouth
against another, yet resist, resist.
We part on a day just like this,
a day that seems as if it will never end,
in an explosion that sends my body
flying through the air
in the white glare of morning,
when without warning, I step on a land mine
and regain consciousness to find
I'm a notation on a doctor's chart that says,
BK amputee.

Now I imagine myself racing through the house
just as Max did once,
only to return to myself, to the bed,
the night table, the canvas in my lap
and my brush, poised above it.
When Max, toothless and so old,
his hair comes out in clumps, when I touch him,
half sits, half collapses beside my wheelchair,
I begin to paint, first a black background,
then starting from the left side,
a white line, beside a red line,
beside a white, beside a red,
each one getting smaller and smaller,
until they disappear off the edge of the canvas.
I title it *Amateur.*
I call it art.

FLASHBACK

For Norman Fox

I'm on my way to work
at the Tackn' Feed shop
of which I own fifty-five percent,
when I hear sirens behind me
and pull over as three cop cars,
an ambulance, unmarked van, and a firetruck zoom past.
Not two minutes later, I start to sweat.
My heart beats rapidly
and I get that old feeling of dislocation
as my truck rocks like a cradle.
I grip the steering wheel the way I always do
when the pit bulls of bad memory
threaten to chew off my hands.
I count to twenty and drive on,
but as I pass the abortion clinic,
suddenly, I am in country again,
snorting pure heroin.
It's setting off flares in my brain,
tracers and those psychedelic snakes
I hallucinate are crawling all over me,
until I jump out of the truck,
which somehow I have driven onto the sidewalk.
I am using the open door for cover,
when Captain Kiss My Ass yells,
"Get down there where Charlie's holed up."
Waste the motherfucker. Motherfucker, I think.
I hear Simpson screaming something
and I am screaming too
and running through the elephant grass and bullets.
Someone steps on a land mine,
but it's nothing to me.
I am focused on my objective,
which is to wipe out the enemy,
but who is he?
"Bud, Bud, you OK?" I hear a voice call.
It's Harley, the guy who works at 7-Eleven.
He says, "Right to Lifers

threatened to blow up the clinic again."
I don't want to know anything about it,
even though I have a personal connection to the place.
"Need some help?" he asks.
"No thanks, man, I'm OK," I tell him, but I am shaking,
as if I am still trying to kick back in Saigon.
My girlfriend squeezes tepid water on my face
from a dirty towel and clucks her tongue,
as if I'm the one who needs sympathy.
"Save it," I tell her, shoving her hand away.
I don't need anything but a way out.
I had it for a while,
but I could not give myself over to the drug.
Even when I was high, I always felt
as if I were up above my body watching myself
pretend to descend into my own hell,
which even the Devil had abandoned
for more fertile ground.
My hell was just a hole in the ground
at the bottom of which the captain waited.
I hated him, but in an almost loving way,
for like a bad parent, he made me what I was
and what I am, despite my settled life,
my wife, kids, a savings account,
and once-a-year vacations to Barbados.
So many men died, because of his ambition.
He'd send us into more dangerous situations
than he had to, so he could make himself
a hotshot with the yahoos,
back at headquarters.
He had one eye on the slaughter
and one fixed on war's end,
when he'd use its career boost
and ascend the ladder of command.
I was just a grunt, humping my ass,
but I could shoot even better than I could breathe.
He needed me, so most times he left me alone
and focused on some other slob,
Simpson, another old-timer and volunteer like me,
Miller, Dean, Johnson, Macafee, Sanchez, or Willoughby,

our latest "FNG." We didn't use his name at first,
but called him Fucking New Guy,
until I said I'd "marry" him
and teach him the ropes.
I'd been in country twice and in the bush
more times than I cared to think about.
I can admit now that I liked war,
but I didn't like killing the way Miller did,
or that kid who fell on sharpened bamboo poles
hidden in a foliage-covered hole.
One even went through his asshole and ruptured his guts,
which spilled all over the ground,
when we pulled him off the poles.
"Like a stuck pig," said Johnson,
as he sat back on his heels,
looking down at the bloodstained bamboo.
Then he used a flamethrower to incinerate them.
"Anybody for barbecue?" he asked.
That set off a round of jokes about the Fourth of July
and by the time we got back to base camp,
we were good and hungry.
The CO didn't join in. He never did.
He hid behind his mirrored sunglasses and his commands.
He could give you a death sentence
with a smile and a handshake.
He'd say, "Men, make me proud"
and if we didn't, next time he sent us on patrol,
we knew he'd have us taking fire no matter how intense,
not caring whether we all went home in body bags,
as long as he survived to receive his medals
from the boardroom generals and jive-ass politicians
who only played at war.

Finally, I get back in my truck,
as the unneeded bomb squad, cops, and firemen start to leave.
I should too, but I just sit
only half aware of my surroundings
and watch as a protester is led to a police car.
I see it is my wife, Pam,
who must have violated the court order

to stay one hundred feet
from the entrance of the clinic again.
She notices me and waves,
just as a cop pushes her into the backseat,
but I imagine I see Captain Kiss,
waving me on toward the lair of the VC
who wasted Macafee and Simpson,
who had just become a short-timer.
Since I am the only old salt left,
the others look to me for some semblance of reason,
but they also realize I'm itching for a confrontation
and the captain has given me permission
to make the VC pay for every shitty day
I've been in my self-made exile.
When Sanchez says, "Waste the sonofabitch"
and Captain Kiss for once is outrunning me,
firing like he really means it,
until maybe he realizes what he is doing
and slows and seeks cover,
I can't resist screaming "Yellow dog" at him,
but he doesn't hear me as I run past,
zeroing in on the hole, where the tunnel rat
is dug in with a machine gun
and God knows it's booby-trapped,
so even if he dies, he'll take more of us with him.
Suddenly, I slow down, until I come to a full stop.
I'm hit, I think, almost relieved
as I sink to the ground.
I'm ready to die. I want to die,
having at last found the peace
that only comes when you cease to struggle
against the inevitable
and intense disintegration of body and soul,
but my survival instinct takes hold
and I manage to get up on my knees
and see the captain as he retreats
even farther from the fray.
I can't get to my launcher,
so I throw the grenade as far as I can
and remember only the terrific force as it explodes,

but soundless and somehow divorced from time,
while I am outside myself,
just swimming in the amniotic sack of destiny.
When I finally drag myself to where I last saw the captain,
there's nothing left but dog tags splashed with blood
and a few shreds of cloth.
I want to cry, but I don't.
I just lie on my back, listening to the eerie quiet
as the bloodshot-eyed afternoon stumbles off
and early evening arrives with the fanfare of rats
scurrying through the grass.
I remember the sapper who attacked the transit facility
the night I arrived in Vietnam.
She wasted four men, when she detonated her grenades.
I wonder why she chose certain death,
when she could have thrown them and perhaps survived?
Should I have done the same? I wonder,
as I hear someone coming toward me.
It's the VC.
I wait for him to take me out,
but he only bends closer and closer,
then he smiles and says, "I see you,"
and raises his arm, pretending to throw.
Then he stabs me with my own K-bar.
The rest is insignificant, is just evac and recovery,
is going through the motions back in the world.
Now I use my family like a magic potion
to get me through the memories
that are more real than the life I lead,
but nothing really eases my conscience.
Sometimes I even pretend the captain
has come home at last
with the ugly past forgotten
and the present rotten with happiness.
Maybe he's a general now too,
or a senator who won't give a guy like me the time of day.
Ain't that the way? I think,
as I choke on the stink of the last twenty-eight years
and have to light a cigarette
and suck it really hard.

I start the truck and head downtown,
where I will bail Pam out of jail
and never tell her about the crime I committed,
which at the time seemed necessary,
seemed like the very essence of the meaning
of the word, *soldier.*

MOMENTO MORI

for Jim & Turner Davis, artists

Twenty years ago, you were the man
who tended my roses, Jim,
but that ended in the garden of friendship,
where nothing grows
so much as serves its time,
frozen in the poses of love.
Those scissors you wielded like a surgeon
cut away that version of me
and now you don't know who I am
beneath my clothes.
My body's changed.
It's grown older
and rearranged itself to suit
some other truth, or lie.
I said good-bye. I meant it,
until I met you
stumbling through the rye again.
I could have let you pass,
but I caught a reflection of you
in a shot glass
and when I raised my eyes
your son was standing there to my surprise.
Now he's the one whose touch
I dream sends me reeling
from desk and chair, to bed
to rest my face on the pillow
where he lays his head,
where I take him on my tongue
like a sacrament,

where I am the paint he strokes on the canvas,
until the image he creates is my face
transfigured by desire,
my body surrounded by flames
and pierced by a single arrow.
I'll die for art, but not for love
and I sense he'll give me what I want,
still I choose to rendezvous
only in sleep,
until he crosses over the boundary of the unconscious
when one day, I run into him
at the Lucian Freud show (how fitting, no?).
Afterward, we go out for drinks.
He thinks he's so daring
when he says, "Damnit, let's go to bed,"
or something more romantic (I forget)
and we do,
though I mostly find lust a bore now.
I'd just as soon mop the floor as make love.
He understands. He knows I go
from one passion to the next
without a fixed destination.
He knows my inclination is to do
my loving with my mind and not my body.
I don't use men. I lose them
in the rough seas of my imagination,
where aroused and afraid,
they give in to my domination,
before they disappear.
Cleverly, he plays the role
of slave so skillfully,
I decide to free him,
but he says, "Beat me, use your fists."
I use a whip instead.
When I draw blood, I stop,
but he begs me to go on
and I do, until my strength is gone
and we lie gasping in the long shadow
of night among the starving,
where you find us, Jim.

At first, you stare at us
as if we were merely objects,
then take up the brush
and paint us
as if we'd died this side of Paradise.

VISITATION

"Heaven and earth.
What else is there?"
Said Walt Whitman in your dream,
then he smiled at you
and disappeared,
but you wanted him to come back.
You wanted to tell him that there was more.
There was the hardsell
you had to give yourself to stay alive
HIV positive five years
and counting backward to the day
your other life was stripped
bare of its leaves
at the start of the war of disease
against the body.
You don't have AIDS,
yet, you know it's coming
like a train whose whistle
you can hear before you see it.
When you feel the tremors
of internal earthquake,
will you do the diva thing?
Will you Rudolf Nureyev your way on stage,
so ravaged and dazed
you don't know who you are,
or commit your public suicide in private,
windows open wide
on the other side,
where your father, Walt is waiting
to take you in his arms
like a baby returning there on waking,

beside the picnic basket
in the long grass,
where the brittle pages of a book
are turning to the end.

STAR VEHICLE (MY SENIOR YEAR IN HIGH SCHOOL)

One loud whistle, then another
blots out the sound of Mother's screams,
as she runs alongside the railroad tracks,
where my best friend Suzy and I sit,
our backs to the oncoming train.
I didn't plan on Mother finding out.
I thought I could just die in peace,
without her interfering,
but she must have read my journal,
which she promised she would never do.
Looking back, I should have known.
Mother is parent to the bone
and not the older sister she wants to be.
She wants control.
The day I told her I wouldn't go to her alma mater,
she told me how much I'd disappointed her.
I was fed up and so was Suzy,
whose father had grounded her for smoking cigarettes!!
Suzy told him she wanted to die cool.
Anyway, we were sick of bullshit rules
that make a girl go crazy.
I don't know why we didn't just drink rat poison,
or hire Jimmy Barnes to do it.
He said he would for the thrill
of killing stupid bitches,
but I abhor boys who condescend to me.
I had high scores on my SATs.
I told him I didn't need his help.
I'd think of something
and he yelled in front of everyone
in the cafeteria
that Suzy and I were cunts,

then Robby, my old boyfriend punched him
and got suspended for two weeks
and that day ended
and another one began just like the other,
but as I was watching VH-1
and RuPaul was showing us all how to be a woman
just like a man,
it came to me that we needed to do something dramatic.
We had to be drama queens
and snap our fingers at the world and mean it.
I told Suzy what we would do
and she was even more into it than I was.
She *wanted* to commit suicide.
She even planned her outfit down to her Calvin Klein thong.
I told her it didn't matter what we wore.
I was already feeling kind of weird about it,
but we'd sworn an oath of sisterhood
and pricked ourselves with pins
we'd dipped in alcohol to kill the germs,
so I couldn't back out. Not then anyway.
I promised myself that I would stop it,
before it was too late,
but before I knew it, I was holding her hand,
as the freight train from hell (downtown L.A.),
rolled down the tracks.
When I tried to let go of Suzy's hand,
she held on tighter
and I couldn't get free,
but as I prepared myself for death
by imagining Brad Pitt would save me,
I got the strength to save myself.
I balled my free hand in a fist
and hit Suzy in the face.
She released my hand
and I got up and ran across the tracks
to my mother, who had fainted,
the way she always does when things don't go her way.
That's when I changed my mind
about the whole thing
and screamed, "Suzy, I'm coming back,"

but just then, the train splattered Suzy
all over the tracks.
I sat beside my mother, rocking back and forth
like a crazy person, or a drug addict,
until the cops and ambulance arrived.
I survived, because I have a well-developed
sense of self-preservation,
at least that's what my shrink says.
Mother told the cops I tried to save Suzy
and nearly got killed myself.
She told them I was a hero.
"Heroine, Mom," I said.
A few days later, I scanned Dad's morning newspaper,
as I dipped my biscotti in my latte,
but Suzy and I were already old news.
Later, I went to Neiman's
and bought a pair of high heel velvet mules
with pointed toes
that made my legs look great,
when I danced for the first time in ages
at the rave held in Suzy's honor.
I was so glad to be alive,
I didn't even need X
and when the hunk with the shaved head came up to me,
I grabbed his balls.
He went down on me later, in the bathroom
at Einstein's Bagels.
They asked us to leave.
I got mad and threw my lox at the waitress
and we ran and ran, until I remembered I'd left my car
in the parking lot.
I got Robby to go back for it
and we smoked some grass behind his dad's house
and made love for old times' sake,
then I made him take me to a strip club,
where I stripped down to my thong.
It was a long night.
Then I felt so sad I knew I was in mourning
and I had him take me home.
Mother and Dad were out of town for the weekend

and I went in their room.
When I looked in the nightstand drawer,
I found vaginal lubricant, condoms and handcuffs!!
I knew I'd had enough. I needed a vacation,
so I crammed some clothes in my backpack
and got to LAX in time to catch a plane to Tahiti,
where I sat on the beach,
letting the sun, not Clairol, bleach my hair
and pretended I was exactly where I wanted to be,
until I was so bored
I booked passage on a freighter.
I had dinner with the captain,
strolled the deck with Mabel,
an Englishwoman and her Maltese, Ralph,
pronounced Rafe
and fucked the first mate
on top of a table in the dining room,
where they served roast beef, duck l'orange
and chicken Marengo
the night before we docked back in L.A.
It was good to be home after three long months
and I was even able to graduate.
I enrolled at USC film school
and had Suzy tattooed on my thigh,
so I wouldn't forget my best friend,
who was able to escape her fate, or maybe found it,
while I live my life surrounded by new friends.
Sometimes I still think life sucks,
but it's better than the alternative,
which never ends.
Thank God a movie does.

PASSING THROUGH

"Earth is the birth of the blues," sang Yellow Bertha,
as she chopped cotton beside Mama Rose.
It was as hot as any other summer day,
when she decided to run away.
Folks say she made a fortune

running a whorehouse in New Orleans,
but others say she's buried somewhere out west,
her grave unmarked,
though you can find it in the dark
by the scent of jasmine and mint,
but I'm getting ahead of myself.
If it wasn't for hell,
we'd all be tapdancing with the devil
Mama Rose used to say,
but as it is, we just stand and watch,
while someone else burns up before salvation.
"People desire damnation, Bertha," she said,
unwrapping the rag from her head
to let the sweat flow down the corn rows,
plaited as tightly as the night coming down
on the high and mighty on judgment day.
They say she knew what was coming,
because she threw some bones that morning.
She bent down to pick up her rag which had fallen
and when she straightened up, her yellow gal
had gone down the road.
"Go then," she called out, "I didn't want you no how."
Then she started talking to herself
about how Old White John caught her milking cows.
"He wrestled me to the ground and did his nastiness."
He said, "your daddy was a slave and his daddy
and I'm claiming back what's mine."
It was July. I remember fireworks going off outside.
When Bertha come, so white
she liked to scared me to death,
I let her suckle my breast
and I said, "All right, little baby,
maybe I'll love you. Maybe."
Mama Rose said she did her best,
but it's hard to raise a gal like that
with everybody thinking she's giving them the high hat,
because she's so light and got those green eyes
that look right through you. She frightens people.
Even men, who're usually wanting to saddle up
and ride that kind of mare, can't abide her.

They're afraid if they try her, they'll never be the same.
The only ones willing are white.
They're watching her day and night,
but they know John swore to kill any man
who touched her,
because lo and behold, he owns up to her.
He's proud of her. Nobody can believe it.
He's even at her baptism.
He buys her cheap dresses and candy at the store.
He hands it to her out the door,
because she can't go in.
He won't, he won't stop looking at her
like it's some kind of miracle she was born
looking so much like him and his people.
It's a warning, or something.
"It's evil turning back on itself," said the preacher
the Sunday cut clean through by the truth,
by the living proof, as Old John stood up in church
and testified to the power of God,
who spoke to him that morning,
telling him he was a sinner.
He died that winter. Horrible suffering, they say.
He had a stroke on the way to town.
His car ran off the road and he drowned.
They say Bertha found him.
They say she ran all the way to town for the doctor,
who told her, "I am not a colored doctor,"
so she went and got the sheriff.
He listened for a while, then he locked her in a cell.
He said he knew she was guilty of something.
Well, after a while, Rose went down there
and I swear she nearly had a fit.
"Get my daughter out here," she said.
"How can you lock up your own brother's child?"
The sheriff knew it was true, so finally he said,
"You take her and don't ever cross my path again."
When Bertha passed him on the way out,
he tripped her with his foot.
When she got off the floor, she said,
"Every dog has its day."

From that time to this is a straight line,
pointing at a girl,
who doesn't even have shoes anymore,
as she runs down the road,
throwing off her ragged clothes, as she goes,
until she's as naked as the day she was born.
When she comes to washing hanging on the line,
she grabs a fine dress and keeps on running.
She's crying and laughing at the same time.
Along comes a truck that says J. GOODY on the side.
The man driving stops to give her a ride.
He swings the door open on the passenger side,
but Bertha says, "Move over, I'll drive."
When she asks him why he stopped,
he says, "I know white trash, when I see it.
You're just like me, but you're a girl. You're pretty.
You can free yourself. All you have to do
is show a little leg and some titty in the big city."
He gave her fifty cents and a wink
and she started thinking she might as well turn white.
She got a job waiting table in a dance hall.
One night, the boss heard her
singing along with the band.
He said, "Why don't you go up on stage,"
and she said, "I play piano too."
He said, "Howdy do."
From then on, she made everybody pay
one way, or another.
She got hard. She took lovers—
fathers, sons, and husbands.
It didn't matter,
but once in a while, she heard her mother's voice,
saying, "You made the wrong choice,"
and she felt the blues
and she let loose with a shout.
"Lordy," said the boss, "you sound colored."
More and more people came to hear her sing,
but they kind of feared her too.
They said, she was too white to sing the blues like that.
It wasn't right.
One night, she got to talking with the boss.

He walked round and round the office, shaking his head,
saying how much he'd lose,
if she stopped singing the blues.
"How often can you find a treasure like mine," he said,
laying his hand on her shoulder,
then he said, "If I weren't so old,"
and his voice dropped off to a whisper,
then he said, "I got the answer now, sweet Roberta.
Go on down to the dressing room and wait."
It didn't take long.
He came in and set a jar on the table.
"What do I do with this?" Asked Bertha.
He said, "you're going to pass for colored."
Suddenly, she was wearing blackface.
Suddenly, she was safe on the other side
of the door she slammed on the past
and it was standing open at last.
She could come and go as she pleased
and no one saw her enter, or leave.
She was free, she was freed,
but she didn't feel it
and she needed it to be real.
She went on, though. She flowed like a river,
carrying the body of a man,
who had himself a nigger, because he could.
She lived. She got old.
She almost froze one cold spell
and she got up from her sickbed
and told her daughter
she got during the change of life
it was time to go.
She sewed a note to her ragged coat.
It said, "*This is the granddaughter of Mama Rose.*"
She put fifty cents in her hand
and went to stand with her at the bus stop.
She would not return, but her child
had earned the right to go home.

When I got off the bus,
a hush fell over the people waiting there.
I was as white as my mother,

but my eyes were gray, not green.
I had hair down to my waist and braids so thick
they weighed me down.
Mother said, my father was a white musician
from another town,
who found out her secret
and left her and me to keep it.
Mama Rose knew me, though, blind as she was.
"What color are you, gal?" She asked
and I told her, "I'm as black as last night."
That's how I passed, without asking permission.

Dread

DREAD

My name is Shirley Herlihy,
but to the lowlifes on my beat,
I am Officer Girlie.
They do not mean to diss me.
It is a sign of respect
that I let them think is ok with me, and it is,
when I am trying to do my community policing.
After my brother disappeared
at the World Trade Center,
the word went out.
The lowlifes even gave me a bouquet of flowers
I could not accept.
They came from the Korean store
before somebody tossed a Molotov cocktail
through the front door
in retaliation for a "situation"
that involved the girlfriend of a drug dealer
shoplifting disposable diapers and Tampax.
The fact is I appreciated the thought
if not the deed.
I mean the flowers were at least a sign
I had not become a cop
turning a blind eye on the misery of the street.
I was known as someone who was tough,
but fair in meting out justice.
God knows it's hard to toe the line
every single time a perp messes up, but I tried.
If somebody's mother needed a ride
to a bail hearing,
my transportation specialist,
Bobby J, the gypsy cab guy would oblige.
I'd say thanks by slipping him
tickets to a ball game, a movie
or some lame excuse for entertainment.
I kept the wheels turning,
so I didn't fall under them.
I only had to use my gun once in two years
against a sonofabitch

who murdered his uncle
and hid his body in a dumpster.
Original, huh?
Stanko, the wino, found him on his garbage rounds.
We cornered the asshole in an alley
behind that shooting gallery
in the building that's now been gentrified
and is home to a decorator, six cats
and stacks of old cool jazz albums.
Anyway, the asshole said he had nothing to lose
fired and missed, fired again
and clipped me in the shins,
but I got him as I went down.
He died, but the paramedics revived him
and now he's in prison.
He's born again and keeps claiming Christ has risen,
as if nobody heard the news.
Once in a while, he calls me to apologize
and proselytize. I let him last time,
even as I sat, holding the telephone,
wishing my brother would come back.
I keep telling myself he's gone forever,
but it's so hard to accept.
He was always rescuing things
when we were kids—injured cats, birds,
even a German shepherd
who had been known to bite without provocation.
I used to tease him by singing,
"Patrick Kevin's going to Heaven."
I wonder if he made it,
or if he's suspended between the life
that didn't mean much to him
and the death that means everything to me?
He was such a good boy.
He would have been a better man, if only . . .
After our parents died
when I was fifteen going on twenty-five
and he was twelve, we raised ourselves.
No one else had the time.
It's a busy world out there

the addicts tell me and I believe them
because I know.
I bet they're lining up at Smitty's
crack house right now to score.
I should be there to arrest someone,
but I've turned in my badge and gun
and come downtown to search this crater
for some sign of Pat,
even if it's only a feeling
that he's still around in spirit at least,
if not in body.
There're just a few of us
who won't give up.
With our shovels, picks and garden tools
we dig among the hunks of steel,
the concrete and remnants of people
who went to work one day
and vanished into our memories.
I dread finding him and dread I won't
as I choke from the fumes less poisonous
than the hope that keeps me awake at night,
but I can't give up.
He'd do the same for me.
Patrick Kevin Herlihy, I repeat under my breath
as I uncover another credit card
and a wallet with something that looks
suspiciously like blackened flesh fused to it.
I turn them in and return to digging
until faint from the effort and fumes, I collapse.
Two other searchers take me by each arm
and help me to a chair,
but I don't stay there long.
After a candy bar and a glass of water,
I'm back at my task.
On the job, I never questioned what I was.
I had my role to play
in the day to day give
and mostly take of the criminals
who inhabited my world,
but this sixty acres is a city of ghosts

and I don't know where I stand with them.
When I arrived this morning,
nothing greeted me but the wind
and a grackle making a din
as it pecked and scratched
at flat, charred patches of ground.
Maybe it's a good sign
that the birds have returned,
a sign of rebirth. But whose? I wonder,
as I stare at my bruised hands.
Last year, I solved the robbery
of a palm reader.
As a lark, I let her read my lines.
She said, "In the future,
you'll find the one you lost,
but it will cost you."
Now as I stand above a hole seventy feet deep,
looking down, I don't see Pat.
When I call his name,
my voice is swallowed up by the roar of machines.
At first, that sound signified the possibility
of finding him
and made my heart beat faster,
but now it's just the white noise
I hear in my nightmares
that always begins at the scene of a shooting
that occurred during a domestic disturbance
between a man and a woman in Queens
that left two teens bereft of a mother and father
and made them cling to one another much too tightly,
so that now the one left behind is frightened
by her utter loneliness
and drinks Irish whiskey at the pub
where her brother, Pat, used to hold up the bar,
promising the patrons he was going to quit drinking
one of these days
and to assorted laughter
call for another round of drinks,
knowing his sister would never let him
sink as low as he wanted to go.

He'd seen the fight. I hadn't
but I was haunted too
although I tried not to show it,
especially to him.
That day when I got home
from basketball practice,
I found Pat cowering under the stairway
as I had so many times before
when our parents fought,
but this time, I knew something was different.
He wasn't crying for a change.
"Are Mom and Dad fighting again?" I asked.
"They were," he said, without a trace of emotion,
then he told me Dad had come into his room,
hugged him and said goodbye.
That's when I knew something terrible had happened.
All the years since, I'd nursed him
through the rough times, the blue funks
and the highs that were too much
and always ended in a rush
of promises to stop drinking.
He worked construction, he'd say,
I wouldn't catch him falling off some scaffolding
high above Manhattan,
even drunk he could maintain his balance.
The truth was he was often unemployed,
but I supported him.
I'd long since moved into our parents' room,
but he stayed in his
across the hall from where they'd died,
surrounded by all his trophies from high school, comics
and posters taped and retaped to the walls.
The week before the attack,
he'd told me he was going back to work.
He'd stopped drinking for good
and I believed him, as I looked deeply into his eyes,
and saw a boy who having barely escaped
the inferno of family violence
would still finally perish in fire's cold embrace.

DELUSION

I watched the Trade Center Towers
burning, then collapse
repeatedly on television,
until I could see them clearly
when I shut my eyes.
The blackened skies even blotted out my vision,
until I screamed and threw myself on the floor
and rolled there as if I were on fire.
That's when I decided to go and claim
my sister's body.
The doctor said I had suffered a psychotic break
and in my delusional state,
it didn't matter that she wasn't there.
I carried a photograph of two women laughing,
one of whom was me, the other a stranger
I met on the street, but I pretended she was my sister.
It became my passport into the suffering of others.
I never took money, only sympathy.
I tried to repay everyone
by serving coffee to the firemen and police.
We shared our sorrow,
ate it like bread.
It was our defense
against the senselessness of it all.
They "wanted" to believe that I was seeking
someone I'd lost
and I absorbed their need.
I understood the power of belief and used it.
My phantom sister gave me the power to deceive.
Since I didn't know what was real anymore,
sometimes I thought I'd died
and was a ghost come back to haunt myself.
I'd catch a glimpse of someone familiar
in the mirror before she disappeared
beneath my face.
Was I a mask the past had taken on,
or some magician's trick gone wrong?

Maybe instead of being sawed in half,
I'd been sawed down the middle
and to the gasps of the audience
part of me had run in one direction
and part in the other.
I searched for my sister,
until at last, the looks of pity and concern
I'd learned to accept without question
made me yearn for escape,
so one day, I packed my suitcase
and faded into the landscape
where it all came back to me.
When I was twelve and my sister was ten,
she drowned in Cape Cod Bay.
At first, we swam side by side
in water so calm and blue
it was almost too beautiful.
When suddenly she sank beneath the waves,
I tried to save her, I really did,
but I couldn't stay underwater long enough.
I could have blamed myself
for I had coaxed her
into swimming so far out when she grew tired,
we couldn't reach shore easily,
but I didn't, I was almost relieved.
She was my parents' favorite
and she annoyed me endlessly.
She would have pulled me under, wouldn't she?
I had to save myself.
At first, I didn't even miss her,
oh it hurt, but like a blister
when you burst it,
then it heals and you forget how it felt,
but I began to dream about her.
Sometimes she cried,
but mostly she claimed she hadn't died at all,
but was simply lost
and finally, I thought I found her
when the Twin Towers came down.

At nineteen, I dropped out of college,
left my family and roamed from city to city.
Sometimes, I took my sister's name.
I played a game with myself.
Who am I today? I'd say, staring into the mirror.
Sometimes like a vampire,
I cast no reflection.
Other times, all I saw
was my wild desire to bring her back.
I was tired all the time.
I quit, or was fired from job after job.
Finally, I asked my parents to send money,
which I used to buy green contact lenses
and breast implants.
I dyed my blonde hair red
and adopted a brogue.
I learned to step dance
and joined an Irish troupe and went on the road.
I did what I fantasized my sister would do.
My mind flew everywhere like a bird on a dare.
I resolved to remain in flight,
but one night, during a performance
my feet simply would not move.
I had to be carried offstage
and lifted into an ambulance.
In the hospital, I chanced to see
the horrible events of September 11th on TV.
The day of my release, I told a nurse,
"I'm well, you know,"
and she didn't even glance my way,
as she replied, "That's what they all say."
On the way to my apartment,
my sister came out of hiding.
"You'll find me at ground zero," she whispered
and I answered, "I know."
"I had a conversation with the dead.
It was all in my head," I said aloud.
No one paid any notice.
I was just another person "with issues"
and on that day in particular

attention was focused elsewhere.
So when I showed up at the lodging
for relatives of survivors,
I had an identity at last
that combined the past with the present.
Still, I couldn't find my sister.
I wondered if she had vaporized,
or whether her body, or part of it
was fused to some piece of metal
I would never see, much less feel.
Maybe she was sealed in a room
beneath tons of debris, I told myself,
then I thought I heard her calling my name
over the cacophony of machines,
the voices of rescue workers,
and dogs barking
when they caught the scent of a body,
only to discover another body part
and slink off dejectedly,
until at last, even they lost heart.
By then, I didn't have to pretend
I hadn't given up myself,
and given in to the grim truth
unfolding before my eyes.
I came to hate the lie of my sister
even as I became a symbol of sisterly devotion.
I knew I wasn't worthy,
yet, I couldn't stop the forward motion,
propelling me toward the ocean
where she drowned
in glass, metal, fire and ash.
When I couldn't stand it anymore,
I said I got word she'd never been there afterall.
I had received a mysterious telephone call
informing me she'd left her job
at The World Trade Center months ago,
but didn't know how to reach me.
A friend had seen her photo on a kiosk
with my contact number on it
and had gotten in touch with her.

Now she was calling to tell me
to come to her immediately,
so I packed and set out,
but after a few weeks in Atlantic City,
I felt irresistibly drawn back.
I rejoined the search,
until someone remembered me from before,
pausing, unable to allow that I had somehow
fooled him and asked why I had done it.
I'd run out of lies by then
and the energy it takes to keep
those multicolored balls spinning in the air.
I only wanted to be somewhere the grief of others
was as overwhelming as my own.
He didn't understand,
so once again I made a narrow escape,
and found my sister waiting on the Red Line in Boston.
She hugged me, saying,
"We should come here more often,
just the two of us"
and I agreed, easing into the seat beside her.
"There's seaweed in your hair," I said
and she replied, "I don't care. I'm dead."
Then she laid her head against my shoulder.
It was so hot, my blouse burst into flame,
I told her I wouldn't let her down, I'd hold her,
but like all the other times, I let her go.
At the next stop, I got out,
but instead of walking upstairs
and taking Amtrak to New York City,
I stepped into the path of an oncoming train,
because I preferred to stay in the underworld,
with all the other missing boys and girls.

FAIRY TALE

The first time I heard the story
of Red Riding Hood,
I was so afraid of the wolf

I dreamed he ate me for dinner.
The next morning,
mother found bite marks on my arms.
Even though I swore they weren't my teeth,
she punished me for lying
by tying me to a chair,
facing the object of my dread—
a woodcut of the wolf in Grandma's bed,
but I knew it wouldn't make a difference
because the wolf had chosen me.
At twelve, I turned to model airplanes
and my dreams became a means of escape.
High above my body, looking down,
I'd find the wolf in my bed,
as if he too had been released
from some nightmare
and finally could sleep.
Eventually, I dreamed of girls,
but even so, my nocturnal emissions
often ended in visions of the wolf
dressed in women's clothes
whispering my name seductively.
I came to him every time he came to me
just like the kamikaze did in nineteen forty-three,
when the United States was at war with Japan
and I was a pilot.
For some reason, neither of us fired at first.
We just flew side by side,
staring at each other
across the great military divide.
He wasn't wearing goggles
and I swear I could see his eyes
gleaming like black opals
and the expression on his face
was the one the wolf wore
the first time he tasted me.
I think we Catholics call that look transfiguration.
I don't remember how long our strange communion lasted
before I fired on the bastard.
I flew through the smoke and flames

of his disintegration sure that his death
had left me changed and whole,
but today, when borders and oceans
can be crossed as easily as tossing a coin,
as I am on my way to San Xavier Mission,
suddenly, I hear an explosion,
while all around me, the desert steams
under an empty turquoise sky
and once again, I feel as if I am a fragment of myself.
The highway stretches forward and back without traffic.
I am alone, yet I know the wolf's returned to haunt me
as I stop the car by the side of the road.
When I close my eyes,
I remember watching with horror and relief
as the kamikaze's burning body
shot from the wreckage of the plane
and dropped into the ocean below.
I made it home in one piece,
at least on the outside.
Now I'm retired, in good health,
relocated to Tucson, Arizona, from Baltimore
and I've returned to the Church
after forty years of drifting between the New Age
and whatever "this" is.
I breathe deeply, open my eyes and start the car.
I drive the few miles to the Mission,
where I learn of a terrorist attack on New York City.
I ask Father Anthony if what I experienced earlier
was a premonition,
but he says, "My son, I don't know."
"A miracle then," I ask.
"Only if you pass certain tests.
You didn't save anyone, did you?
But if you saw the Virgin, or a saint . . ."
"Only a wolf," I answer, "and a dead man."
"Was the dead man a good man?"
"Maybe once upon a time."
"So was Adam before the Fall," he says.
"Perhaps it was Satan you saw, for this is his work."
"Yes, Father," I say, but I don't believe that either.

The kamikaze was only a man
and the wolf, I must admit at last, is me.
"You aren't the wolf," he says mysteriously . . .
"I'm not?"
"Don't you remember I absolved you of all that?"
"No, I'm getting old," I answer.
"So are we all, but some of us moreso.
You know the wolf is not necessarily evil.
To some Indian people it is a protector spirit."
"But what could the wolf protect me from?"
"Yourself?"
"I'm not convinced of that," I say.
"Then come have coffee," he says.
"We can chat about this latest manmade disaster
and wait for the Second Coming with bated breath."
"You are so eloquent, Father,
but I'm not in the mood for conversation."
"I'll just pray, until I run out of words,
then I'll howl."
"Have you noticed the absence of birdsong?
It's as if they know of the tragedy.
All right, all right I'll go."
"You know the way," he adds,
laying a hairy hand on mine
and I glimpse behind his benign gaze
the face I know so well.
The reports say people jumped to certain death
when the jets rammed into the Twin Towers.
Rather than let death come to them,
they went to him,
their clothes billowing in the wind,
making them look like the kamikaze
in a fiery tailspin.
I kneel, staring at the altar,
trying to connect the dots of my life
and not getting anywhere,
as mother looks at me with a wolfish grin
and pinches my cheek,
encouraging me to repeat with her,
"The end."

RELATIVITY

Mama says she was lost,
says she asked directions from my father
and doesn't know how they ended up in bed,
or how they created a baby from one afternoon,
a chance meeting at a streetcar stop
in the Japanese neighborhood of Denver.
She was married.
When she told him she was pregnant with his child,
he said, "Go home to your family."
The rest is history, is my story
and I don't know how it ends,
but I hope it's painless when it does,
unlike the end of their affair
which left her gasping for air
as he boarded the streetcar home
to his family and a deep sleep
untroubled by dreams of souls to keep,
but my mother was another story,
Catholic, seventeen and married,
abandoned by the man
she describes as being kind to her,
but how kind could he have been
when he left her to fend for herself,
left her at the top of the stairs,
where she calculated that a fall
might end it all
and sent herself tumbling down them,
only to realize when she came to at the hospital
that she had survived and so had the baby
that was growing inside her
like the truth she could not hide.
When she confessed to her husband, he beat her.
While he was out drinking,
she called her mother and father in Tucson.
They sent her uncle Bill
to take her back home.
She says Uncle and she rode the bus,
not talking until they were out of Colorado.
Uncle had cried when he saw her.

He was that way, you know.
He didn't like women, they said,
he was one of those men,
but they didn't hold that against him
so he was dispatched
to bring my mother and her bastard back.
The family decided that they could hide it all
by allowing everyone to think
I was the husband's daughter.
They didn't worry about the future,
or what that lie might mean to me.
On my birth certificate,
it says he's my father,
but I always knew he wasn't.
The two times I saw him,
I realized my mother was lying,
knew I was the daughter of another,
but I was afraid to ask her about it
and get to the bottom of those stairs
where wracked with guilt and despair,
she finally owned up to her "sin."
She'd never do that again, she tells me,
at least I think that's how she put it
when she told me the truth
or the version of it she'd decided to share.
She says it as if she's talking about someone
she only dimly recognizes
as if I was only a detour on the way
to her real life
and that's what I can't reconcile.
When she said she was just a stupid girl
I thought about how much it had cost her and me,
but I couldn't escape the feeling of displacement
of reeling from the shock of recognition
that doesn't come from finding out
who you really are,
but who you are not,
neither a love child, nor a hate child,
just something that happened
while she wasn't looking.
Her husband was twenty years older.

He ignored her, she said.
He had a girlfriend on the side.
She'd seen them together
and she'd promised herself
that she'd never be unfaithful,
but see how hard promises are to keep, she said,
shouldn't we let sleeping dogs lie?
I'm one big lie, I thought
and she said, "I did it for your own good."
I said, "You should quit while you're ahead
and admit you were ashamed,"
and she said, "That's not true,"
but I knew it was.
Even today, I'm a stranger to her.
When she looks at me, she sees him,
hears him ask her if she's cold
in her thin, wool cardigan, cowboy shirt
loafers and Levis,
her long hair done up in Shirley Temple curls.
He smiles because she's too old
for that hairstyle,
although she's still a girl.
He asks, "Are you lost?
She answers boldly, "Not now."
He was Japanese. He was studying physics
like Albert Einstein, he told her.
When I look in the mirror
sometimes I think I can see his face
imposed over mine,
although it's only an outline really
with a bare fact, a detail
my mother doled out grudgingly.
I truly only see what he left
going faster than any $E=mc^2$ formula
could take him,
escaping fatherhood like any other man
who hadn't planned on staying long,
my otōsan, traveling light,
traveling at the velocity of darkness.

FAMILY

The old man sent for Papa,
but he wouldn't go.
That's what they tell me.
I don't know.
He had land to give him.
He was on his death bed,
but Papa wouldn't go.
Papa said, "Die like a dog, Old Man."
He said it in the shed
where he kept the horse tack.
He said it when he fed the horses.
He said it in bed like a prayer,
then he kissed the only picture
he had of his mother, fell asleep
and woke up another day
and they sent word again.
The Old Man was calling out for him,
but Papa said, "I got a hen's neck to wring.
We're having baked chicken for dinner,"
and he went in the barn
and came out with eggs still warm from laying
and he took them in the kitchen
washed off the shit, put them in a basket
and went to sit on the front porch.
He rocked back and forth in his glider
and Mama brought him a glass of hot apple cider.
"Where's that chicken, John?
Nevermind, I'll do it myself," she said.
"The way he treated my mother," said Papa.
He remembered riding to Texas in a wagon
from Oklahoma when he was five
with his Choctaw mother
and his white father.
An older brother left behind,
because he resembled Choctaws more than Papa did.
"That," he went on, "was a time."
The Old Man on a bay horse,
just staring at him,

until Papa waved,
then turning and riding off.
His father, Charles's silence at dinner,
biscuits and a basket of fried chicken
sent from the ranch house
and a teddy bear with all its fur nearly gone.
"That was mine," said his father,
"now it's yours."
Papa nodded and picked up a chicken leg.
He ate ranch beans, potato salad
and washed it down with buttermilk.
Then his mother put him to bed.
Her long black braid had come undone
and he touched her hair
and it made a sound like silk rustling
in his dreams anyway.
The next day, his father took him to see cattle grazing
as far as the eye could see and further.
He saw a pond for fishing, horses and a bunkhouse,
a doghouse, an outhouse his father once used
and he met a lot of people—cowboys, two cooks
a man who took him up in the saddle of his horse.
That was his uncle, but he didn't know it then.
He died in the Great War.
He didn't see his grandfather.
His father took him in the kitchen of the ranch house.
"You be quiet as a little mouse," he told him.
The cook gave him hot chocolate and a book about the ABC's.
When his father came back, he just said, "Let's go, son."
He didn't return to that house,
until he was twenty,
after his father got killed when a steer trampled him
and ran clear to Abilene,
before anybody could catch it,
at least that's what they say.
Papa didn't know what would happen,
so he started packing.
Then a message came from The Old Man,
whose name was never uttered in their house.
John went that time.

He didn't know what he expected to find.
I'll tell you what he didn't, The Old Man.
The foreman had a letter for him.
It said, "I need a good drover."
He talked it over with his mother,
but she was ready to go back to her people,
so he took her home to Oklahoma,
where he met his brother
and Mama and went back to Texas
with his new bride, a job
and a life this side of respectable.
And so they lived that way for fifteen years.
Grandson and grandfather,
who couldn't put asunder the divisions of race.
Papa gets up. He walks to the gate,
opens it and just waits
for God knows what,
then he steps back and shuts it.
He remembers again the Christmas presents
sent from the ranch house,
always one for him, nothing for his mother
and smothers the urge to kick in the door
of the ranch house
pour gasoline on the Old Man, light it
and watch him burn to a cinder
with a smile on his face.
The same kind The Old Man wore
the day they first came face to face
and The Old Man rode off.
It had no love in it, it had no hate,
but it had kinship.

THE SAGA OF CHARLIE SMITH

For my great-great-grandfather

I had my first Choctaw woman when I was seventeen,
got tired of her, got me another.
I wasn't like my father, who settled for one wife,
and like him, she was Scotch Irish.

They were Catholic, but in desperation,
they had me baptized
by a hellfire and damnation preacher who evangelized
but I wouldn't break my pact with the Devil
who made my desire for red women
such a raging fire.
They almost died when their boat capsized
on the Red River.
They were going to Texas to get away from the Indians and me.
I wouldn't leave, nosiree.
I was born in Choctaw County, Oklahoma.
Back then, it was Indian Territory.
That's what counts in this story.
In those days, you lived the Indian way.
It was easier if you made peace
with the red man, give him a hand
when he needed it and he'd give you one.
You took a wife, raised a bunch of half-breeds.
Nobody made much of it,
unless you made somebody mad
and things got said,
things that could leave you dead,
but by and large, you worked the land
and tried to live like a Christian.
Sounds simple, don't it?—
a few rules to follow
before you got dropped into the ground,
but my second Choctaw wife
wouldn't do nothing I said.
Had to hit her sometimes, hit her in the head,
so she'd understand
what I was trying to teach her.
Nickname was Annie.
She had an Indian name I can't remember,
but I do remember how she would sit on my lap
and bounce up and down on it. What a girl,
but she was wild.
Packed up her rags one day and left me.
I come in from checking on the cattle,
stove was cold, nothing left for Charlie to do

but make bacon and eggs,
twice in one day, mind you.
Soon enough, I got word where she was,
loaded my six-shooter and went to get her.
I found her with a Freedman.
That's what they called freed black slaves.
I said, "Come on out, you black sumbitch.
I'm itching to kill you."
He come out shooting, all the while
she was crying.
Meanwhile, I was shot through my thigh,
blood running into my boot kinda tickled me
and hurt too, of course.
I musta blacked out, because when I came to,
she run at me with a knife, screaming,
"You killed my daddy."
Well, I just about soiled my pants.
She had never said a word to me about a daddy.
I thought she didn't have one.
She didn't even look like one athem mixtures,
looked full-blooded to me,
but maybe I just couldn't see it, being a white man
and not used to how they turn out.
I mean, I had seen some of them.
They looked like any other coloreds to me.
"I'll be," I said, then out come her uncle.
I knew him. He was part white.
"What the hell?" I told him, "This is too confusing.
A man ought to know who he's shooting, oughtn't he?"
He raised holy hell about it, then whispered, "Good shooting,"
to me under his breath.
I just wanted my wife to come back.
She did a few days after the funeral,
caught me in bed with the redheaded daughter
of that Irish pots and pans mender,
who used her to get work.
She knew how to make a man feel like a man
if you know what I mean,
not like my first wife, Iola, who lay there
wincing the whole time.

Annie cursed me in Choctaw. I knew what she said,
but I kept it to myself.
The redhead cried, "You going to let that squaw
talk to you that way?
She says she's going to cut it off."
"Why Moira, I didn't know you could speak Choctaw," I said
like it was just an ordinary observation,
as she dressed
and left me trying to defend myself.
A few days later, the tribal police come to my place.
They asked me to ride with them in a friendly way,
but I knew they wasn't.
They was relatives of Annie's.
I told them I'd come after I fed the cattle,
then saddled up and rode hard into Texas.
That ride made me a fugitive from justice,
but Indians don't mess with white men in Texas,
so I became what I had always been,
a white man who had lived among Indians,
but had not become one of them.
I had tried. I'd married their women
would have had children then too,
but the first one, a bastard, was stillborn
and my fourth, or fifth wife, a Cherokee, got rid of one
by using some remedy her mother brought with her
when she walked the Trail of Tears.
I did not hold that against my wife.
I thought she'd change her mind,
but she said she was too old,
said I wasn't worth a damn and she was right.
I strayed again. Found myself another Indian gal,
a Choctaw mixed with white.
She was fourteen. I was sixty.
I thought she'd conceive, but she was barren
and died from TB when she was sixteen.
After that, I met Fannie, a full-blooded Choctaw,
who finally gave me two sons.
They both hate me.
I don't know howcome.
I only know I'm an old man now.

Looking back on ninety-five years with some remorse.
A woman is not a horse you can trade, sell or shoot
when you get tired of her.
I realize now that it's too late
a man can learn from his mistakes.
A few good women is all it takes.

DISGRACE

I was drinking scotch and water
when my daughter got home.
She was wearing the graduation dress
I bought her at JCPenney.
It looked like it had stayed on her,
and I was relieved,
because I had imagined her
lying on the backseat
of a beat up Ford
as the Martinez boy put his you know what
you know where.
The dress was too old for her,
a black, velvet sheath
with a big satin bow in front.
I told her I wouldn't buy it, but I did.
I shouldn't have.
Now I tell her, "You disobeyed me."
"I told you to be home by twelve midnight.
I don't care if you just graduated
from high school.
You are seventeen and living under my roof
and it is three o'clock in the morning.
Guess I'll have to teach you a lesson,"
I say quietly, although I want to yell.
That's when I trip over the vinyl hassock
I bought at Levitz Furniture half-off
Christmas in July sale
and fall flat on my ass.
"This is nineteen sixty-five," she says,
"not the Stone Age."

"Don't sass me," I yell finally,
as she runs in her room and slams the door.
"And don't slam that goddamn door.
It gives me a headache."
These days you can't tell a girl nothing.
She thinks she knows everything.
Got those Beatle records, them Rolling Stones
and what not.
All those white men. I don't know
what's gotten into her.
She's going down a dangerous path
on roller skates, yes she is
and I'm all that's standing between her
and disgrace.
Ever since she started men'strating,
I have dedicated my life
to keeping her from getting pregnant
out of wedlock.
All a woman's got is her good name
and there's always some worthless man
waiting to drag it through the mud.
I should know.
I didn't turn up with no bastards,
not exactly, no, but I could have
and yes, she only knows half the story
about that sonofabitch first husband of mine,
old enough to be my father,
left me alone so he could run around
with a white waitress, what was her name?
Did I ever know it?
Anyway, left me at the mercy of another man,
left me with her.
I plan to tell her the whole truth one of these days.
She's already suspicious.
Who wouldn't considering how she looks?
Took after her real father.
I just tell everybody it's our Indian blood.
"She's Indian," I say,
if anybody asks me about her,
but if you really "look" at her,

you see the Japanese.
You see Mike Ogawa, that's who,
on his knees,
taking off my penny loafers and socks,
see him kissing my toes,
so I tingle all over and go weak.
I know I shouldn't,
but I can't even open my mouth
to let his tongue in,
just have to lie back
and feel as if the whole world
is one big candy apple,
red and juicy just for me,
until reality comes knocking at the door
nine months later.
What a sound.
After Mike leaves me the last time,
I see what I've done
without the blinders on,
but it's too late.
I don't want her to end up like that.
I want her to come in the kitchen,
while I make a grilled cheese and tomato sandwich
the way I used to when she was a little girl
and it was the two of us against the world,
not just her against me,
but she won't because now I am her enemy.
I've only tried to make her see how empty
what she thinks is love can be.
That Martinez boy is half like her,
Mexican and Negro,
not a bad combo as it goes.
They'd have pretty children,
but I know he'd hurt her.
Pretty men are useless.
She needs a toothless old fool
she can control,
but some of them are cruel too
and use a young girl, yes they do.
I should let her get her kicks

on the old Route 66 of heartbreak, I guess,
but I am too old to clean up the mess,
no she's going to college.
She'll make something of herself, unlike me.
I let my chances disappear between my legs
more than once and look at me now,
doing housework,
not making enough money to dress my girl
the way she deserves.
I ought to tell her about her father,
just call her out here
but I won't, it's too soon
and tomorrow I won't speak to her either
when she gets up the courage
to ask me to pass the sugar,
as we eat our cornflakes in a silence
as loud as a slamming door
and footsteps going downstairs
on which later I take a "fall,"
to get rid of her,
but only succeed in scaring myself
into this reluctant motherhood.
After we finish, I finally croak a few words,
as if I haven't spoken for a long time.
"Dicks don't have no conscience," I tell her
and she gives me a look that asks,
"What are you talking about?"
"I mean," I pause, thinking it should be clear.
"Mom, I'm just taking out the garbage," she says,
as I put away the past
like a wedding dress.

GREETINGS FRIEND

Choctaw, Cherokee . . .
It was all the same to me
when I was ten.
All I knew was we were Indian,
part anyway.

I couldn't tell by looking at myself.
I just saw a mouth with front teeth missing.
I always wore a red velvet shirt like a Navajo
a cowboy belt, jeans, cowboy boots
and my hair in pigtails.
When I went outside to play,
I'd whoop and holler
and pretend I was a warrior
defending my people,
until my mother called me
and my Siamese to dinner.
He ate beside the table
on the floor, of course.
Afterward, I'd go outside again
and look at my horse, Queenie.
I didn't ride because I was scared to,
but I gave her sugar,
then I stood on a stool
and scratched her head above the white star.
Sometimes she whinnied and galloped over
when she saw me.
Other times, she just ran away
as if she didn't want to be bothered
by little girls that day.
She was like my great-grandfather, John.
He lived with my great-aunt
and spent his time sitting in his room.
Once I asked him what he was doing
and he said, "Chewing on the past."
"How does it taste?" I asked.
He said, "Like sawdust,"
then he didn't say anything else.
He mostly kept to himself,
a cigar box of deeds in his lap.
I mean ashes,
because he didn't own the land anymore.
A few years before,
somebody burned down his house in Oklahoma
after he found oil.
He said he knew who'd had a hand in it,

but he was too old to fight them
and asked my great-aunt to move
him and my great-grandmother, Maggie,
to Tucson, Arizona,
which is where I was
and where he sat, a can of tobacco spit
at his feet,
the smell of it and the musty odor of old people
mixed in with something else
so suffocating I used to have to run outside
and take deep breaths
if I stayed too long.
He'd always say, "Go on and play.
I'm tired today,"
but one time, he called me back.
He said, "I got something for you,"
and he gave me a photo of an Indian man.
He said, "that's my brother.
He's named after me."
I wondered how that could be, but I didn't say so,
then he said, "Don't you see the resemblance?"
I said, "Sort of,"
and he just snorted and bit off some tobacco
and started talking about the past,
but I wasn't interested
and he said, "Go on then.
Take care of that picture,
you'll need it someday."
I was so happy to escape,
I kissed his wrinkled cheek
and didn't even need to breathe
fresh air once I got out of there.

Now I look at the photograph
and try to feel something about it,
but I can't and I can't even claim
that being fifty-three has given me
some perspective on what John was doing
when he gave it to me.
"Must have been a whim of some kind," says my mother.

"You know how old people are."
Still it worries me sometimes
that I can't find the reason,
can't even find out what his brother's name really was,
unless John wasn't teasing me back then.
"I wonder if they were twins?"
"No, couldn't have been."
"John was older," mother tells me
and, "He lived like a white man."
I wonder what she means by that,
but when I ask her,
she just goes back to smoking her cigarette
and says, "Let the dead stay dead.
Anyway, I'm black and I'm proud.
I'm not an Indian anymore, if I ever was."
But I remember when she used to dress
like a Navajo too and go to powwows
and all her friends were Indians, or part.
She married black men, except for my father,
but that's another story
and I won't bother with it now.
Like Queenie, I don't have time.
I'm busy searching old census records,
land titles and such,
trying to reconstruct what was once
a living, breathing entity,
but now I realize was John's sawdust.
As I sit in his room,
which is long empty,
because when he died, they burned all his things,
I wish he'd come back, so I could ask him
what it was like to be robbed of his birthright,
if that's what it was.
But maybe he didn't think of his land that way.
Maybe he thought he was just its caretaker.
I don't know, but being so close to it all
makes me feel if I just call his name the right way,
he'll lean down from heaven,
or wherever he is and say,
"That's right, that's it. Now go on and play."

But I'm chewing on nothing but air and I know it
and my mother is saying how we're Choctaws
and we're better than these Arizona Indians
and I say, "I thought you were black,"
as she goes back to coughing just like John used to,
until she says, "Shit, who knows what I am?"
When I look in the mirror now,
I see a little girl
who can't be anyone I know,
who long ago, met Tonto at the drive-in
and said, "How" and raised her hand in greeting
and he said, "How"
and moved on to the next car,
leaving her, leaving me even then
with a slight sense of dislocation.
I remember how proud we were
that an Indian was there to meet us,
although John said we'd have been better off
staying home and going to bed early,
because a real Indian
would never say "How,"
he'd just know what to do.
I guess that means I'm not real either.
I guess I'm just pretending
and should give up and move
and let my house burn,
let my oil earn another man's living,
but I'm not giving up.
I won't be dust.
I won't just sit here,
too old to do more
than pore over charred papers
and rue the day Columbus arrived
just in time for the big giveaway.

GRANDFATHER SAYS

"Sit in my hand."
I'm ten.

I can't see him,
but I hear him breathing
in the dark.
It's after dinner playtime.
We're outside,
hidden by trees and shrubbery.
He calls it hide-and-seek,
but only my little sister seeks us
as we hide
and she can't find us,
as grandfather picks me up
and rubs his hands between my legs.
I only feel a vague stirring
at the edge of my consciousness.
I don't know what it is,
but I like it.
It gives me pleasure
that I can't identify.
It's not like eating candy,
but it's just as bad,
because I had to lie to grandmother
when she asked,
"What do you do out there?"
"Where?" I answered.
Then I said, "Oh, play hide-and-seek."
She looked hard at me,
then she said, "That was the last time.
I'm stopping that game."
So it ended and I forgot.
Ten years passed, thirty-five,
when I began to reconstruct the past.
When I asked myself
why I was attracted to men who disgusted me
I traveled back through time
to the dark and heavy breathing part of my life
I thought was gone,
but it had only sunk from view
into the quicksand of my mind.
It was pulling me down
and there I found grandfather waiting,

his hand outstretched to lift me up,
naked and wet
where he rubbed me.
"I'll do anything for you," he whispered,
"but let you go."
And I cried, "Yes," then, "No."
"I don't understand how you can do this to me.
I'm only ten years old,"
and he said, "That's old enough to know."

THE SECRET

You stand so still beside my bed,
the pillow raised above my head
while I pretend to be asleep.
I can barely keep from laughing,
but I don't want to stop playing.
I'm having so much fun.
I won't betray myself by saying,
"Mommy, see I'm still awake.
I was only fooling you,"
as you take a nickel
from your robe pocket
and lay it under my pillow,
whispering, "Willow, do you know
how much your mommy loves you?"
I know you did before the "incident."
That's what Daddy calls it.
I think it had something
to do with my baby brother, Danny,
who got taken up to Heaven
when he was three and I was eight.
I just remember his bed was empty
and you were crying beside it that time.
Afterward, Daddy took you to your bedroom.
You stayed a long time with the shades drawn
and the maid dressed me.
She combed my hair,
prepared my lunch and shook her head

when she heard your name.
Then one day I came home from school
to find you sitting on the stool
in the kitchen,
chopping carrots and celery
so you could make your famous stew.
I said, "Where's Ethel?"
"She's gone," you answered
and I said I didn't like her anyway
she smelled like wet wool and cabbage.
We had dinner like a family
but we weren't the way we used to be.
Daddy didn't notice, but I did
how you hid your tears.
When I heard you crying and went to help
you'd yell, "Are you spying on me?"
I began to stay in my room.
Other times, when I came home from school,
I'd find you prowling the hall
like a caged lion.
Back and forth you'd stalk
all the while talking about Danny
as if he were still here
and not in the grave.
I knew that's where he really was
because I'd seen him in his little casket,
then watched as they lowered it
in the ground
and heard the sound of your screams
in my bad dreams that night.
Grandmother said I should have stayed home.
I was too young to go to a funeral,
but you said, "She's got to learn that life
is just dust in the end,"
or did the reverend say that and not you?
I seem to remember adults there,
but no other children, except cousin Johnnie,
who is older than me and gets an allowance
and never sees his mother on her knees,
scrubbing the floor which isn't dirty,

because the new maid cleaned it
before she left an hour ago.
Something is wrong, but I don't know
how to tell Daddy,
so I tell my dolls and my teddy bear.
They think I should do something
and I say I will
when I am ready.
Now they are mad
and won't talk to me,
because they think I don't value their advice.
They say I'd rather ask my computer
which is only a machine.
I did log on to a Web site for teens
whose parents had died,
but it didn't help.
I tried to find one for dead brothers and sisters,
but I only got locked out by this thing
Daddy put on it for my protection.
Now I sit, facing the wall,
while Mommy calls out Danny's name,
as if he can answer.
Maybe it's a game she's playing
like the one she plays with me,
the one I pretend not to see.
Maybe Danny's only playing dead too
and there's no gash in his head,
where he was struck hard
with a glass decanter that shattered,
leaving splatters on the walls and carpet
and a trail of red down the hall
that I followed to find Mommy
lying on her back,
glass embedded in her hands.
When Daddy came home from work,
they locked me in my room
and when I came out,
everything was different
and smelled of disinfectant
and Mommy wasn't anywhere

and Danny simply wasn't there—
no clothes, no toys,
no awful smell of boy remained.
Ethel said our apartment was like a tomb
and turned on the TV, opened the curtains
and told me to make all the noise I wanted,
but after Mommy came back
I had to keep quiet.
I couldn't even chew cornflakes too loudly,
so I'd hold them in my mouth,
until the milk softened them,
then I'd swallow.
Sometimes I'd gag
and Mommy would send me to my room
where I would sit
until I learned not to disobey.
Today, she made me pray for forgiveness,
but I don't know why.
I didn't do anything wrong. Did I?
I asked and threw my glass of orange juice.
It smashed against the refrigerator.
One piece stuck in my hand
when I tried to remove it from my hair.
After I started to cry, Mommy did too,
then she said, "It's not you, not you."
Everything was fine,
until Daddy had to drag her away from my bed.
"Your mother's tired," was all he said.
The next day, she was gone again.
Ethel was back
and I decided maybe I should pray,
so I knelt in front of my dolls and Teddy
and confessed my sin,
because I was ready.
They told me they always knew the truth.
I can't hide anything from them.
I tried and failed and Mommy knows too,
but she'll never tell.
Cross my heart and hope to die
I never will either.

INTERCOURSE

for John Kennedy, Jr.

The water is a cold fire I swallow,
thinking it tastes like blood,
as I rise to the surface.
I'm saved, I think, as my head
emerges from the waves,
then everything disappears in a gray haze
that smells of smoke and sizzling flesh.
I choke, spit out bits of bone.
I'm surprised to see a mermaid
sitting on a smooth black stone.
I tell her I'm lost
and she throws me a rope of long, blonde hair,
but when I grab hold,
she pokes me with a trident
and I fall back into pure hopelessness.
I drift that way a long time,
until I find myself in your bedroom.
I inhale the perfume of your sleep,
a combination of baby powder and almond oil,
trying to keep from waking you as I breathe deeply,
but you open your eyes
and I am seized by the need to confess
all the things I've ever kept secret,
but I can't remember what they are,
so I settle for idle conversation.
I mastered the art of seeming ordinary, I tell you,
but you don't respond.
Is that why you don't recognize me, I continue,
content to hear the sound of my own voice,
though it's filled with weariness
and a chilly intimacy,
which seems to increase
with each breath I take.
"I rose from the dead just for you," I say finally
and that seems to move you,
as a tear slides down your cheek
and seeks refuge under the sheet,

pulled up to your chin,
as if it can keep me from getting too close.
Didn't you cry for me over green tea and poppy-seed cake?
Didn't you make a pilgrimage to the botanical gardens
and sit meditating over my fate,
as if you could make sense of your own life
by summoning mine, or am I mistaken?
I loved how you stared at my photographs, I say,
and endless film footage of me
leading my life in the public eye,
as if I had no idea I was being watched.
My inamorata, I'll do anything, I whisper,
as I take your hand
and press it against my erection.
At last, you seem to wake
from your enchanted sleep,
then wrest your hand from mine,
asking, "How can you dress like this?"
Is that any way to talk to your prince?
I admit I'm not wearing Armani,
but what difference does it make now?
You ask if I have proof I'm who I say I am.
You can't believe I'd appear to you
wearing white chinos, white opennecked shirt
with the sleeves rolled up,
my feet bare, my toenails painted dark red.
I turn my head in profile.
See. Death only enhanced my beauty.
I'm still John.
I'm still living on in your dreams,
as horny and ordinary as any guy on a first date,
who can't say, or do anything right,
but feels he must prove he can.
You're not amused.
You think you can do better
and I sink into a puddle of saltwater,
as you finally relent and call my name.
It's too late. I came and went
in the same instant it took you to realize
you'd captured your prize only to lose him

as he slipped between your thighs,
but could not penetrate the sealed landscape,
where celebrity creates an alternate reality.
There fact and fiction lie
one atop the other fucking furiously,
when one surrenders unconditionally,
the other dies.

TRUE LOVE

I absorb you through my skin,
then exhale you like a breath held too long.
I inhale again, air scented like cloves, oranges and musk,
by the candles I bought just for tonight,
as you slide your fingers inside me,
pull them out and wipe them on my thigh.
My fluid dries in the breeze
from the fan that does not cool.
Ninety-five degrees and nothing
to ease us back from the precipice,
where we stand, staring down.
We end here tonight,
or descend from the heights of passion
to become a couple.
You look into my eyes,
trying to read my desire,
as if it will tell you what to do.
You put your hand in the fire
and now it's burning you,
turning you into another one of my possessions.
It's what you want. If you didn't
you wouldn't beg to be poured into my mouth.
I press your face down
and say, "That's where I am."
You get up after I'm done, wash and dress
and I lie watching you,
waiting for you to give me a sign you'll come back.
"You're destroying me," you say.

I can't stay away from you and it's too much.
I can't work, or think about anything
but how sweet you taste
and that place where you put your hand last time.
"You mean up your ass?" I say,
delighting in being crass,
provoking you, a pastime of mine.
"I won't let you make me the villain of this B movie.
Why don't you go home to Mommy,
but you can't fuck her, can you?"
That gets to you. I knew it would.
You slam the door on the way out
of our favorite hotel room
in Bisbee, Arizona.
Our vacation in hell, if you ask me,
but you love the atmosphere,
love the "primitiveness" of it.
No air-conditioning, dial phones,
an old-fashioned iron bed
and a small black-and-white TV, no cable.
Just you, just me.
"Nothing between us and our lust," you said,
but there is, isn't there?
It's eternity. It's the thing always out there
when people start caring about each other.
It smothers love eventually,
yet we need it.
We pursue it single-mindedly.
I lie in bed contentedly, despite my unease,
thinking maybe you freed yourself from me this time,
until I hear your key in the lock,
then I turn, facing the mirrored bathroom door
and pretend to be asleep,
imagining how tomorrow you'll be so glad
I didn't see you raise the heavy, glass ashtray
above my head for a few minutes,
before you put it back on the table
and admitted to yourself at last
that you belong to me.

RUDE AWAKENING

The first time I saw Clotilde,
she was standing in the window
of an Amsterdam brothel,
her negligee discreetly buttoned
from head to toe,
so I had to use my imagination.
I liked that, liked how she beckoned me
with one long, scarlet fingernail.
"Follow me," it said and I obeyed.
Before I met her,
I taught high school English in Rapid City
and coached volleyball
and most of the time
I didn't even think about my nights
lying alone in bed, smoking,
watching the red lights of my alarm clock.
Last July, I got an insurance check,
because I wrecked my car
and I decided to use the money
to do some things I'd always dreamed about.
My buddy, Art, the Assistant Principal
and I went to London, Rome, Paris
and I allowed him to harass me
into going to see the prostitutes of Amsterdam.
He said, "Frank, are you a man?"
I answered, "Yes, I am,"
and so we went to take a look and look we did.
He was sensible.
He partook, but did not take out
more than he put in,
but then he didn't fall in love
and have to spend so many nights
waiting for his beloved to get off work
and do for free what she was paid to do
simply because she loved me
and not because she wanted my money.
I swear there was nothing to make me suspicious
and it was so exciting with her

that I did not acknowledge what I knew
deep in my heart
and so in my mind escaped total complicity
in the thing that came to be my ruination.
Clotilde's gone now,
she's just the breeze
that chills me this autumn afternoon
when instead of teaching,
I'm lying in bed, trying to understand
why I chose to accept the disgrace of losing my job
and not to fight, not to present myself
to the school board as a victim of her deceit
as an answer to the complaints
about the company I was keeping.
Art, being the SOB I'd once mistaken for a friend,
decided to tell the secret
I had not failed to share with him,
so overcome was I by passion.
I never thought we'd end our friendship
over that thin, slip of a girl
just because she had a penis.
I ask you, what is wrong with the company of men?
If I had read the guidebook that said,
"If you visit one of the women,
we would like to remind you
that they are not always women,"
I wonder now if I would have faced it all sooner
and left my darling back in the window,
posing as if for a Rembrandt tableau
in which a slightly overweight, middle aged man
pretends to practice the art of letting go
and does not notice
what is so obvious to those
whose vision is not obstructed
by the rose-colored glasses
behind which with eyes closed tightly
he kisses the throat of his loved one
and runs his tongue over the apple there
and knows everything at once.
Don't we all want a little mystery

with our romance,
even if it is accompanied
by a rude awakening,
when you find in your hand
the kind of surprise
that might disgust any other man,
but only made me wonder at fate
and how it sends us the mate we always wanted,
if only we could admit it.

GENDER/BENDER

for Chip

Men used to call me "Beauty."
They all wanted me
and I let them run their hands
over my body
and taste the anisette of it,
but they meant nothing to me,
while you mean everything.
I asked my friends for help.
I even asked my mother.
I said, "Is he my soul mate,
he can't be, can he,
isn't it a mistake
and how can I make it go away?"
He can't give me what I want.
He loves me in his way
which is to say
within the limits of his sexual orientation.
The one experience he had with a woman
when he was seventeen
was a disaster, he tells me,
as he takes my hand out of the blue.
We are getting ready to go to a party
and like any other couple,
we stand in front of the mirror,
checking our reflections for imperfections.
True, I have stood with other men,

both clothed and naked,
but never in love like this,
in love enough to make me wish
I were a man,
so I could stand naked with him,
running my hands over him, erect and quivering,
before licking him from neck to feet,
then back up to meet his lips in a kiss
that nullifies all other kisses
and defies the limits of our bodies.
I could wear a strap-on dildo (why not?).
They make them so lifelike now.
Would he know the difference
if he were blindfolded
and didn't touch me?
Would he somehow feel the subtle presence
of a woman assuming the disguise
of a man's desire?
Once a fire's lit,
it burns until it's out.
Could he stop me
once I put my tongue inside his mouth
even when he tastes my lipstick?
Or maybe he'd think I was a cross-dresser,
a transsexual,
or some other hypertextual combination.
Would I be me, or just a version
he could tolerate
for a furtive and exciting assignation,
a vacation from himself perhaps
when he relaxes into a new identity,
not knowing who is he and who is she,
only knowing me,
as I sit astride him,
as he lies face down, moaning into his pillow,
"What a man. You are so powerful.
And sensitive."
I know I should give up
and accept the fact that he is homosexual,
so clinical, but accurate,

so unromantic
and lacking the thrust of poetry.
Love is just love,
until it's physical,
then often it turns cynical and violent.
I'm better off without that loss of dignity.
But maybe I "should" drink that poison once again
and on the brink of dying
send my spirit flying into him,
but ooh la la I mustn't forget we're friends,
not lovers, not enemies,
just in between extremes,
safe in our dangerous dreams.

FIFTY-THREE

"I never thought I'd end up a hard blonde," I said,
"Did you?"
My friend, Sue, looked at me, just looked,
then went to pee
and I settled down to think about it,
but first, I ordered another round.
"Bartender, I mean Brad," I yelled,
over the hell-raising boys
bellied up at the bar, "Fill 'er up."
This round's on Sue, who's back
from the restroom now,
hair combed and sprayed
and there's a chalky place under her left eye,
where she put too much concealer,
but I'm too depressed to tell her about it
and I just lick salt from my lips
and knock back another shot of tequila.
"That shit'll kill you," says Sue,
as she downs another scotch on rocks.
Scotch on cocks, I call it,
but she doesn't get it and I let it slide.
She's my best friend now and then

when I'm beside myself
and about to do something terrible.
She can always tell
and says, let's get the hell out of town,
which means let's go down to the Shamrock Bar,
where the drinks keep coming
like I used to,
before the change got through with me.
Now I have to fantasize
like nobody's business
just to get set and go.
Ask my last boyfriend, that no good sonofabitch,
who ditched me for a younger, dumber version
of guess who?
Boy is he in for a surprise
once her eggs dry up
and she starts to look a little tired about the eyes,
her hair starts thinning
and when men look past her
as if she isn't there.
I'm here, though, like an itch
that won't go away
and here I'll stay
on a stool at the end of the bar,
where I can see everybody who comes in,
hoping one of them will take me
down memory lane and leave me there.
Twenty-three and raring to see what's next,
as I sit on some guy's face,
but every hair in place,
as I yell my own name,
because I love myself too much
to ever love anyone else.
But that'll never happen now.
Now I sit watching the shitty night unfolding
as fast as it can,
knowing I won't be holding anything in my hand tonight
but another drink and a bottle of Percodan,
daring myself to do it one more time.

PASSAGE

for Allen Ginsberg

Sunflowers beside the railroad tracks,
sunflowers giving back the beauty God gave you
to one lonely traveler
who spies you from a train window
as she passes on her way to another train station.
She wonders if she were like you
rooted to your bit of earth
would she be happy,
would she be satisfied
to have the world glide past and not regret it?
For a moment, she thinks so,
then decides that, no, she never could
and turns back to her book of poetry,
remembering how hard it was to get here
and that flowers have their places as people do
and she cannot simply exchange hers for another,
even though she wants it.
That's how it is.
Her mother told her.
Now she believes her,
although she wishes she didn't.
At fifty-three, she feels the need
to rebel against the inevitable winding down.
She already feels it in her bones,
feels artery deterioration, and imagines
cancerous indications on medical charts
she hopes will never be part of her life,
as she turns back to the window
to catch the last glimpse of the sunflowers
that sent her thoughts on a journey
from which she knows she will never return,
only go on and on
and then just go.

LULLABY

Run my child. Don't delay.
The beast is beating on the door
with rifle butt and fists.
Soon his boots are stomping
on the floor, as if he's cold
and trying to warm his feet.
He hasn't had a thing to eat for days
and tears bread from your sister's hand
before he shoots her in the head
and smashes all the dishes.
His mouth full, he chews
as he ascends the stairs
two at a time and finds me
calmly sitting on the bed.
"Waiting for me?" he asks,
as he hurls a stone
that strikes me in the face,
breaking my jaw,
then proceeds to set fire to my body,
after which he walks back downstairs and outside.
The hound howls as the neighbors
steal what's left of us.
We're dead afterall.
Who cares whether or not we suffered
or even that they once called us friends,
because in the end they agree
we got what we deserved for being born.
I hoped you would survive,
but you die anyway beside the road
your body frozen to the earth
until spring,
when your bones are discovered by the hound
who buries them with other bones
he's collected as he roams the countryside
masterless now and wild.
He's forgotten he once was companion to a child,
who used to scratch him between the ears.
Now that spot is inflamed

and he shakes his head and rubs it against a tree
beside the stream where we picnicked
and he stood on his hind legs,
almost dancing as he begged for scraps
of boiled ham, dark bread and deviled eggs.
Now when he hears the sound of voices,
he growls, covers the bones quickly
and hides beneath the burned-out shell of a car
until they fade
like all the voices that once made us family,
but could not save us from our destiny.

THE BROKER

Twins are good luck.
In my country, a boy and a girl especially.
Two boys equals double support,
but two girls I am sorry to report
are looked on as burdens.
Of course, sometimes the stars
are inclined to bestow
more bounteous fortune on a family
than they might ordinarily
and twins of any and/or either sex
are blessed by being born
under a sign
that is cause for rejoicing
rather than for mourning.
Your twins, fortunately, are a boy and girl.
You cannot in all the world
find any two more compatible with you.
They are not from my country, no.
I acquired them, shall we say, in Mexico.
They speak no English,
although they know the words,
"please," and "thank you,"
which I taught them,
because I felt it might

make them a bit more acceptable
to a respectable person like you.
Americans appreciate courtesy.
I know that now that I am an American
and no longer let astrology,
or superstition rule my life,
no, I let my daily planner do that
and it is telling me
that I have another appointment
in exactly thirty minutes,
so if you're ready
we can retrieve the children.
They will be so grateful to receive you
and will repay you a thousand times
for choosing me to be your procurer.
That word does not offend me,
because it describes perfectly
the service I provide
for discerning customers
who want a bit of the exotic in their lives.
The downpayment you wired to my bank
is earning interest
and I appreciate your advice on investments.
One has to think of the future,
even if one finds it unpleasant.
I used to live from day to day,
but I realize that isn't the way it is here,
where fear of starvation
or some other tribulation is less common
than among my countrymen.
Where are my keys?
Ah, here they are glittering like stars
above the ocean
the night my brother offered to stake me with—
Oh, yes, I know you're anxious to get going.
You're a busy person.
So am I
and what is worse than hearing boring stories
about someone else's struggles.

I know, I know it is difficult
to juggle your duties.
I have the same problem myself.
Anyway, come children,
come say goodbye to uncle.
What? Oh, it's just a term
one uses in my country.
One learns to do what one has to
in order to make things run smoothly
don't you think?
Remember if you find that you desire
another foray into uncharted waters
I am at your service.
All sales are final.
Thank you.

THE CALLING

I promised I'd be good that day
and go to missionary school,
but the bad man still came to punish me.
My mother begged him to spare my life,
but he said, "Woman, I am Africa
and Africa takes what it wants."
He opened a box and she looked inside,
then she screamed and fell to her knees.
Before I knew what was happening,
pain shot a fiery bullet into my arm.
When I came to, I was surprised
for my whole body told me I died
when death shook my hand.
My mother burned the stump to cauterize it.
Is healing agony? It must be, I decided,
as I lay in the strange quiet of morning.
Not even a cock crowed,
no women went to get water for cooking,
no scent of plaintains and stew
blew into our hut.

I shut my eyes and tried to ride
the waves of nausea,
flowing through my body
to someplace where suffering did not exist,
but it was useless.
Again and again, I returned to the place
where my hand, clenched in a fist
lay in a box with other hands
in various states of decay.
When my mother shook me awake,
I knew what I would do.
"Get me a knife," I told her.
I began to practice slicing melons
with one hand,
until I could take my place
beside the man who's like a father to me now,
as we wander around, demanding reparations
in pounds of flesh.
In the villages, they call me "The Chopper,"
and they say it with respect.

THE WHITE HOMEGIRL

My mom liked back roads, side roads,
high roads and low.
She didn't know much, but she knew go.
Once she got started, she wouldn't slow down
until she was out and she was out a lot.
I understood, though. She got depressed
'cause people fucked with her, people did
and she'd take a break, relieve some stress
then she'd be fine for a while,
get clean, get a job.
They couldn't tame a girl like her, like me,
but they tried. She'd tell me
to be strong like the brothers
who could give her what she needed,
the ones who only sold

and didn't partake of the product.
When she scored, I'd wait around for her outside.
Sometimes I'd find another kid
in the same typea situation.
Tyronne was last time.
He helped me with my homework
while mom was whoring inside.
Anyway, that was a long time ago, like twelve years.
I was ten then. I wasn't scared
when the big shit finally happened and Mom OD'd.
I got put in a foster home.
Boy was I ever glad to move outta there
when I came "of age."
I'd always been of age. They just didn't know it
and now I don't do no dope, I don't 'ho.
I work at Jack n' Box, Taco Bell, you know
until I get restless, then I rolls
with my homies.
You can always find a few discarded like condoms
by their parents who maybe got caught up in somethin'
they didn't know how to get out of and you,
you just along for the ride.
Like Tyronne, Baby Ruth and Chantel, my homies
we just going, well, that's my moms, that's my pops.
We don't make excuses, I mean I didn't.
Now I'm the kind of woman she would have been,
made for friendship, not sex,
with my flat ass, my flat chest
and a big mouth
that gets me in trouble
I can always get out of,
'cause I'm smart
and know how to start something and finish it.
See me "rope a dope" around the coke, the "herine,"
the mainline to nowhere.
Honey, I been there
and I'm not going back,
not even to get my mother's body.

THE GREENWOOD CYCLE

after the events surrounding the Tulsa Riots

1. Conjure

I thought I was dreaming,
when I saw the sky fulla black smoke,
but I wasn't, no, 'cause I pinched myself
and it hurt
and I knew we were gonna suffer
for somebody's sinfulness.
"Just like Jesus," you said, Mama,
when you screamed,
"Run, daughter, run,
white men are comin', they got guns."
I said, "I see 'em, Mama, I see,
they ridin' up and down the street
throwin' torches on rooftops, on porches,
on the poor Negro trying to pray
while the flames eat him up
they so hungry.
Mama, we can't get away."
"Run on, daughter," you cried, "hide if you can
from the white devil,"
but he wasn't no devil, he was a man
and he was evil, yes, he was,
but he wasn't supernatural,
he didn't have no power to conjure like I do,
when I conjure you,
crying, "Don't look back, or you'll turn to ashes
and fall down among the dead in Greenwood."

Now I'm alone
and I don't say nothing 'bout it to nobody,
just fix me a hot toddy
and sit rocking in my rocker
and think about you, Mama,
turned to dust
wrapped in a dirty sheet
with a body lying on top.

"It ain't Christian, is it," you whisper,
"to be murdered like this and just forgot?"
I rock in time
to the ticktock of the grandfather clock
you dragged from the burning house,
because it was your daddy's,
give to him by the old master
when your daddy got freedom.
For some reason, it didn't burn up
just charred a bit,
a piece of wood pried off it.
When I got up the money,
I went and bought it off the junkman,
who thought it was worth something.
It was, but only to me,
rusted, permanently stopped
at the hour and the minute
that cost me you.

2. Sanctuary

> *"Is the world on fire?"*
> —SISTER OF MR. BEARD, survivor

I said, "Brother, the world's on fire."
He said, "Liar,"
but Daddy said, "Y'all climb on up higher
in that tree so only God can see you,
not me, or the white man running thisa way,
guns blazing, burning up everything.
Can't see nothing through the smoke,
can't breathe, choking like I got two hands
around my throat.
Je-e-e-sus, Je-e-e-sus."
"Brother," I whispered, and he said, "Hush,"
as a hot wind rustled the leaves
and the white man ran past,
screaming something about niggers and too much—
"What'd he say, brother?" I asked,
but he turned away.

"Lookayonder," I heard him say,
just as a loud crack and a popping sound
got mixed up in my head.
When I climbed down that old tree, I said,
"Brother, are you dead?"
He just stared at me,
then outta nowhere someone grabbed my hair.
Daddy had braided it for me that morning
and tied a ribbon on it
and said, "I'm warning you don't take it off,"
and I didn't, but it come off anyway,
when the hand jerked too hard
and got a fist fulla red ribbon
and I started running myself.
Wasn't nobody else but me around after 'while
in the dark, back in the back of somebody's house,
I mean underneath it,
where a dog was hiding too.
It was a hound dog with two pups.
You know how mean a new mother can be,
but she didn't growl, or nothing,
just gave me the eye
and went on back to nursing
and didn't do nothing when I got real close
and stroked her fur and closed my eyes.
I woke to her sighs.
The pups' eyes weren't open yet,
but they moved their heads
when I started to crawl outta hiding,
but then I heard crying, I heard a shot
and moved on back
and got close to the dog and those pups.
I knew from that moment on
I was hound Mary's daughter
and I would never leave.

3. The Rescue

I seen trouble coming from a long way off.
I seen it this morning in a bubble of blood

when I cut my finger on that cup I broke.
Nobody had to tell me about it.
I could see things. I had second sight.
Got it from Mama, a full-blooded Cherokee.
"Son," she'd say, "you got one foot in Heaven
the other in Hell
trouble gonna find you
wherever you dwell.
It's gonna come in fire.
I know secrets I better not tell
and you will too, when the time comes."
Here it is—
a Negro boy running fast as he can
a white man behind him
with a noose in his hand.
My daddy was Negro too.
Should I do something 'cause halfa me
could also swing from a tree?
I don't know what to do
til I remember Mama telling me
about the long walk
when so many died on the Trail of Tears.
She said the old folks told her
nobody could believe Andrew Jackson
would make them leave their home, but he did.
The white man takes what he gives.
He's got two faces and both of them smile
while he plans your destruction.
"He don't like Indians, but he hates Negroes," she said.
"You got looks and hair like your mother
you're lucky that way,
defer to the white man, stay out of his path."
"But I can't Mama," I say out loud,
"Can't let a child die like this.
It ain't right, is it?"
She answered, all right,
well, it was the wind,
but it was her voice talking through it.
I got in the wagon, all hitched 'cause I was going somewhere
and turned my mules in the path

where the white man was running and stopped there.
Gave that boy enough time to hide someplace.
White man cursed, pointed his gun at me.
"Sorry Mister," I said,
"these mules got minds of their own."
"Ain't you part nigger?" he said to me,
then he shot my mules.
I knew he'd die in his sleep.
I saw the sowing he'd reap
and that released me from my hatred.
I buried Brandy and Brandywine
took a long time, said a few words.
One day, that boy came to see me.
He had a scar running down one side of his face.
He said, "Mister, I'm cold and hungry,
can I stay at your place?"
I said, "Yes, come on in the kitchen where it's warm.
Lemme look at your face.
Maybe I got something that'll help,"
but he said, "Nothing will."
I filled his plate with pinto beans, bacon, cornbread,
filled his glass of milk to the brim,
then we said grace.
"Where's your mama?" I asked
and he said, "Dead,
Yours?"
"Same. Pitiful, isn't it?
You aim to move on, or stay?"
"Don't you know?" he asked.
I said, "Some things, not others."
He said, "Your mother was a witch,
that's what people say."
"Naw, she wasn't, she just saw things."
"I ain't too black for you?"
"I am too," I said.
"No, you ain't," he answered,
"but you'll do."

4. The Sheriff's Explanation

I deputized a lot of men that day.
I didn't say, "Are you men in the Klan,"
when they raised their hands
and swore to uphold the law.
All I cared about
was whether they were willing to die.
If they did so in the service of the white race,
I could live with that.
I could not live with the disgrace
of allowing Negroes to get away
with rape, murder and worse.
If we didn't stop them now, I thought,
we'd have to later.
Yes, innocent died,
depending on how you look at it.
You couldn't tell who was what.
Miss Mary, old woman
used to cook dinner for us
when I was a boy
got caught in the middle of gunfire.
I drug her body out of the way of trampling feet,
least I could do,
but see, she was one of them.
That's what it came down to in the end.
I threw her body in the hole with the rest.
I stood there awhile,
watching the others bury that sad affair.
Mary was a kind old girl.
She liked to tickle me and make me laugh,
but I couldn't say that, could I?
She was as black as the iron skillet
she fried chicken in, her face gleaming
like it had been polished with a jeweler's cloth.
She called me her baby
and she rocked me to sleep,
but I didn't say a word when that old boy
hit her body with a rock
and said, "Another one dead,"

and told me if I needed any more help
he was ready.
I didn't have anything to say. It was over.
From then on, we avoided talking about it
the way people do when they're ashamed,
but we weren't ashamed, no, not that.
We were justified.

THE PSYCHIC DETECTIVE: IDENTITY

I follow the blood trail from the front door,
down the dark hall with the pristine walls,
only to find upon entering the kitchen,
the kind of crime scene I can sink my teeth into
if that's the right term to use
and it isn't and I know it,
but back to the action, or my reaction
which is not to show it,
but to go about my business,
because I am a professional
and this is not a confessional,
but I repeat, a crime scene
complete with corpse
slumped beside the sliding glass door
in the patio, set up for a party,
judging from the paper plates, styrofoam cups
on the picnic table under colored lights.
Who did they burn for tonight, I wonder,
then I don't because I won't let myself.
I have to focus on the dear departed
now entering a state of rigor mortis.
I sniff the air. There it is,
the smell of death,
or is it my own sweat, my own fear
beaten down to its knees,
so I can do what needs to get done,
so I can walk through blood,
as if it's nothing but a slight inconvenience,
so I can show this corpse how bad I am,

a man with a badge and a gun isn't afraid
of anyone and by God I'm not, I tell myself,
as I shut off the water in the sink.
Did the killer get thirsty
from all that dirty work?
Did he take a drink, then sink his teeth
into her, because that looks like a bite
on her right thigh and there on her breast.
Did he break the rules this time
and mix business with pleasure,
which is why he got so mad he broke the pattern
of his attacks and mutilated her,
or was it another monster who attacked,
having read enough about the other
to want to imitate, then outdo him
and embark on his own
secession from the human race?
But who am I kidding? It could have been anything
the devil, a dog or a devil dog
ordering him to do his bidding
and not the cold, calculating killer
who left her with her pubis artistically exposed,
because he's an artist, I suppose,
at least he thinks he is
and like any artist, he has an ego
as big as Texas, and a tattoo of a rose
on his shoulder. That's the only description
we've got of our homicidal lothario
and that's why they call him "The Florist."
He makes his fatal delivery
of one American Beauty Rose for each killing.
There are five beside the body
in their little containers of water.
I know it's water, because it's been tested
and will be again, but it's plain old H_2O
I'd bet on it
and nobody bets against a sure thing, right?
Anybody in Vegas can tell you they do all the time
and I'm just blowing smoke.
I'm waiting for my partner

to poke his head in the door
and tell me there's another body this time,
which I already know, because I'm psychic
and sensed the absence of completion, of letting go.
In the garage, on the front seat
of the old Dodge Dart,
a body, rather, parts of it
are laid out like cuts of meat.
"Where're the flowers?" he asks,
but I just stare, then point.
There it is, there
and it is. Body parts are laid out
in the shape of the rose my partner couldn't find.
He's getting symbolic on us, I say,
wiping a spiderweb from my face.
He'll be harder to trace now,
because he knows one mistake
and he'll fall through the ice
of his own existence.
He has no regrets now.
He's conquered his conscience
and come to a place where all is killing
and killing is all.
I know my partner thinks I'm bullshitting.
"Stinks in here," he says,
then steps out for some fresh air,
but I'm ok where I am.
I can think here. Like him
I can see the girl coming up the walk,
talking to her mother.
She's sixteen. She's carrying a birthday cake.
There's a gap between her teeth.
He's heard it's a sign of appetite
and he wonders if that's true.
Maybe she'll prove it,
if he does it right.
I get dizzy all at once
and lean against the fender.
I don't want to see anymore.
I just want to shut the door on the evil

that greets me each day with its pants down,
saying, "Look at it, look at me
and see yourself."

THE PSYCHIC DETECTIVE: FANTASY

The victim is lying on her side
as if trying to hide the imprint
of the boot heel that smashed her cheek.
As the river runs through her wounds
(and there are many)
I am coldly examining her body this morning.
"What do you think, Bob?" I ask my partner.
"Do you think she was out shopping?
See that empty shopping bag there
the one from that fancy mall."
"Who cares?" he says.
"She's dead, end of story."
It isn't ordinary as crimes go,
because she's so mutilated.
He hated her naturally,
because he imagined that she was his mother,
or some other female who wronged him
and he's in payback mode,
cracked her skull maybe with a bat,
probably his kid's. "What do you say, Bob?"
He shrugs. Psychology is not his thing.
He likes putting it together
like a math problem he can solve by adding one plus two,
but that doesn't work with psychos.
They hide from the average crime solver.
Somebody like me has to go down into hell with them
and bring them back,
even though they're radioactive with an evil
that clings to your skin.
I'm still hot from the last crime.
Hear the crackle and pop
as I pass through the mind of this killer.
There he is on his knees, his eyes filled with a red glow.

He has to pee and does into the water
that runs over her shattered face,
then he zips up, he leaves
just as the sun rises as big and as orange
as those lollipops
his mom used to buy him
when the first urge to destroy
made him tear apart his toy rabbit.
No, it was her, naked, her big breasts
swinging over him that first set him off,
as she bent down to say good night
as he lay in bed,
the odor of alcohol and a fight with his dad
suffocating him, making him reach up
and pinch the nipple inches from his face.
His mom said, "Suck on it, go ahead,
if you're man enough."
He wasn't then, but he is now
and I'm on his trail.
I'm going to swallow him
like the whale did Jonah.
Who am I kidding? He's gone, Bob.
I won't catch this one,
because he's disappeared into the ether
of ordinary life.
Can't you feel it?
This kill wasn't planned.
It was some kind of posttraumatic thing
where a scent, a sound, maybe a glance
threw him into his murderer's trance
and he entered his mother's spread thighs,
his eyes closed tightly
as he felt those breasts press against his head
like two feather pillows, so soft, so . . .
Then he came out of it
in his driveway.
His rosebushes, his azaleas,
the big cedar tree
and the kid's swing reassured him
that what had happened

was only a fantasy
and he told himself so over and over,
even as he cleaned a few remaining drops of blood
from his hands,
then watered his rosebushes
and greeted his wife with a kiss
when she came home from the store.
He did not acknowledge, or go near that door
behind which his mother
said, "Just once more, son, once more"
and he tried, he really did,
before he fell asleep,
only to wake in his own bed
and tell himself he'd had a bad dream
and leave it at that
and leave us with another unsolved murder,
another body to send to the morgue
to be claimed by relatives
who'll never have another peaceful day like his
when it's hard to believe he's the one who's alive
and not on the other side
with that girl he met at the mall and his mother
beating on a door
even the psychic detective can't open.

THE PSYCHIC DETECTIVE: DIVINITY

He stepped out of the dark.
He *was* the dark
with his chloroform, his duct tape.
He'd been waiting since dawn,
but he really hadn't been, maybe an hour
after a long hot shower,
steam seeping into every pore of his body.
The body wash after,
damask rose and sandalwood.
He liked to smell good.
It countered the other odor just enough
to soothe and calm the prey

until they recognized him for who he was.
I knew the smell mixed in
with the thin metallic odor
on the victim's clothes
folded so carefully
and laid beneath her head
and in her hands a rosary
of large black beads,
the kind the nuns at St. Anthony's
wore on their wide black leather belts,
when I was twelve
and doing time in Catholic school
which answers questions possibly
about the villain of this piece.
Perhaps the victim's death
helped ease some guilt
he'd carried with him,
while talking with friends,
wearing a slight smile,
a twinkle in his eyes
for this was a guy of guys,
not the type you'd imagine
who would kill
until something unleashed the will to murder.
Was it seeing the nuns
gliding down the esplanade at dusk,
the musk of sanctity
too much for him to bear
as the memory of some incident
returned to him with such a vengeance
he had no choice but to act and save himself!
She was the sacrifice he made
to his depraved self
and he is, believe me.
Father Thomas told him so
in confession when he was thirteen
and after a night of touching himself
he let go at last
when he imagined how it would feel
to choke his little sister.

He confessed
and was given absolution.
Father Thomas said,
"One hundred Hail Mary's, Kevin
and ask your mother to come see me."
His mother never went to Mass.
His father did
and the priest hadn't said to ask him,
so he said nothing about it,
only avoided the confessional
and when his parents separated,
he never went to Mass again.
Kevin often caught his father
looking at him in such a way
it made him wonder
but then one day his father was gone,
taking his little sister.
He stayed with his mother
and made the best of it
and never wondered much about
that fit of adolescent sexual confusion
or whatever it was
that had made him confess in the first place.
Better to keep quiet about such impulses,
about the riot of feelings
which assualted him
for years until the night
they overwhelmed him
and overcame the obstacle
to the desire he'd tried to ignore.
It was a fire, it was burning him
like the need to preach and convert.
Bob laughs and shakes his head
and asks me if I've been drinking
and says, "He's just a warped little shit
who gets his kicks by killing.
Don't you get tired of being a willing conduit
for their sickness?"
"I do, but I swore I'd use my gift to help others
and if this is the price, then so be it.

I have no choice anyway.
When I tried to stop, remember,
you called me back?
You needed my expertise to catch
that guy who liked to slice, dice
and can his victims.
Remember how we found the pantry,
the smell?
Who could stand still for that?"
Bob doesn't answer,
just waves to the forensics people
to come do their stuff
now that I've profiled the perp
and am ready for further study
in my own way,
which is to say
by tracing him backward from today,
then forward into the gray afternoon
descending on us now,
when he climbs the steps of the cathedral
stands inside the nave
for the time it takes to say
one hundred Hail Mary's,
then simply walks away.

THE PSYCHIC DETECTIVE: DESTINY

A nightlight in the shape of a bear
burns in the center of my darkness.
It's clear acrylic and inside, a blue bulb
casts a pale blue light in the room,
where I lie awake,
my twelve-year-old insomnia,
a warning of future sleepless nights.
In the rest of the house,
the lights are out.
My mother is asleep
in her room across the hall
and in the twin bed next to mine,

my little sister also sleeps,
although occasionally she says a few words
I can't quite catch.
They're like snatches of a song
you can't forget,
you can't remember either, yet . . .
They haunt me now,
as I kneel in the cathedral,
where I was baptised
and where the memorial for my sister
was conducted.
I say memorial because she was—
her body was never found.
But to achieve a sense of closure
(those were my mother's words)
the family, friends and concerned citizens
were herded into church
to listen to the priest say a few words.
He looked like a bird of prey.
I mean the way he hovered over the pulpit,
his crooked beak of a nose
and furrowed brow so vulture-like,
as he used his words as if somehow
they could conjure a body out of sound
and place it in front of us.
He said she was there in spirit,
so I thought she hadn't gone to purgatory afterall.
She wasn't bad enough to go to Hell,
well, I didn't think so.
I didn't know. I did know someone
had entered our room.
I'd heard stealthy footsteps,
the pause outside our door before he entered
and shut my eyes, barely breathing,
hoping the flutter of my eyelids
wouldn't give me away.
I wasn't afraid.
I'd been waiting all night.
I knew I'd be all right,
oh, I'd seen that too.

Don't ask how I knew. I just did.
I like the term second sight,
because it emphasizes that you "see,"
but with another kind of vision.
I heard my sister sigh,
then heard a deeper muffled sigh,
felt a hot breath against my cheek,
a chuckle and a voice whispering, "Don't peek."
I didn't dare.
"I don't need to," I almost cried,
but realized I'd be lost too,
if I didn't play dead,
so I lay still until dawn,
when I turned over and looked at the empty bed,
then fell into a deep sleep
and dreamed I understood the words
my sister had mumbled the night before
to wake finally to my mother's screams.
"It was the boogeyman," I told her,
but she didn't listen
and I chose to keep silent,
although I knew he'd taken my sister
and buried her alive in his backyard.
I'd even gasped for breath that morning
over breakfast alone at the table,
while the police asked my mother
whether I were able to tell her anything.
I tried, but I couldn't breathe,
so she put me in her bed
and I lay there until darkness covered me
like a baby blanket.
Now as I kneel without praying,
I am looking for a different boogeyman,
but he won't come inside.
He'll just stand with his hand
suspended above the holy water,
which he will not touch,
a slight smile playing about his lips,
because he thinks he's clever.
He thinks it's all clear now,

that he can go back to how it was,
before he decided to go for broke
and let out the monster
who had urged him to choke his sister years ago.
He thinks he's safe from discovery,
because he stands beyond
the outstretched arms of the statue of Christ
upon the altar where I kneel,
but he's wrong.
I gave up hiding long ago
to seek absolution for not saving my sister
and with each case I take,
I hope I'll reach some closure of my own.
I'd known the boogeyman would come,
but I was only twelve.
I saved myself, but I couldn't save her,
or could I? That question haunts me
as I ruminate on my past actions, on my fate,
which is to wait for my sister's abductor
again and again
to say, "Take me too,"
and pray, "Hail Mary, full of grace,"
before I suffocate.
Bob taps my shoulder and whispers,
"We got him."
I only nod and return to my rumination,
but he doesn't leave.
He kneels beside me
and I feel something emanating from him.
It coils and uncoils around my heart
like a snake.
I stare at him
and he asks, "What's the matter?
What's going on with you?"
I say nothing, but I'm lying.
I have "seen" something
in between Bob's conscious and unconscious
and it's mean and hard as a black diamond
as anything I've ever encountered
on my latest quest for forgiveness.

"What do you see?" he asks again.
"Nothing. . . . Nothing," I lie once more,
then I say, "What happened to you
when you were a child?"
"I was never a child," he answers cryptically.
"I live for now. That's how I make it.
You should too, but you won't.
It's got you by the throat."
"Not it," I say at last, "he has."

THE PSYCHIC DETECTIVE: INFINITY

"I'm packing it in, Bob," I say,
"I'm tired of 'seeing' things,"
but he just laughs and runs gloved hands
over the slash marks on the body
he is studying to find a pattern
by reading the cuts made
when the perp attacked with a hatchet
and pure malice.
"I don't want to interrupt your tête-à-tête,
but this was jammed inside her," says the coroner.
"It is a page from the Brothers Grimm."
"Whoo-who a clue," I say, but I already knew
this killer's into fairy tales,
because he thinks reality has failed him.
"You'll never guess what else I found," he adds,
bending down and looking inside her.
Suddenly, I feel embarrassed and turn away,
then turn back and say, "It's round and metal
and when you shake it, it rattles."
"You *are* good," he says, removing the object.
"Do you think he made her insert it,
or did he do it himself, after he killed her?" he asks.
Before, I think, after he took it from his mouth. I add.
"His mouth?"
"He did it to fill her with his hatred, not just to kill her,
but to humiliate her first,
then as if quenching a thirst, drank in her hurt."

"See all the blood," adds Bob,
"the contusions? . . . Maybe he beat her with a belt, or—"
"Maybe his fist," says the coroner, sighing
and removing his gloves,
as he prepares to turn his attention elsewhere.
"Lunch?" he asks,
as if we could eat now and we decline
as we begin to define this killer by his actions.
"First one?" Bob asks.
I nod and say, "He's been thinking about it a long time,
then he snapped."
"In other words, the usual occurred."
In the parking lot, Bob says, "No semen because—"
"—Because this guy's not an ejaculator,
at least not in the body of his victim
and not on her either."
"Maybe he's impotent, or uses an article of
clothing," says Bob
and I tell him I'm beginning to think
these killers are really demons,
but he says, "They're all too human. You know—"
"—Because I've got second sight
which more and more means I can't see
what is right in front of me,
like the reason you are looking at me funny," I say,
"I mean funnier than usual."
There's blood in your eye, dare I say it?
It's my fault for noticing things. I can't help it.
The feeling that tells me you have something to hide
is stronger than ever.
"What is it, Bob?" I ask.
"You drive this time," he says
then out of nowhere, he tells me,
"Leave it alone."
"What?"
"You know," he tells me,
getting in the driver's side after all.
"He's underground," I say.
"A basement?" Bob asks.
"Too obvious."

"A tunnel," we say in unison.
When we find the murder scene,
we get more than we bargained for,
because we discover the body of a man,
clutching a book of fairy tales in his right hand
and a gun in the other.
"Blew his brains out, oh brother," says Bob,
"another narrow escape from justice."
"If you say so," I tell him, but I don't know.
"He could be burning in hellfire now," I say.
"I wish I could be sure."
"Just assume," says Bob, "you'll sleep better if you do."
"I don't sleep you know that. Neither do you."
"For different reasons," he says.
"Whatever you say," I tell him, stepping out of the way
of the coroner, who's just arrived.
He's pissed because it's almost five
and he's got tickets to a concert.
He's taking his neglected wife, he tells us
and that we owe him.
We say we know, then wrap up and go.
Bob's off to the Bahamas for the weekend
and I'm thinking I will see some movies,
if I can handle
the violence on-screen,
but Bob asks me
how I can do my job since I'm so squeamish
and I say it's different,
but I don't know how, then I say
"Don't let what happened to your mother
ruin your good time."
He looks as if he wants to hit me,
but starts the car instead.
"When I was fourteen my father killed her,
after he raped her in front of me.
Satisfied now?" he asks.
I don't answer. I can't, because I might tell him
I know what else happened.
No, I'll just let that pass into the ether
like the victims who to us are neither alive, nor dead,

just in transit forever,
but Bob says, "You know, don't you?
A murder-suicide was really two murders,
but one of them was in self-defense."
I just tell him I can't see anything.
"Liar," he says, "you know what it feels like
to lose someone to violence.
It's what makes you sensitive."
"Maybe," I say, as my cellphone rings
and I hear about the terrible things
that happened to a five-year-old girl.
"We're on it," I say, signaling to Bob.
"Better unpack your toothbrush," I tell him
and it feels good to avoid the truth
if only for a few hours.
"The two of us are something," he says
and I answer, "We're as warped as they are."
"We aren't," he says,
"we only want to be forgiven for our sins.
Instead we end up hiding them
among the crimes others have committed."
"I've heard your pet theories before.
They're nothing more than excuses you make,
because you can't admit that you're addicted
to solving crimes, or trying to.
We're both hooked on mutilation, strangulation, decapitation,
should I go on? . . . I've heard this before too.
Whatever happened stays in your past.
I never asked to know your secrets, Bob,
the last one spooked me is all,
made me want to erase my memories
and replace them with scenes
straight out of greeting cards.
Instead, I see a boy
about to shoot his father through the heart."
"That's why we're partners," says Bob.
"We understand how a lucky shot
can set you free."
"Or imprison you for eternity," I tell him,
"but that's just me being optimistic."

"Come on cowboy, let's ride
and forget your toy pistol
you won't have to shoot anybody this time," I say,
as the car peels out of the lot at such high speed,
it rises off the street and we fly
like the body of a girl
hurled from an apartment building
into the murderous air.

No Surrender

MOTHERHOOD, 1951

Dear Saint Patrick, this is Peggy,
Or maybe it's Pegeen to you,
Well, I'm really Stella Mae.
Peggy's my nickname,
But anyway, will you please tell me
What to do about the rattlesnake
That's in my room?
I know it's there,
But I can't find it anywhere I search.
I've ransacked the closet more than once,
Because that's where we found the skin it shed.
I even put the cat in there and shut the door,
But he only went to sleep on my new dress
Which he had clawed from a hanger.
My grandma, Maggie, says you drove the snakes from Ireland
And they came here to Arizona.
She's right, you know
For didn't a rattler kill our cat, Blackie?
There he was beside the porch, stiff as a board
And Baby Florence saw it.
She's only three and doesn't need to see death like that, not yet.
If you can, let her believe for now
That we will live forever.
I'm pregnant again.
I know I've sinned
But I am paying for it.
Don't make my girl suffer
Because her mother used poor judgment
And got herself in trouble out of wedlock.
My mother's disappointed in me.
My father doesn't care
And says I don't have to marry
Just to have a name for this one in the oven.
Father says there's nothing wrong with our name
And will serve the babe as well as any other,
But Mother is determined to give this one a legal father
Like Baby Florence has, but only on paper.
She doesn't have a father either,

But she's got her granddad, he says
And goes to work. He is a barber.
Mother is a cook and she works longer hours,
So I'm here with Baby Florence
And that infernal snake all day.
Outside, the new cat, dogs, chickens and hogs
Roam about the yard,
But they can't help me, can they?
I keep praying, but you don't answer.
I guess you've got no time for me,
So armed with a shovel,
I go in the closet once again
And succeed in smashing a wall.
Bits of plaster fall on my head,
But I don't mind.
I'd rather be dead than never find the thing
That crawls about the room
Without fear of discovery.
This morning, I woke up to find a coiled imprint
At the foot of my bed.
They say I am protected from harm
Because the Virgin Mary put her heel
Upon a snake's head and crushed it
For the sake of all pregnant women.
I am safe, I say to myself, and pray for mercy
And recall the dead baby diamondback we found last fall.
It glittered like a tiny jeweled bracelet.
I almost picked it up,
Before I remembered my own warning to my daughter
To never, ever pick up anything suspicious.
The diamondback was like the lust I felt for him.
It glittered so beautifully
I had to pick it up and wear it for a while,
Then like some Lazarus, it came to life,
By striking me with its poisonous fangs,
Leaving me to pay for my crime
Once by lying to myself
And twice for good measure.
Now I must suffer for my pleasure.
I curse, slam the wall again

And feel pain radiating from my navel
Down through my bowels
And am not able to get to the telephone
To call my mother.
I hear a splash and all of a sudden,
The snake darts from the hole I made in the wall
And crawls forward to slake its thirst.
I grit my teeth, but stand stock still
As the pain gnaws at my vitals.
I try to show no fear
As the snake takes a long drink of my water
Then slithers away,
But not fast enough to escape,
As screaming with pain and rage
With all the mother instinct I can muster,
And in the Virgin Mary's name,
I raise the shovel and smash the snake,
Crushing its head,
As I double over and fall beside it
On the red, concrete floor.
For a while, a ripple runs through its body,
Then it is still.
When my pain subsides, I fall asleep
And dream I'm dead
And hundreds of baby snakes are gathered at my wake.
They crawl all over my body
And I try to shake them off,
Until I realize they're part of me.

At Saint Mary's Hospital, the nurses and my doctor
Tell me how courageous I am
And the nuns even come to visit me.
They claim I have performed a miracle
And should be canonized.
Saint Peggy. "How does that sound?"
I ask Saint Patrick aloud
When left alone to hold my child.
I smile at her and tell her she is blessed.
The nuns have gone off to light some candles
And in the chapel

They say they're praying for special dispensation
But I don't need that and neither does my girl.

Back home, after a few days, I realize
That I made a mistake in thinking I could take away my sins
And in a state between agitation and rest,
I remember something I had forgotten.
As I lay beside the snake,
I saw a tiny bunch of eggs spill out of her
And realized she was an expectant mother too
And simply wanted a drink to soothe herself
One desert afternoon
When mothers must decide to save
Or execute their children.

THE INHERITANCE

Mother, when I survived eviction
By the skin of my very white teeth,
I arrived at your front door
With four cats in a twenty-six-foot U-Haul
Packed to the ceiling.
You stood on the back porch steps,
Underneath the yellow bug light
Wearing only a long cotton nightgown.
You had not thought to put on a robe.
I was embarrassed,
Although I tried not to show it,
As I introduced you to the grad student
Who drove me to Tucson from Scottsdale.
Once I got the cats inside,
I went back out to bring in a few suitcases
And found the student smoking.
I was about to ask him to stop,
When you came outside and told him
"Come on in with that cigarette,"
Shyly, he declined.
Although you'd told me your three-pack-a-day habit
Had given way to one, I didn't believe it,

As the heavy odor of smoke
Emanated from the house.
"Mother," I said, "this must be the only house in America now
Where smoking is allowed."
"I'm going to stop," you told me halfheartedly,
As the three of us stood under the light,
As if conspiring some way to insinuate the cigarette
Back into all our lives the way it had been
When I was five and asked for a puff
To which you answered, "Okay, but don't inhale."
How strange to think those words
May have saved me from your fate.
Emphysema, oxygen tanks, hospitalization
And the final lie you told me on the telephone.
"I've really quit smoking now," you said,
"And I'm doing fine."
I didn't doubt you that one time, but I should have,
Should have known you'd never give up your cigarettes.
The proof was before me on the floor years later,
When I found your body
And the oxygen bottle beside the pack of cigarettes
As if you'd set them side by side
In order to decide which one was more important
And finally chose the one whose odor so infused your clothes
I had to throw them out,
Remembering the night you gave me sanctuary
And how like a phoenix
I rose from my own ashes.
If only you could have too,
But one day you would make your bed of tobacco leaves
And lie down to sleep forever,
Leaving me only smoke to call my mother.

DISCIPLINE

It was Vegas. It was 1954, one hundred fifteen degrees in the shade
    and my half-sister,
Roslynn, was on her knees, begging Mom not to whip her. She said
    she didn't mean it

As tears streamed down her cheeks. She was getting what she
   deserved, because she had

Taken a hairpin and scratched the toes of all my mother's shoes, plus
   ripped out all her

Dress hems. I'd known she was up to something in the closet.
   I'd been told to watch her,

While Mom went off to play the slots with a girlfriend, but I
   preferred to read about

Sir Lancelot, while Roslynn did the deed and now I was going to
   pay for it, because according

To Mom, I hadn't done what she'd told me—"Watch your sister and
   don't let her do anything

Wrong." Ha! As if I could control the little monster. Still, I was
   going to pay in a big way, but I

Wouldn't beg, or anything else to let Mom think I was a baby like
   my sister. No, I said to myself

As Mom grabbed the heavy tooled leather cowboy belt with the
   copper buckle that had a

Longhorn engraved on it. As she swung that sucker down, I saw my
   chance and ran out

The screen door and down the dusty unpaved street. After a block,
   or two, I realized I had nowhere

To go, but back to face the rock 'n' roll, so I took the scenic route
   through the park, by the kiddie

Pool, then I thought of my grandmother who just might save me. I
   stood quietly on her front porch

A few minutes, hoping she'd open the door, but I suddenly
   remembered that she was working some party

Where the high rollers tipped big. She was a cook and my mother
   was an army wife. My stepfather

Was stationed in Korea and he couldn't help me either, so I moved
   on with a scene from my

Favorite cowboy movie, *High Noon*, playing in my head, the one
   where Gary Cooper goes

To the shootout and proves what a man alone can do, but I was a
   little girl and I remembered when I was

Four and playing peekaboo with my mother, right after Roslynn
   was born. When she asked me to stop,

I wouldn't until she threw a tin of baby powder and hit me in the
   right eye. As I screamed in pain,

She said, "I told you to leave me alone." Yes, she did, and she always
    meant what she said. I hung my
Head, as I stood forlornly in the yard. When Mom opened the door
    and said, "Get in here," I got. It was
Over quickly. I licked my wounded pride and later, pinched my
    sister until she cried. When she
Complained, Mom said, "That's tough. You have to learn to take
    your punishment."
I was only seven and I had already learned enough.

SISTERHOOD

For what it's worth,
I left the convent.
But I never left the Church.
It's true, I left Ireland in a hurry too.
You could say I broke the habit,
Or to quote my da
"I pulled a rabbit out o' my arse"
And realized I put the cart before the horse
And wasn't going anywhere,
Certainly not to Heaven
With my sparse faith.
I'd come late to thinking
That when I beat my breasts three times
And said my prayers, no one was listening,
Not even Father Patrick in confession,
Who did his own magic trick
Of pulling forgiveness out of thin air
For you can do all sorts of things
When nothing's there to stop you.
Everywhere I looked I saw forms that evil took
And all of them were pleasing,
All bent on deceiving poor wretched Catholics
Into believing that an Act of Contrition
And a few Hail Marys could save them
From the very things they craved,
So one day I said to Mother Superior,
"I'm leaving."

On the ship to New York, I tossed my rosary overboard.
Sure and didn't it float upon the water
A full three minutes before it sank?
I almost fainted,
So I went back to my cabin, lay down and fell into a deep sleep
And dreamed of slaughtered sheep bleeding and bleating,
Until I screamed myself awake.
Soon after I arrived in New York,
I bought another rosary
And kept it under my pillow and didn't dream at all,
Maybe because it seemed as if my life was a dream.
Alone in the gloomy rooming house in Brooklyn,
I made peace with myself
And stopped wondering how I would survive
My separation from Christ's side.
No longer His bride, no longer free to hide
Behind His sanctity, I was beside myself,
Until I joined a community of former priests and nuns.
I moved into their brownstone, having found a home at last
Where I could pass for being just another Colleen
Who'd dreamed of a better life in America.
I was only twenty-five in nineteen sixty-four, you see
And didn't know how cruel men could be,
But I learned soon enough
When I lost my virginity, or I should say, gave it away
To a scoundrel who left me pregnant.
By then, I was a practical nurse.
I treated women left in the lurch by other scoundrels,
Yet, I fell for one myself.
One day at work, I miscarried.
A week later, I called my da and told him.
He only asked, "Was he Irish, lass?"
"He was black," I answered.
"Black Irish, that's all right," he said.
"No, he was black American," I said, "you know, negro."
"You mean you did it with a blackamoor?" he shouted
And hung up.
Soon after that, the scoundrel came round again.
He brought me roses
And got on his knees and proposed.

I was frozen to the spot.
I could not speak, but finally just laughed
As defensively, he said he only wanted
To make an honest woman of me.
I told him God had already tried
And look what happened.
I'd hurt his pride, but I thought so what?
I'd lost my child and anyway,
What kind of father would he have been?
He was perpetually broke
And a stranger to responsibility,
Admittedly to be expected
Because he was a fiddler in an Irish band.
"What's that black fellow doing here?"
People would ask the band members
And if he overheard them,
He would say, "I'm Creole from New Orleans."
He was a handsome devil indeed
Who didn't need a wife.
"What you need," I told him, "is me out of your life
So I'll take my chances with dishonesty."

After a year, I decided to move west.
I tried San Francisco, L.A. and finally, Las Vegas on a whim
Where one night when I was two sheets to the wind,
I put a quarter in a slot machine
And to the accompaniment of ringing bells,
Coins poured from its orifice into my hands.
They comped me for the night
And wouldn't you know
That in the penthouse high above the desert,
I found my God again
With an Elvis record playing on the stereo
And in the very bosom of sin,
Where I lay my head that morning
When at last I fell asleep?
That afternoon, I received a call to join a gentleman
Who'd seen me the night before.
"I'm not a whore," I said, then instantly regretted it.
After apologies on both sides,

I decided to accept the invitation.
Anyway, it was only the other side of the casino
Where the permanent residents resided.
At last, I was led into his room
And to my astonishment, the man standing with his back to me
Suddenly turned and instantly, I knew who he was.
"Ma'am," he said, in that faintly southern accent
I'd heard only the night before
And there he was in person,
Overweight and wearing a white jumpsuit,
Snakeskin cowboy boots and enough jewelry
To open a store.
He bade me take a seat on the black leather couch
And I sank deeply into it as if it were fabric.
"Gotcha," he said. "Soft, ain't it?"
I agreed, trying to keep my amazement at bay.
"I watched you play," he said, "you're lucky,
I can tell. Can't I?" He asked the guy
Who'd brought me. He nodded yes
And while they waited expectantly,
I only said, "Not really."
"Honey," said Elvis, "I'm never wrong.
Ask the Colonel."
At that, I noticed a man
standing in the shadows of the room.
He came forward then
And stared at me as if demanding I agree
And finally, I did.
"Now," said Elvis, "let's eat."
So we did. Late lunch, I guess you'd call it,
A distressing amount of food appeared
As if by magic
And he ate so much I feared he would explode,
But after a self-satisfied belch and a wink,
He said, "I think I'll take a nap.
Feel free to stick around and hey, take something
As a souvenir, something that says, The King, you hear?"
"I was a nun," I blurted.
And he said, "Hon, I knew there was something about you.
You were playing with Jesus."

I only smiled. I didn't know what else to do
And after a while, I left.
As I walked through the casino,
I knew I was going home.
When I set foot upon the auld sod,
I didn't feel like kissing it.
I hadn't missed it. Much.
But when I tasted the salt in the air
And savored the faint, sweet flavor of melancholy,
I realized I was back to stay for good.
Next thing I knew, I was in a pew,
Praying my heart out,
Praying I had enough strength to undo the past,
But the past cannot be undone,
Only lived through.
I remembered watching the blood flow down my legs
And begging Jesus to save my baby,
But also thinking it was my punishment
For leaving the Church.
How could I go back now, I thought,
As I sat daydreaming
About an existence full of meaning
I'd imagined being a nun would give me.
Had I been too young to understand
That self-sacrifice was part of the plan,
Had I let myself be enticed by the world,
Then abandoned by it, or to it?
I couldn't tell.
My life was like a tightly woven black cloth
I couldn't see through, but could feel its weight
Upon my body as I kneeled down,
Praying to the Blessed Virgin
Who stood beneath the Cross when she lost her Son.
Had the awful memories of His death ever left her thoughts,
And had I returned to bear witness to my own poor truth?
Oh, reckless youth, I murmured,
Covering my face with my hands
When suddenly, I heard a baby crying.
At first, I thought its mother would quiet it,
But the crying continued and finally,

When I went to see what could be done,
I couldn't find anyone.
"Hello," I called, but receiving no reply,
I started to search the pews
Which led me to a corner near the confessional
Where I found a baby,
Dressed in a christening gown.
I tried to soothe her by cooing like the doves
Who lived above my room at the convent
And soon, she quieted.
When I took her to the rectory,
The priest said, "A foundling,"
But I said, "A miracle."
He disagreed and said, "A sin."
Then looking hard at me, he said,
"She's your daughter, isn't she?"
I answered, "Yes, I was only trying
To do what was best for her."
He said, "But you're not a girl.
You know that life is full of disappointment and strife.
You have to rise above your troubles.
We'll pray for guidance."
"But Father," I gently protested, "it's time for her to eat."
And so I made my escape to motherhood,
Or was it a retreat?
Then I knew what I would do,
Although I did not know how I would manage.
You could say I took her in, or rescued her,
Or maybe she rescued me.
When I went to see my da,
Cradling the baby in my arms,
He asked, "Is this the black one?"
"That was long ago. She died, remember?"
He said no, he was getting old,
But anyway, this one didn't look black at all.
"Are you back to stay?" he asked.
"I am," I said. "Is that all right?"
"I wouldn't mind the company," he answered,
Including the baby with a nod of his head.
"What's her name?" he asked.
I told him, "Faith."

WOMANHOOD

People assume I was named after Saint Michael, the archangel,
Because they think why else would a girl be called Michael
Unless she were a nun,
But I was named after my father, Michael Gavin Daugherty,
And he was neither angel, nor saint.
He was a lousy bastard underneath the smiles
And camaraderie he saved for his mates
Not Ma and me.
No better than a slave to him was she,
The real saint of Delancey Street in nineteen forty-five.
Next stop was Hell's Kitchen,
But they had to leave there in a hurry
As Da offended someone
And took his wife and young son on the run to Boston.
I wasn't born yet and only heard about it recently
When the old crowd gathered at his wake.
They made me take their hands
And stand in front of the coffin
Singing a sorrowful tune I merely hummed
Because I didn't know the words.
I'd heard it often enough when I was a kid.
Usually, he was drunk when he sang it,
Or sad, or both.
He had bad luck, he'd say,
Explaining away each lost job
And finally, settling for sweeping up at a bar
In the Combat Zone,
At home at last among the thugs, hookers and druggies
Who dragged their tired bones
To this macabre celebration of a wasted life.
He was a writer once in Ireland.
He wrote stories and poems that glorified the poor.
He was middle class, but he could pass through any door
And be welcome, but that was long before
He set foot upon the golden shores of America
Where his life took a sudden cruel turn to tragedy.
His mother died back home in Galway
And he was too broke to go to the funeral.

Ma was sick too, pregnant and jaundiced.
My brother died the spring
They welcomed me into the fold.
I was three before they settled in a rooming house
In Dorchester.
Ma went to work at a department store in Boston
And Da got more and more involved in the sporting life.
I guess playing the horses was more interesting to him
Than a wife and a kid who hid from him when he came home
Red-nosed and loudly singing that infernal song.
"Michael, my boy, come to your da," he'd shout,
Squeezing me in a bear hug.
I would try to break away, but he'd hold on
Until Ma would shame him by saying,
"She's a girl, you fool."
"What happened to my son?" he'd ask
No one in particular
And Ma would answer, "You killed him."
That's when the tears would start.
He'd cry as if his heart would break,
Then he'd take a swing at Ma
And end up falling down,
Where he would lie so still
You'd think he'd died
And gone to the hell she prophesied he would.
There he'd lie, then rising finally, leave us for days
Only to return sober and unshaved, smelling of liquor
And the faint perfume of betrayal.
Ma wouldn't speak to him
Until he begged her forgiveness,
Then they'd declare a truce for a few months.
He'd be the perfect husband and father.
He wouldn't even call me "boy."
I'd be his daughter
And wouldn't get a taste of beer
When he watched *The Honeymooners*
And wouldn't hear a dirty word.
I thought if that was what it was like to be a girl,
I'd rather be a boy and get to swear and drink,
Spit and piss outside on a dare

So I welcomed his lapses sometimes,
Although Ma didn't.
I'd get to wear pants and a cap
And dance on the table at the bar
And have strangers tell my da what a fine son he had
And with a wink at me, he would agree.
Breasts and menses put an end to that
And I was back where I started in the womb.
I was trapped in an all-girls' Catholic school.
My da became my father
And I became a bothersome claim on his time.
Often he would complain that he had two females to complicate his
    life,
As he stingily handed out Ma's weekly allowance
For groceries and incidentals.
He said I was an endless drain on his expenses
Until he aimed me in the direction
Of the boy he called the young fool, Anthony Santoni,
Not exactly the boy he had imagined for me,
But he gave his blessing anyway
In the summer of my eighteenth year.
I added Mrs. to my name and became Michaela
Because Anthony thought Michael was too masculine.
After five years, two miscarriages,
Adultery on both our parts
And a yearlong separation, we divorced,
Of course without the blessing of the Church
But with the cursing of my father
Who said I'd disgraced the holy state of matrimony.
I worked my way through college
And got a bachelor's degree in elementary education.
I couldn't sustain a relationship
And drifted in and out of love.
Sometimes I wondered whether I were guilty
Of something terrible, rather than the usual
Crimes of the heavy heart
By being condemned to be alone.
Then I thought I was cursed
Because I had been given my brother's name.
I decided he hated me

Because I was alive and he was doing time in Purgatory.
I suffered privately,
While my career blossomed like a rose.
I became principal
And thought I was invincible
Until I felt its thorns prick me
And I fell into a poisoned waking sleep.
A parent sued the school
Because of a cruel teacher and won.
I'd done what I could, but not enough to get rid of him.
He had tenure, was well liked, jovial,
Talked of his sexual conquests, one of whom was me
And to make my story short, I was fired, not he.
He became principal
And I got a certificate in geriatric health.
I make home visits and tell myself
I'm doing something useful and good,
But I would give it up if I could join my da
For a beer and a song,
Have him call me "boy"
And make me feel that I belong in the world
That never had a place for girls named Michael.
Afraid I'll fall into the trance of living life
Without ever taking chances,
I chugalug my beer
Then climb on a table and dance,
Waiting to hear what a fine lad I am,
Father, son and daughter, one, at last.

WIDOWHOOD

The word "remains" is no match
For the reality of a piece of skin
Taken home in a plastic bag,
Marked with a number taken from a tag
Tied to the armrest of the airplane seat
Where you died
When the intense heat of an explosion
Fused the back of your head to the metal frame

And tore the rest of your body
Into more pieces than the puzzle
You had been working on for months.
It's still unfinished on the desk
Where you left it two years ago.
I haven't had the heart to move it,
Or should I say, the nerve?
Your business papers, your last cigarette
In the ashtray you set behind the Chinese vase
As if you could hide the smell
By placing the evidence well out of sight.
The first night I spent alone
I combed your office as if searching for the bomb
That took you from me.
Yes, the dog was with me, but he only watched
As I opened desk drawers,
Even looked inside your books on banking and finance
On the outside chance that I would find some evidence
That would make your murder more personal
Than it really was because you were simply a victim of our times,
One of two hundred seventy people
On a red-eye to oblivion.

As always, you did not wake me when you left
And out of love, I pretended to be asleep
So you could keep the illusion
That you were being a thoughtful husband
And you were once in a while
Like every man whose inner child is sixty.
You were never a child.
You were always too responsible
And while you respected others who weren't,
You could never abandon yourself to irresponsibility
Unlike me, even though I had my work too.
I knew how to relax and let the world go on without me.
You weren't giving in to my demands for company
And told me so earlier that night
When we had a silly fight about your business trip,
The fourth that month.
Facetiously, you said, "Cedric will keep you company,"

And I responded, "He's a dog, although he's sensitive
And all the things you could want in man's best friend,
But then, he's man's best, not woman's, isn't he?"
I don't know how I've survived without you.
I only know I'm trying to without much success.
I finally told our families and our friends
I didn't want to see them anymore
And after four or five months
They seemed to accept that I was beyond their help
And suggested grief counseling.
After a few visits, I abandoned that too
And began to grieve for you without restraint.
Then one gloomy Saturday afternoon,
A faint desire stirring in me for our favorite latte
Sent me to the corner coffee store
Where I bought four hundred dollars
Worth of exotic beans, a new coffeemaker,
Coffee cake, imported coffee cups and saucers
And once done, went next door to the Italian shoe store
Where I bought a pair of thigh-high boots.
You would have loved them—
Pink patent leather
And I would not and would never wear them
Only set them in a chair
And stare at them
As if a stranger left them there by mistake.
I wish my shopping were all it takes
To come back from despair,
But it's such a long way I know it can't.
If I counted it in dog years, I think it would be clear
How long it took me to arrive
To stare vacantly at my BlackBerry
After the party calling me ends our conversation.
It seems another piece of your body has been found
And I've been asked to come to hangar 515 to retrieve it,
But this time I won't go.
I was polite, but I said, "No."
Only silence greeted my refusal,
Followed by the argument
That I needed it for closure,

But what I need is to know why you, why me?
I have to check the question box
As if I do and graduate into a life without you.
At last, as if hypnotized, I stride past the accusatory boots,
Cedric following with his chew toy in his mouth
To stop at your desk
Where I pick up a piece of your puzzle, then another,
Taking apart what's left of our life together,
Then I throw them all out the second-floor window
Into the backyard
Where they seem to writhe into a shape
Too horrible to contemplate.
I had forgotten, or made myself forget,
How much you loved old jet planes.
The puzzle was of a Supersonic.
How ironic, that you would die
Inside a twenty-first-century descendant of that type
And yet, so very right.
I cry out and fall to my knees.
If this is release, if this is life, I think,
Then let me die, then I sob
Until cleansed of my tears, I rise and make dinner—
A small Caesar salad, steak, grilled vegetables
And chocolate cake I cannot eat,
But feed to Cedric who dines happily at my feet,
His doggy indifference a kind of rebuke
As I prepare to take a ride to receive
Another piece of your body.
If I weighed them all
I think I'd have a pound of your flesh
So literal and so bereft
Of literary connotation
That I feel as if I'm falling
Through the air beside the pair of shoes
You promised you'd bring me.
They survived miraculously intact.
They set back of my closet in tragic magnificence.
They are not mine.
Still, I claimed them,
Then I was afraid some relative of the dear departed

Would ask for them
And I started to think I should turn myself in,
And be identified as a grieving widow
And, lately, a thief to be reviled,
But after several days,
I began to realize it was one lie
I would never be called upon to deny
And I set them on the silver tea tray
On which you used to serve me Sunday breakfast
When you decided I deserved to stay in bed,
The *Times* spread out on it, while I read aloud
From the Style section.
We were nothing, if not au courant
In our thinking and our behavior.
At forty, we were past the age
When we had to participate in every event
Our social standing dictated,
But we kept in the loop,
We kept ourselves apart, but not outside.
Now I hide from it all.
I've disappeared into the tall grass of endless mourning
Where dire predictions and warnings of disaster reside
And only come out to bring you home.

This afternoon, I completed my gloomy task,
Intending to break my voluntary exile
By attending a wedding
Until I realized I had forgotten to buy a gift.
I could not attend without one,
So there it was.
I'd managed to absent myself from that too,
And somehow ended up in Little Italy
On my way to see an art show
That had as its theme
Death by violence.
It seemed like something I could handle
And I'd escaped causing a minor scandal
By showing up at a society wedding
Without a gift, which technically
Should already have been given anyway,

Although I knew mine would have been accepted
Mainly out of pity which I would have hated.
As if punishing me for my attitude,
The Feast of San Gennaro greeted me.
I mean it was in full swing
Outside the gallery which was closed.
I got dizzy while trapped in a crowd of onlookers
And managed to collapse
Into the arms of a woman also wearing black.
She helped me to a café
Where she ordered two Pellegrinos
Which we sipped without talking
Until I felt a bit better.
She was older, maybe sixty-five,
But her eyes twinkled with unbridled youth.
"You okay now, my dear?" she asked.
"My husband's dead," I shouted
Over the sound of the parade,
Then I said, "I'm sorry."
"Don't apologize," she told me kindly,
"Widows have to stick together. I'm Janice.
See, I still wear my wedding ring,
Although Sam's been gone ten years."
"I'm Maeve," I said, as tears welled up in my eyes.
I tried to stop them, but she said,
"Go ahead and cry. You have to,
Otherwise you'll just get sick,
At least that's what my mother told me
Before she died suddenly a month after my husband.
Now how's that for a one-two punch?"
I had to admit I couldn't top that.
When she asked, "Have you had lunch?"
I told her I hadn't.
Then she said, "Let's do."
When we parted that afternoon,
I began to admit to myself, though unwillingly,
That I could never go back to the evening
You proposed as we sat on the deck,
Arms wrapped around each other
To fend off the cold November wind.

"If I die before you do," you said, "go on living."
"How could I?" I asked.
Now I know, as I drive home,
The plastic bag containing your bone fragments
Beside me on the seat,
Accepting that this is just another step
In the sweet eventuality of letting go.

LIBBIE

*The mother of the little "folornity" was killed while fighting in the
Washita battle, and the captive women were given charge of the baby.
They took every opportunity to drop it in the snow on the march, and
our officers had to watch vigilantly to see that the squaws did not
accomplish their purpose of leaving it to perish along the way.*
—Elizabeth Custer

When the General introduced me to the papoose
Whose mother had died during the Washita campaign,
I claimed the right to name him.
"Folornity," I exclaimed, upon receiving into my arms,
Wrapped in a fragment of gray threadbare army blanket
The orphan whose light skin
Proclaimed him a half-breed.
Although a scout who accompanied the General
Told me that Cheyenne children could be light-skinned
And that he would darken when he grew older.
I did not believe that soldier of misfortune
As he was known to embroider truth
To suit the circumstances of a situation.
But he did count the Cheyenne among his relations,
Having married at least two squaws.
"I know," he said, "'cause I have got a child of my own
By the last one.
She done left me and taken the boy,
But I hear you can't tell he's half-white
And me, I'd probably walk right past him
And not recognize my own flesh and blood.
A funny thought, ain't it, ma'am?"

"Well, I guess I ought to be going," he said at last.
"I need to rest afore the General sends me out again."
"Too much excitement," I said, half in jest
And half seriously,
Which I think surprisingly, he sensed
As he reached to take the child.
But while I acquiesced,
I still resisted, at least my hands did,
But I think I hid it well.
"Take a good look, ma'am," he said,
As if he realized that I was hiding how I felt.
"This little whelp's not long for this world.
They are going to let him die.
Why should he stay alive when all his family has died, they reason.
They think it's better if he joins them on the other side, so to speak."
"How barbaric and cruel," I almost shouted.
"It cannot be. I'll tell the General
Who warned me it could be they'd do the deed
When his back was turned, the savages.
Leave him with me then awhile."
I did not smile when I said it,
I only let him know my heart was not as frozen
As those women who had been given sanctuary by my husband.
"I fear you've tarried here too long," I whispered,
Then realized the scout had gone and left me with the child.
"Come back," I said aloud while pressing him against my breasts
That had not and never would nourish a little one,
Because I could not conceive,
At least I believed I could not.
I never entertained the thought
That it was the General I ought to blame for my barren womb.
I wondered was it guilt that made the General suggest
I take more than an interest in this child
And visit with him while the General went about his duties?
No doubt he worried about me
And wished to make me happy,
Although I wasn't sad at all.
I'd call myself content in every way that counted.
I'd never be a mother to a child,
But the General was my child as well as my husband,

Brother, nephew and father who knew me better
Than I knew myself.
I did not need anything, or anyone else.
As I lifted the boy, I thought
What if I smashed his head?
I'd just be doing
What the other women would
For his own good.
Just then, the General came in
And saw me with the boy lifted in the air.
"There, there," he said in the soothing voice
He sometimes used for his horses and his dogs
After he had abused them
And was feeling repentant.
"He's better off dead, isn't he?" I said
And he agreed by nodding slightly,
Then politely taking hold of my arms until I lowered the boy.
"Now give him to me," he commanded.
"All right, all right, all right," I sighed,
Imitating him by using the only cusswords
He was allowed to say in my presence.
"There is someone here you should meet."
"Who is it?" I asked.
"You'll see," he said, walking out with the boy.
I followed him
And watched as he handed Folornity to an old squaw
Who took him reluctantly and spat three times
As if to cleanse some evil from him
And I was at once shocked and intrigued
To see a mulatto woman dressed in buckskins
Much like my husband wore when he was feeling jubilant.
"Miss Easter Waggoner," he said, letting her get too close to me,
I mean so close that I could see the faint mustache
And dark chin hairs
That made her look like some kind of circus freak, at least to me.
"I sho am hairy, ain't I?" she said, extending a hand I would not touch.
"The best cook aside from our Eliza this side of the Mississippi,"
Said the General, "aren't you?"
I could not imagine eating anything she prepared.
"I ain't cooking much these days," she replied,

Stepping back to stand beside the General.
"I come to see if I could be of service in some other way, but maybe
    not.
You know I've got my son to think about.
His name is Charlie Smith
And I was wondering if the General
Could use him as a scout,
But the General says he don't need none,
So I guess I'll be on my way.
I just wanted to pay my respects to you, ma'am,
For I am an old friend of the General's."
"From when?" I asked sharply,
Having guessed there might have been more to it.
"Oh, he seen me on the trails a'cooking for some Texans.
Afore that I served that rascal John Smith."
"You mean the squaw man?"
"I do, the despoiler of my youth
And father of my son, although he denies it.
His lies are second nature. Ask the Cheyenne.
They'll tell you he can be friend and enemy at the same time
And you can't find the dividing line between the two.
He called me a nigger," she said, "but I am half white
And between you and me some Cherokee mixed in,
But I am called a mulatto and I am proud to be.
I ain't no darky."
I did not say anything to that.
I was shocked at the disdain she seemed to have for blacks
And shrank from her in horror.
The General, sensing my discomfort,
Proceeded to end our one-sided conversation
By saying she should stay for rations
And take her leave in the fashion in which she arrived,
That is, in a covered wagon, pulled by mules.
"I brung some fabric," she said, eyeing me as if I were a piece of cake.
"You could make you a new dress. It would please him," she said,
Smiling but all the while I felt as if she were sticking a dagger in my
    heart.
Maybe I was losing my mind, I thought,
Imagining some rivalry with this creature
Who was no threat at all to me,

So I agreed to look at her wares after a nap.
The General slapped her back as if she were a comrade-in-arms
And said, "I knew you'd do the trick."
"What trick?" I asked his back
As he strolled out with her.
What had she got that I hadn't? I wondered,
Then I had to admit that it was freedom
And the thought hit me so hard I sank to my knees
And stayed there so long I thought they were bleeding
When I finally rose,
But it was only perspiration
From the numerous petticoats and underwear I wore to keep me
    warm.
She was harmless, harmless,
Unlike that temptress Monahsetah.
Later, when I went to see Easter, a handsome young man
With light golden skin, brown hair and a hawk nose
Descended from back of the wagon,
Watching me through gray eyes.
"You the Gen'ral's missus?" he asked.
"I am," I said, ignoring the hand extended to me
As I had his mother's,
But he left it there so long
I finally laid mine in his
And found it calloused and warm.
"You look like your father," I said, "except for your nose."
"Heard that before, but he claims my mother's a whore
And I could be anyone's bastard.
Pardon me, ma'am. I didn't mean to—"
"Don't apologize," I told him. "It is the correct term."
"Well now, I'll just let you peruse the merchandise.
When you find what you want,
I'll give you a good price on it."
"Eureka," I said gaily in no time at all,
Handing him the very bolt of cloth
His mother had described in a whispered aside
As she took her leave from me.
Red silk with cabbage roses woven into the fabric
And with silk threads that gave it a sheen
As if a thin layer of water had settled on it.

"It's beautiful," I said. "How much?"

"It's a gift," he said. "I'll settle up with Mama."

"No, no, I can't," I protested. "It wouldn't be right."

"What's wrong about it?" he asked, staring into my eyes.

I was hypnotized.

"I could stay another night," he said,

Releasing me from my trance.

"There's a dance," I blurted, before I caught myself and stammered

"I mean—"

"No white woman could dance with me," he said, winking
    conspiratorially.

"What if the Gen'ral said it was all right?"

"He couldn't. He wouldn't—"

"I'm only teasing. Another time then."

"Yes," I said, "indeed. I'll leave you to your packing up.

Say goodbye to your mother for me."

"She taken that baby."

"What?"

"That Cheyenne orphan."

"Folornity?"

"That his name? Don't forget the cloth," he called,

As I walked off in a daze.

Why should I care? I thought. I ought to be glad he's rescued,

Even if it is by two—two what?—uneducated mulattoes?

I turned back. "Were you baptized?" I asked him.

"I can read a bit," he said, "a priest taught me."

"You're Catholic?"

"That ain't it, just Christian I'd say. Is that okay?"

I looked away from him

As my eyes teared.

"You cryin', ma'am? I'm sorry to distress you.

I thought you'd be relieved

Because the Gen'ral said you'd be pleased

To see the orphan with a family.

Everybody needs some peoples, even if they evil.

They still family and can be redeemed by Jesus Christ."

"You're right, of course," I sighed. "Be good to him."

"Got to. He my brother now.

Anyhow we going to Texas. Mama claims she got relatives there,

But I don't know.

I think she just wants to go somewhere new is all.
She got what she calls wanderlust. I got it too.
Ain't nothing for us in Kansas but tears.
These Indians are suffering."
I might have argued with him, but instead I took my leave,
My head spinning with the news I had received.
The next morning, the wagon was gone
And so too the orphan born of grief.
As I stood forlorn beside the deep ruts
The wagon made the day before,
I swore to myself I'd try to keep from crying from despair.
That night, I'd calmed down enough to be the hostess
Of the General's celebration dance.
The officers were dashing, the ladies elegant in their finery
And I was relieved to be dancing with my darling boy.
I felt as if I were a young bride again
When everything was possible,
Then suddenly the face of Charlie Smith appeared to me
And I swooned against my husband,
Who could not have guessed
That just for a moment,
I saw myself sitting beside that boy on a wagon,
My breasts heavy with milk,
My belly swollen with a child
While I held another in my arms.

When I came to, the General said,
"You fainted clean away. I was so worried."
"I'm fine, fine," I told him, trying to sit up in bed,
But he gently held me back.
"What did that black boy say to you?"
"Charlie? Why nothing."
"He made you a gift of fabric."
"He made me a gift, that's all."
"I may play cards awhile. You'll be all right, won't you?"
"Of course. I'll sleep well," I lied, knowing I would not,
But keep constant watch over my thoughts
Lest they escape.
Suddenly desperate to be reassured, I asked,
"What comes after all of this?"

"Why everything," he answered.
"Now I'll say good night," he continued, as he leaned down
And sealed my betrayal with a kiss.
But I had not been unfaithful.
I'd only had a brief fantasy of motherhood,
My only tryst was with a baby, not a man,
While the General plays his hand in every way he can.
Of course, when I hear the rumors, I try to ignore them
But they torment me.
Even in my sleep, I see him in a torrid embrace
With his Indian princess.
Tom sensed my distress and tried to lessen it
By taking his brother's place.
I feared the sacrifice he made for me
Was but an excuse to further his rivalry
With the General.
"Stop it," I told him only last week
As I sewed while he sat at my feet,
Entertaining me with ghost stories.
"Ah, she's just another Sallie Ann," he said lightly,
But I saw a tremor in his hands,
As he reached up to brush away a strand of hair
That had fallen across his face.
"Time to cut my hair," he said jauntily,
Though I could not see any joy in his eyes.
"Shall I get the shears?"
"My dear, you take me for granted," I told him,
Standing abruptly and walking away.
I had not spoken to him since that day
And when we danced,
He did not say a word, only held me stiffly at first,
Then when the General cut in,
He made no mock protestations, only released me
Into his brother's arms again.
That's when I swooned and found myself
In my bedroom
With the General's gloomy visage looming over me
Until I smiled and stroked his cheek awhile.
"Shall I shave?" he asked.
I said, "No, the beard makes you look so distinguished."

"Not old?" he asked, passing his hand over it.
"Doesn't it scratch you?"
"Yes, but I don't mind. I'm not the kind of wife who complains.
You know that."
"Yes, I do. You are an angel, the angel who saved me from myself."
"Hardly," I said.
"You'll miss the whelp, won't you?"
"I will," I said, "but you know best."
"I wish I did," he answered, leaving me,
With my heart beating as rapidly as a bird's.
Was I dying, I wondered,
I couldn't tell, I thought, then I fell asleep,
And woke to see my beloved watching me,
But was it love I saw in his expression
Or the pity one feels for an invalid?
"Do you think I don't love you anymore?" I asked,
Unbuttoning my gown.
"Of course not. Only the Cheyenne put a curse on me
By dumping ashes on my feet
And I am filled with so much emptiness,
I dare not sleep tonight."
"Then we will stay awake.
Here take my hand.
I'll keep you safe, my dear," I said,
Trying to cheer him.
"Just lay your weary head upon my milky breasts
And you will see your soul's unrest
Is but the afterbirth of victory."

BROTHERHOOD

I stare down on Southie
From my ivory tower.
It is the blue hour,
Blue of navy blazers and navy slacks
Worn with white button-down shirts
And polished black oxfords
As blue as I am afterschool
With Sister Margaret

Who used to let me erase the blackboard
After I had written
"I must not talk in class" one hundred times.
She told me I must ask permission
To go to the bathroom.
I must stand with my hand over my heart
When I pledge allegiance to the Flag
And mustn't brag to the less fortunate
When I come back from Christmas vacation
And I must stand and kneel and stand
And say the rosary and genuflect
In front of the Virgin Mary statue
At the foot of the stairs
Up to Father Donovan's office,
Where my brother's waiting with Mother and Father
Because he hit another boy and bit him too.
He won't do anything they tell him.
He promises he will,
But he never keeps his promises.
He enjoys inflicting pain,
But he rarely shows it
As he dispenses punishment to fit the crime
He thinks you've committed.
He believes in justice,
Maybe not your kind, or mine, but he does.
He'll bust your arms with a rock,
Knock you down and stomp on you.
I've seen him do it,
But I'll never tell anyone
Who it was he threw into the Charles
And who didn't come around anymore.
The family packed up and moved
And that was that
And it only showed the neighborhood
My brother was someone to be respected.
He was. I've got the scars to prove it
And the mad loyalty that comes from total devotion.
He had the gift.
He could sniff weakness
And use it against you.

I let him do it. We all did.
Now that he's on the run
The police want me to abandon him
And appear at some hearing
To tell them what I know about his supposed offenses,
But I won't. I can't.
He's blood and that's all that matters now
And back when it ran into the street
Outside Pete's Diner
When I got a shiner instead of him,
By taking on Pat Ryan
Who was threatening him with a baseball bat.
Pat knocked me to the sidewalk
And the two of them walked off arm in arm,
Laughing at me
Because they thought I was too serious and so boring.
Years later, they would hang Sully
From a meat hook in the diner's freezer
And say they ought to have done the same to me.
Sully's death took a while,
But my brother had time then, and style,
Something I never had in my tweed jacket and corduroys,
My pockets filled with torn packets of sugar,
Pennies and pens without ink.
It was a miracle I could even dress myself,
But I could think.
I thought myself here, didn't I,
High above my brother's life of crime?
We both had the will to succeed.
That's all we ever needed,
But look at us now.
How did we end up here?
Was it justice finally catching up with him,
Or just a few loose ends
He thought he could tie some concrete blocks to
And drop in the Charles
Just like in the good old days?
Those days are gone and so's the old sod
That's not so green anymore
And we are not so poor

As when we listened to "Danny Boy" on the radio
In our shared room
And made farting sounds,
Giggled and dreamed of drowning in chocolate cream
Instead of plain old hot water.
I ought to tell the police he called
To ask if I would squeal on him.
He said, "You weak little shit,
Remember Easter, 1967 and the diamond earrings
I gave Mother?
You knew they were hot and you told Father.
I got detention, remember?
They called it the summer of love,
But it wasn't love coming off the old man's belt
And it wasn't love that made me a man;
It was something you don't understand,
You academic little prick."
I kept silent because he needs to say these things to me.
What else can he do now that he knows he isn't invincible
But wound me with words?
They aren't fatal after all
And only hurt like hell at first,
Then like Saint Stephen's arrows
Produce a kind of ecstatic and dramatic sacrificial thrill.
I first encountered it as a kid
When I wrote a hundred times,
"I won't, I won't, I won't,"
But Sister Margaret said, "You will,"
Then before she told me to erase it and go,
She said, "Your brother needs you to defend him."
I tried to take the blame that time.
He never forgave me.
He wanted the world to know he wasn't a punk
And he would show them, oh, how he would.
Now we're middle-aged,
Bearing the curse, not the luck, of the Irish
On our shoulders like crosses.
We know that loss is just the outcome of living,
The dross that's left after you turn gold back into iron
And end up in Rio with a mulatta, who's got a habit,

But he doesn't care. He's flying blind
And I am right behind him
In my imagination anyway,
But he's really at South Station,
Having mastered the art of hiding in plain sight.
When I get there, the frigid air heats up
And I start to sweat,
Knowing that as he steps from the blue shadows
He's going to give me the bullet to the back of the head
He always said he'd deliver just like the bread man,
Knowing it's one promise he's going to keep.

MANHOOD

"Jesus, Kev," says Ryan, "you spent your morning
Writing a story about shaking down a priest.
What's the matter with you, as if I didn't know?"
"'Twasn't me," I said, "on my knees
Giving head in the rectory, was it?
It was Kathryn Mallory.
I saw it all, then went to confession
Where I said my Hail Marys very fast,
So I could ask Father Murphy
What he was doing with his fly open
And Katie's head pressed against him
Like she was listening to it.
The silence on the other side of the booth
Was so thick, you could you know—
I thought he'd fainted
And I was getting up to go
When he called me a malicious troublemaking bastard
And I said, 'Father, you got it right at last.
I'd pay up fast if I were you.'
'How much?' he said finally
And I said, 'Three hundred and that's not pennies.'
He said, 'Can you wait 'til Monday?'
And I answered, 'Sunday afternoon would be better.'
'That girl's a temptress,' he hissed.

'If you don't watch out, she'll get you too.'
'Thanks for the advice,' I told him,
'But I've already been tempted twice and given in.
Sin is so delicious,
Better than the special dishes
Widow Cavanaugh serves the men and boys
Who crave a bit of naughtiness
The wife or girlfriend will not provide.'
He slammed the grate shut.
I stood up, doffed my hat
And grinned at the widow
As she entered confession's maw,
Only to emerge like me
Refreshed and free of sin.
I had hung around. What else did I have to do
On an afternoon with a few coins in my pockets
When the door to the confessional opened.
Didn't the widow wink at me
And didn't I wink back?
It's a free country
If you can pay for it.
We Irish escaped the Great Potato Famine
And hard times,
Only to end up among thieves,
In New York City,
For isn't the rent we pay exorbitant, Ryan,
The food at market overpriced.
The poor pay doubly, that's the truth,
That's life and then some."
"Jesus, Kev," says Ryan, "we're just laid off.
No need to be so negative.
That famine happened so long ago."
"No it didn't. The past is today
And to quote the writer,
It's how we live now," I say
As I get off the floor
Where Mike Monahan knocked me down
After I poured ale on his head.
He swung round and pounded me.
As I sank to my knees, I felt a tooth loosening,

Then I got to see stars at noon.
A small price to pay for the privilege.
"You artists," Ryan complains, as we go outside,
"always living in your heads.
You'll wind up rich, or dead."
"Maybe both," I say. "Want a toke?
It's fine shit and it won't give you a hangover."
"I just says no to dope," claims Ryan,
Throwing a bottle in the alley
Behind the Shamrock, our local watering hole
Where we are often found holding court.
"Did you like my story then?"
"It shows promise," says Ryan,
"Then again, I'm no critic.
You going to write this one down?"
"If I can remember it," I say, certain I won't,
Certain it will float away like all the others.
"You are not a failure, Kev, although you try to be.
Why not succeed at something?
You don't want to work construction all your life, do you?
I've got a wife and kids and I can't do anything else,
But you could, you could," he says, and goes home,
Leaving me to fill the rest of my day
With my own unwelcome thoughts.
Sometimes I amaze myself and do write my stories down,
All the while wondering if anyone would buy them.
I don't know, maybe I'll make a million dollars
And spend it on booze, floozies and horses
And all the useless artifacts of contemporary life.
I'll bow-wow like a good dog
When I am fed a treat
After I perform the trick of engineering my defeat.
Back in the bar,
I call for another whiskey.
"No more for you today," says Danny, the manager.
"You can't pay."
I say, "Is that the only reason
And not because I might hurt myself, or someone else?"
"Be reasonable," he says. "Go home and sober up."
"I am home," I say, surveying my kingdom.

"Don't you know I've returned
From the eternity of clean living to be here?"
"Go on," he says, moving down the bar
To fill a glass.
"Pass it this way," I call, as I fall on my face,
My head spinning, my stomach beginning to heave.
As I am dragged out the door,
I shout, "Wait, I have another story to tell,"
Then I don't say anything at all.
I just lie on the sidewalk
Until the nausea passes, then I sit up
And assess my options,
Finally admitting to myself there aren't any.
Back home, I spy a letter in the mailbox.
A bill, I think at first,
But when I take it out,
I am shocked to see it's a letter from *The New Yorker*.
My hands shake so much
I have to take a drink of the cheap wine
I keep for emergencies
Then sink down on the patched beanbag chair
My last girlfriend left,
Along with a pair of thong underwear
She abandoned because I bought them.
"Keep 'em," she said, throwing them at me.
I was drunk, of course
And fell past her down a flight of stairs.
She stepped over me as she escaped
What everyone assumed would be her fate—
Being the caretaker of a failure.
I tear the envelope, having almost forgotten about it,
Then I wait a few seconds before I read.
I can't believe they want to publish my tripe,
I say out loud.
I don't even remember sending it.
I can't even recall the story they describe
As a riveting look at the dead-end lives
Of some guys named Kevin and Ryan
In all their pathetic, petty and triumphant glory.
I did not even change our names

And we are not innocent, or penitent.
I crave the limelight, but I'm afraid of it
I think, taking another drink.
In fact, drinking until I pass out.
When I wake this time,
I realize I've been hallucinating.
There's only a cable bill
And a threat to disconnect.
I get up, stumble to the shower
And let the hot water burn me
The way I'm sure hellfire would.
Afterward, I make some coffee
And vow to stay sober for a day, or two,
Or at least until Ryan arrives
As he does, right on cue,
When I'm about to go down to the Shamrock.
I think Monahan is saving my seat upon the floor
And I'm sure if he isn't, someone else I'll needle is.
On the brief walk over,
Ryan talks for a change
And I listen as long as I can contain myself.
"These stories you tell don't have endings.
Why is that?"
"Because the cat ate them."
"Don't joke. I'm serious," he says.
"And I am broke. Can you spot me?"
"You know I will," he says.
"The stories aren't meant to end."
He says, "The gist."
"As soon as we get there," I say,
"I'm going to pee."
"You mean you're going to peek into the ladies' restroom."
"That's the gist of it," I say.
"Indeed!" he says as we continue in silence
Until he adds, "They sealed the hole."
"Now what'll you do for entertainment?"
"It might have been my arraignment,
But now I guess it will just have to be
The continuing decline of me."

In the bar, we laugh and raise our drafts,
Throw some darts
And do what passes for a night on the town
Without the womenfolk
To hound us into submission.
We fathers, sons, brothers, uncles, and husbands,
Confused and sputtering into our glasses,
Paralyzed by what passes for living
In the age of terror and misgiving.

FATHERHOOD

I am at the "Great Brooklyn Irish Fair" of 1978,
Sitting on a curb with my husband
Eating boiled potatoes,
When a stocky, red-faced man standing nearby
Asks, "Are they good?"
We answer, "Yes," in unison
And the man smiles, nods and staggers away.
This is supposed to be a celebration of Irish heritage,
But to me, it's a combination flea market, street fair
And drunken family picnic
With food stalls, where people sell funnel cakes,
Hot dogs and Polish sausages,
Things we might eat at another time
But do not speak to us today,
Thus when we find the stall that advertises
Only boiled potatoes, we stop and purchase two without butter.
My husband, Lawrence Michael, at least looks Irish.
He's dark-haired, pale-skinned,
Sunburns easily, but rarely drinks alcohol, or beer
And doesn't fit the Irish stereotype,
While I am multiracial
With Irish on my mother's side.
I come from a family of heavy drinkers
And tale-tellers and I am Catholic,
But I don't look Irish at all,
Yet fall under the umbrella of Irishness,
Especially with a potato in my hand.

I guess the man smiled at us
Because we weren't ashamed to admit
The potatoes tasted good,
Or maybe it proved we were Irish or something like it.

Perhaps he divined in me a story
I was told once in a while,
The one that changed each time I heard it.
Usually, a drunken male relative
Would start his version at Christmas gatherings
Giving it a wicked spin,
Then forget it and begin a new one next holiday.
He'd tell us how lucky we were to have such a fine dinner
And ungrateful sinners that we were
We ought to bow our heads
And thank not God, but A. J. Malone
Who would have starved but for pluck
And half-decent luck
When digging secretly in a neighbor's field,
He found four shriveled potatoes
He didn't steal, but borrowed
And so had a fine Irish meal slightly leavened by sorrow
For hadn't his neighbor said "What's mine is yours"
Before he died, leaving a wife and ten children beside themselves?
Well, they had help from her family, he told himself guiltily
As he ate enough to get to town,
Pushing a wheelbarrow of his poor possessions—
A hat for Sunday, a threadbare corduroy jacket
And a package from a hated relative
Which when he finally opened, he found inside a wallet
Of cowhide, a steerage ticket to America.
"Want to go?" my husband asks, interrupting my reverie.
I say, "No, I'm here to demonstrate some Irish pride"
And when the parade of ordinary folks
Start walking behind the bagpipers, step dancers
And guest Puerto Rican salsa band, we join them.
We made jokes about this whole affair
And really only came to get some laughs,
But now, we are magically transformed and grasp hands
In honor of our ancestors who came across the sea,

Who couldn't have imagined
There'd be a place for someone like me in their history,
But nevertheless, open their arms
and with "cead mile failte"
welcome the great, great, great-granddaughter of A. J. Malone
who traveled long ago from Derry
to the Texas prairie to marry,
beget nine children and grow old,
having sown his wild seeds among half-breeds,
who bore his name with pride and shame,
knowing that whatever they became,
they would remain his children.
I can hear him whispering to me
above the music and the noise
of this conglomeration,
"Aisling, Aisling."
In Gaelic, that means vision, or dream.
It means I see him staggering away,
Having given me this day my daily bread
Among the living and the living dead.

FINNEGAN AWAKE

Am I daft? I wonder as I shake myself awake from a dream
In which I've seen a photograph of James Joyce's family,
At least that's what the faint handwriting
On the white border claimed
But as my eyes traveled up from there,
I was puzzled to see only darkness
Where I thought I would find the kind of portrait
Popular at the time, from which people stared gravely,
As if daring the photographer
To capture what was only a small glimpse
Of the bitter fruit we call kinship.
Perhaps there was no mystery after all
And I'd been sent a message from beyond by Joyce himself
To help me learn what he knew all too well.
Family is heaven and it's hell so entwined
You cannot tell one from the other,

But must dwell forever in the dark eternity between the two.
Yet, I knew that wasn't quite what he had in mind.
I imagined it was because my surname's Finnegan,
But then again what difference does that make,
I wonder, wishing I could divine my dream runes like some Druid
Who knew it would do no good
To unmask what should stay hidden,
To "develop" the negative.
Better to take a sedative as I do
And sink into a deeper kind of sleep
And not dream, not finally understand the "meaning" of things,
Which after all are meaningless
Outside the context of life, death, sex and the rest of it.
Yet, as I wake a bit hungover, late for work
And hearing my helpmate, child and Rover
Beginning to take their places
At the breakfast table and beside it, I'm glad I failed
At my attempt at divination
And lived to tell the tale.
When I go to breakfast, my girl, Maggie, tells me
She's got something to show me.
It's her latest watercolor which lies upon my plate,
But all I see is a large black square of paint,
So I ask, "What is it then?"
She answers, "Jonah swallowing the whale,
Or it's you setting sail for Panama in a gale.
Aw, it's silly."
But I say, "No, it's our lives reduced to ashes."
When she asks, "How do you know?"
I say, "A great Irish writer told me so."

A CIGAR IS—OH, NEVERMIND

They said all you have to do
Is follow the bouncing Betty, I mean ball,
Well now, maybe it was something else.
Oh yeah, read the teleprompter, they said,
If you lose your way, I mean place,
On the straight and narrow path

The Lord ass-kicked me into taking
And here I am in front of the cameras again
Trying to explain that when I was a young man,
I didn't worry about tomorrow.
I was very fortunate.
Sorrow had never knocked on my door
And if it had, I wouldn't have answered.
I had enough on my plate of grits,
Well, okay, whatever it was
Was on a plate.
I hate to rush you
But I have matters of state to attend to
So you'd better get on with it
And ask the question you've been dying to, uh, um—
Ask?
Wait a minute, I will say,
Sometimes a kiss is justa kiss, uh,
Or is it a cigar?
Well, you know what I mean.
You've seen it on the news
Just like I have.
I sure didn't read it in the paper.
I don't have the patience for it.
I like somebody to read to me;
It helps me focus on the important things
Like—uh, what was I just saying?
I'm kinda preoccupied right now.
Got a lot on m'plate.
Did I say that already?
You can't make hay without, you know—Grass?
Sometimes when you have a date with destiny,
You run a little late,
But you get there.
There's no disgrace in that.
I think the disgrace would be if I let a buncha—
Uh, let someone tell me how to govern.
I have the best teacher anyone could.
I don't have to tell you, well, maybe I do,
I started at the top of my game,
Well, both of them.

See these hands?
Steady as the rock of ages.
That's all you need to know.
Can I go now?
I mean I can go now.
Okay, okay, one question. What's that?
Sorry, we're out of time
And we all know time waits for no man.
Put that in your pipe and toke, I mean
Smoke it.

I'M THE ONLY ONE HERE

I was smuggled to America
inside a ship's container.
Once a day, the first mate opened it
so we could breathe fresh air.
Then one day, he didn't come.
Two more days passed without mercy.
Someone died. The smell was awful,
but my strong will prevented me
from giving in to despair.
I had been on despair's doorstep so many times
I was immune to it.
I had one rope of sandalwood incense
which I burned
despite the entreaties of a few
who were still conscious not to do it,
because smoke would make things worse.
I simply pretended not to hear the cries for air
that had begun to accompany the hum
of the ship's engines.
Suddenly, when even I was too weak to move,
the door opened
and the first mate appeared with a black eye and sparse beard.
He said he'd failed to come to us
because he'd gone ashore, gotten into a fight
and been jailed.
We were hungry, low on water, filthy

and willing to barter anything we had
which was nothing once we'd paid our passage.
Two women gave him something I hesitate to name.
They became our lifelines.
Each time he sent for them
they returned bruised with scraps of food for us
and blamed us for their bad fortune
as if they had forgotten we were truly in the same boat.
By the way, I forgot to introduce myself. I am Manesh.
In New Delhi, I was a scholar of philosophy.
I lost my job at university because of a rival's jealousy.
An old story, but with a twist. He was my brother, a scoundrel,
who had me declared dead
and moved into my house.
A bureaucratic nightmare thus ensued.
When at last I'd gotten the declaration proved wrong,
he had me declared dead once more.
Unable to go through the process again,
I let him move into my house,
whereupon he exiled my wife and child to the maid's room.
While my remaining rupees paid my way
to this gloomy afternoon in New York City
where I drive a taxi
and recall my sad journey and its cause
as if it were a dream,
recall the bodies of my compatriots
as if they were but pieces of debris
washed ashore beside me.
I remember how I tore my fingers, trying to escape the container,
but that, too, seems unreal to me.
Of twenty people, only three of us survived
to be hustled into the back of a van
by a clean-shaven man with a bald head.
Now I live with other illegals
And am grateful to have down the hall a bathroom
All of us must share, one telephone on a wall,
Occasional hot water and the smell of cooking food
Twenty-four hours a day.
All I possess to call my own
Is the forty dollars I earned today

And a videocassette of *Taxi Driver*, dubbed into Hindi
That I purchased from a street vendor
Two weeks after I arrived.
I set twenty dollars aside to send my wife,
The rest must tide me over for a week.
I will not eat lunch, I will keep driving
To meet my goal of simply holding on
Until I save enough to bring my family here,
Unless this, too, is a dream.
I confess I can no longer tell.
For instance, Robert De Niro
Drove a taxi like I do, although it was in a movie,
But to tell the truth, it seems more real to me
Than my attempts at living do.
I must admit I haven't picked up anyone
Who looks like Cybill Shepherd,
But I've driven a prostitute to a few shady assignations
And today, even to one very upscale building in Tribeca,
Where she was refused entry.
I had agreed reluctantly to wait for her
Because she was a regular customer
And watched her argue with the doorman,
Until he shoved her hard.
She spun around and around on her very spike heels before she fell.
I noticed she was bleeding from one knee as she hailed me
With her gruff man's voice,
But having waited long enough
And not wanting to get involved,
I had no choice but to leave her standing at the curb,
Her once very white fur parka, stained
And the dark eyeliner smudged by the tears streaming down her face.
I could have intervened, made up some story,
Perhaps even pretended to be her pimp,
But it wasn't my place.
I am just a taxi driver,
So I sped away, my headset on,
Listening to a conversation between two other drivers
Who had seen a naked woman getting into a taxi.
I didn't talk, I only continued to listen,
My thoughts drifting back to *Taxi Driver*

And the sad fate of the pimp and his mates,
Who paid for their jobs with their lives
As people sometimes do,
Who have not realized the difference between illusion
And the unadorned reality of existence
Which is illusion too.
One must endure cycle after cycle of death and rebirth
Until one is simply reabsorbed
Into the infinite light of the universe.
Ah, such cold comfort to me now.
Having stood on the brink of death, I think
As I pick up my next fare.
"Where to, sir?" I ask in my best Americanese.
When he doesn't respond, I glance in the mirror
And see a face I vaguely recognize
And feel a not unpleasant chill run up my spine
When he says, "You talkin' to me?"
"Yessir," I answer, "I mean it's just you have my brother's eyes."
"Don't look at me," he says,
"Look straight ahead and drive."
When we arrive at his destination,
As if possessed, I shout, "Here is,"
Turning to face my enemy
And he calmly answers,
". . . a man who would not take it anymore,"
Handing me the tip as he slams the door.
"Here is . . ." I say, merging into the roar of traffic
Before I pull out my semiautomatic
And start shooting anyone who touches my brother's whore.

THE STRANGE JOURNEY OF ULYSSES PARADEECE AFTER A HURRICANE

"It's your imagination," said Mama Paradeece.
"You can't feel nothing below your knees."
"That may well be," I answered,
"But I still feel something tickling me."
She said, "Son, doctor done cut off your legs,
You may as well accept it now and go on.

Anyhow, you don't listen to Mama.
You never did, smoked that dope,
Run out on your wife and kids,
Now look at you
Laid up, black and alone,
Ain't got nobody, homeless, penniless and old."
I said, "Mama, I ain't black, I'm Creole like you,"
But she said, "That ain't the way the world see you.
Might as well get used to it. I did.
Anyway, your white blood ain't going to save you today."
"What you talking about?" I asked,
But Mama Paradeece had disappeared,
Leaving me alone in the hospital hallway.
After 'while, the wind howled like a dog,
Walls shook, lights went out
And it took all my strength
To raise up and look down the hall
Where I seen water pouring through the door
And a nurse's aide wading toward me
With a strange look on her face.
She said, "Mr. Paradeece, I'll get you out somehow."
But I could see she didn't know what to do
So I said, "Save yourself, 'cause they done black-tagged me.
I'm hopeless and that's the truth.
It's no use trying to rescue me,"
But she said, "Take this, old man."
"What is it?" I asked.
"It's a life jacket from my boat.
My husband brought it to me before he drowned
'Cause I couldn't hold on to him. Now I got to go."
As she waded away with a sigh and a faint goodbye,
I knew I was going to die, so I closed my eyes.

Lord have mercy, I'm still alive, I thought,
As I floated into the street beside the body of someone familiar,
But I couldn't quite make out who
Then it came to me. It was the nurse's aide,
Now bloated and as dead as Mama Paradeece.
How long had I slept, I wondered,
Holding on to the life jacket,

As I bumped up against a tree whose branches snagged my robe
And tore it off me,
But I held on to the life jacket anyway.
When I heard somebody call to me,
I couldn't open my mouth
And I couldn't let go of the tree either
So I just held on until it got stuck on something
And I broke free.
That's when a water moccasin swam up to me.
I swear I heard him speak.
He said, "Do you believe in Jesus?"
And I said, "Occasionally. You gonna bite me?"
"What happened to your legs?" he asked.
"I got diabetes, doctor had to amputate below the knees."
"Why you want to live then?
Why don't you let me put you out of your misery?"
About then, I heard a shriek
As a big old bird, look like a hawk, or something
Sank its beak down on that snake.
I couldn't help myself, I screamed
And filthy water liked to drown me
When suddenly, two arms wrapped around me
And pulled me onto a porch.
When I caught my breath,
I saw a man with a flashlight bending down to look at me.
"That a dress you got on?" I asked.
"See," he said to a Chihuahua in a fruit basket,
"What happened to this old man,
Lost his legs in this cruel storm."
"Naw, they gone before this," I whispered,
But I don't think he heard me.
"Come on, old fellow, we got to get you a beer. How's that sound?"
I nodded, as he held a beer can to my mouth
And I just about choked.
"Ain't you got no water?"
"Not to drink," he answered.
"Lemme rest a minute, then I'll take me another drink," I told him.
"What do you think is gonna happen to us now?"
"We going to survive, pop," he said,
"Otherwise we going to die.

Either way, I'm dressed for it."
I said, "I guess you are."
Then I slept and when I woke, it was daylight
And he was smoking a cigarette and holding the dog on his lap.
He was wearing a camouflage T-shirt, jeans, combat boots
And a cap that had *Vietnam Veteran* on it.
"Funny," I told him, "you don't look old enough for Vietnam."
"It's my dad's cap," he said. "He's dead now. Alcohol."
"That's sad," I told him, but he just said, "Water's rising.
We better head up to the roof. I'll carry you," he said,
Putting the dog in a leather pouch he wore
Strapped across his chest
And lifted me onto his back.
Somehow we made it and there we sat three days
Without food or water
When at last, we heard a helicopter.
He stood up and waved his T-shirt over his head
As the sound grew louder and louder.
"Well goddamn," he shouted,
As it flew right over us.
"I second that. It's no use, is it?" I said
When miraculously, a rowboat floated up beside us.
He climbed in first, then half carried, half dragged me
Into the boat. Didn't have no paddles
So we just drifted wherever the water took us,
Using our hands to push things aside,
Until a few cans of pork and beans floated toward us
And a loaf of soggy bread which we ate,
Not worrying about germs, worms or anything
But food, food, food. He had a Swiss Army knife
Which he used to open the beans
And then we had a feast.
After that, I fell into a deep sleep
And when I woke, the boat was on fire,
I mean the oil in the water was
As the dog barked and struggled to get away,
Biting the man something awful
As he struggled to hold on to it, but finally, the dog got free
And jumped right into the flames.
I tried to paddle with my hands,

But I was afraid they would catch on fire
So I stopped, watching helplessly
As the man followed the dog into the water,
Whereupon he himself was engulfed in flames,
Leaving me alone with the terrible smell of burning flesh
And the vision of a man on fire to carry me to my own grave.
Who would save me now, I thought,
As the boat suddenly floated away from the flames
And into the path of a larger boat
Where strong hands lifted me onto the deck.
"Thank you, sir, oh thank you," I murmured,
Thinking I had seen him somewhere before as he disappeared
Behind a stack of boxes of food and emergency kits.
"Who is that man?" I croaked, and a voice answered,
"You've been saved by an actor come all the way from Hollywood,"
And I said, "Good God," as I passed out again.

Now I live in Tucson at the Villa Del Sol Rest Home.
I have my own room and a pair of prosthetic legs
The actor gave me and sometimes, I use them
But I don't go anywhere,
I just stand in my room, staring out the window at all that sunshine,
Wondering why Mama Paradeece doesn't come to see me anymore,
But I don't miss the scolding and arguing,
The holding on to nothing but emptiness
That was her after-death interference in my life.
I've done enough of that.
These days, all I want is to sit in my wheelchair
And spin around on the dime of a time
I heard the sirens wail
As I looked into the one-eyed storm.
Once I sailed without direction
Yet I reached my destination anyway.

VIOLATION

When I wake up, pain shoots all the way
from my butt to my brain.
I don't know what's up,

but I know what's down around my ankles,
my underwear, dude, my underwear.
I wonder where I was last night
then I remember doing vodka shots
at the graduation party until I got cross-eyed
and somebody said he'd drive me home
and somebody else said they'd come along,
at least that's my recollection
as I try to vomit away my shame.
There's dried blood staining my underwear
so that must mean—
Whoa, now, whoa, I think,
then I don't, I just cut them up
and flush them down the toilet with the puke.
All my towels are dirty,
so when I get out of the shower
and reach for my roommate's,
I find his towel rack empty
and I remember he graduated too
and must have already moved out
and I'm going to have to air-dry,
unless I can find something clean
other than my last pair of socks
my mom washed for me
when I went home over spring break
instead of going to Vegas
like my friends did,
but I stayed home
so my mom could make me pancakes for breakfast,
big juicy hamburgers for lunch,
steaks for dinner
and apple crunch cake for dessert.
God, it hurts down there
and when I wipe my ass,
I see it's still bleeding.
I need help, I need my mom,
but I can't call her about this shit.
She thinks I'm perfect,
she thinks I'm the bomb,
but I'm not, I'm a moron

who got raped by somebody.
Was it Zach, my roommate? I wonder.
Has he been hiding his evil intentions
behind a blonde with big tits,
who always sits on his bed
with her legs spread and no panties.
Lindsey, smooth and pink
and drinking the shots along with me last night.
All right, I remember that much now.
I remember how mad Zach got
when I shot my hand up under her skirt
and didn't even touch anything
before she jumped down off the barstool
and found her official fool.
I apologized, but Zach
just said, "It's cool" and winked
and set another drink in front of me
and without thinking, I told him
he ought to dump the bitch,
but he said, "I've got plans for her,"
paused and added, "and you."
Now what do I do?
Am I some girl that I have to call the rape line
and get all emotional and go to the hospital
for a rape test and get photographed
and asked so many questions I can't answer, or don't want to.
No, I am not.
I am a man goddammit
and I can suck it up.
I've just got to stop the blood.
Maybe ice will help. Yeah, right.
Wrapped in a dirty towel
and pressed against my ass until it's numb,
until I am, until I can come clean.
It was a scene all right.
The three of us in bed.
Her giving me head until I passed out
right before I saw Zach shooting me a look
that said anything was possible,
at least that's how I remember it now,

as I notice the bleeding has stopped
and I can't feel a thing that isn't normal
as I pack up
and say a not so fond farewell
to the day I graduated from college
and the night that made it unforgettable.
Well, hell, what's this? I say out loud,
bending down to pick up a gift I find by the door.
It's wrapped in mylar
and tied with a big red bow
and there's a gift card attached.
It's addressed to me.
When I open it, I find a big dildo
and I go, Wait a minute.
Just then, the phone rings, or should I say, sings
and I answer, "Yo, dude."
And he goes, "Yo, yourself.
Did you get your present?"
I go, "I don't know."
He says, "Yeah, you do.
Lindsey had it gift-wrapped,
but she was so trashed
I thought I should call you and ask
if you found it."
"You fucker," I say, "you violated me."
"Violated," he says, "violated.
It was a joke, that's all.
Lindsey's in film studies, remember?
She's got access to makeup and stuff."
"Makeup?"
"Fake blood, dude.
You didn't think it was real, did you?"
"Course not," I lie, hoping my sigh of relief
doesn't give me away.
"Anyway, good luck, you jerk."
"Same to you, dickhead."
At least I think that's what I said
as I hit the end call button
then have to sit down and take it all in.
But why does my ass still ache?

Did Lindsey, or even Zach take liberties
they would never say they did?
Did they stick that thing up there
and forget they'd done it?
The only way to know for sure
is to take a trip to the emergency room.
I'm working up the courage
when suddenly, I get the urge
and hit the toilet
and when I am done,
I find the biggest damned turd
I've ever seen.
I mean I cannot believe it came out of me.
I think maybe I shouldn't even flush,
just leave it, or better yet, put it on YouTube
if they would let me.
Probably not, I decide as I try to flush it.
Of course, the toilet overflows
and that thing rises to the top of the bowl
like it's hollow inside
and just before it drops on the floor
the toilet backflows with a loud whoosh and it's gone
and just a faint throbbing remains in my asshole
but I can live with it.
I could not live with the other
even though I said I could
which makes me wonder how women do
and just for a minute, I hate men
myself included
then I do what my ex-girlfriend said,
the one who read all those magazines for women
like O and shit accused me of,
I compartmentalize it, dude
and move the fuck on,
until about a year later
when I am cruising the net
and read a hard-news headline
about how some gay guy got raped
by a so-called straight man
and all of a sudden, my heart starts thumping

and I break out sweating
and I feel like I'm getting a heart attack
and I realize it must be PTSD
or something like a panic attack.
The shit is whack.
I have to get back to my old self,
but how can I do it, I wonder
and that's how after a lot of soul-searching and worse,
I get the nerve to talk to someone
anonymously on a hotline type of deal
and eventually, I mean like another year,
I become a hotline volunteer.
No, I didn't turn gay,
but that's the way I'm dealing with the feeling
that I got violated no matter
what anyone else might say.
I'd call Zach and confront him about it,
if I knew where to reach him, but I don't,
so I just hope he's changed too
and realizes like I do now
that rape is not a joke.

BOOTH

When I aimed my derringer at the impostor
Seated where a bullet would find him
And tear him from the frail arms of his wife,
Giving him a life eternal,
I did not think my own, become infernal,
Would hurl me like a thunderbolt
Into Charon's ferry.
I did not think his life would be so celebrated,
While mine would be relegated to infamy.
Did I perhaps in my wild haste
To prove my loyalty to the states he murdered
Become unhinged?
Revenge was all to me,
"Absent doubt, avaunt thee," I cried out
While Lincoln rose from the dark sea

Of my sleep like some Leviathan
Whose very breath fouled the air I breathed
And from which I now receive only a burning
In my throat and eyes
As all who once supported me
In my crazed conspiracy against plain injustice,
Turn aside and flee,
But I will not, I cannot be less than I am,
A man who demanded his place
Upon the stage of nationhood
But could not wrest it from the hands
Of those who could have saved it from destruction,
Yet chose to follow that butcher down to hell,
Where I am bound instead.
They say when I performed,
Flames shot from my eyes.
If only they had.
I could have burned the Confederacy to victory.
Now defeated,
Must we concede our sovereignty to tyranny?
Say "Never" and be brave sons of the South.
Do not give in to doubt,
But cling more steadfastly to your dream of freedom
And I who have kissed death full upon the mouth,
Will leave you and make way for some other patriot
To prove his mettle,
While like the king in the poem,
I, ". . . silent, upon a peak in Darien . . ."
Gaze upon what might have been
When slavery was not a sin
For men to judge, but God alone
And what I owned was mine.
Now all I was dissolves in death's quicklime
And futility's metronome keeps time
As if it matters anymore.
I am only a poor, wretched assassin now
Taking my final bow without applause.
"The cause, the cause was just," I whisper
As near the same place where I shot him,
A bullet pierced my skull too

And strangely joined in death,
Abe Lincoln and John Wilkes Booth
Let the bloody truth wash over them.
". . . useless, useless . . ."
To imagine that by doing what you think is right,
You won't incur the wrath of gods and men.

THE HUNT

Yellow dog Pete came to greet me
Teeth bared, hair standing on end
Like he seen the devil
But he just seen the slaves run off
And was trying to warn me, that's all.
I called Black Bob, Issum, Laura
And Flora, but hell and damnation,
They were gone too,
Leaving me two useless babies
And no mammy to nurse them.
I knew what happened,
Knew the minute those Seminoles
Came to Indian Territory with their slaves.
"Gave them too much freedom if you ask me.
Now, see," I said to Florence,
My Choctaw wife and helpmate,
"Now we got to go get them."
She didn't say a word
Almost like she hadn't heard what I told her,
But she was like that.
Already had her sun hat on,
Pants on under her skirt,
Six guns strapped to her like a man.
She said, "Hand me the whip"
And I did it. I always did what she said.
I knew from experience where I stood
When she was set on doing something.
It was no good trying to change her mind,
So I climbed on my horse
And we rode over to her uncle's.

There we met up with some Paddy Rollers
The Cherokees had sent to catch their slaves.
They were Irish like me, but red-haired,
Foulmouthed and foul—smelling
And their Cherokee companion couldn't hide his disdain
Each time they claimed to be experts at hunting slaves.
All the same, we went along with them
To find our property.
We had to catch them before they got to Mexico,
Before they got free.
If you ask me, freedom's overrated,
But I've never been a slave,
Unless you consider marriage a form of slavery.
Marriage to Florence was give-and-take.
Mostly, I gave for harmony's sake.
She was royalty, or something, I don't know,
But they all owned slaves, all those civilized tribes
In the Territory and that bunch
Of Choctaws and Cherokees in Texas
Where Florence came from, all of them kept cattle and chattel,
Horses, hogs, chickens, and dogs for hunting.
In other words, they were rich in their fashion,
So I didn't see anything wrong with marrying an Indian.
Why everybody thought the slaves were mine,
But they were hers
And she was going to bring them back.
I knew just looking at the way she sat her horse
She was determined
And I was too, just not as much.
I tried to stay awake, but finally, after twenty-four hours
In the saddle, I cried, "For chrissakes, stop and take a rest,
Take a shit, or something as long as we get off these horses."
Miraculously, they listened to me, the Paddys and Florence,
But I could tell she was mad.
Of course, that went away when I pinned her down and had my way.
Then I went to sleep.
When I woke up, she was gone.
Left me a note on the back of a runaway slave poster.
Yes, she could read and write.
She'd been taught by Methodists.

Anyway, the note said she'd be back directly.
A Cherokee had sent a message
About where the slaves might be
And she was going to have a look–see.
She took the others with her.
I was relieved. I didn't want to see the slaves' faces
When they got caught,
Didn't want to whip them, though I knew I had to
Being the master and all.
'Bout midday, I saw riders coming my way.
Pretty soon, I knew who they were
Because I recognized Flora and Laura
Who looked white.
They were blonde like their Scottish father.
Florence didn't say much,
Just told me the rest of them got away.
We rode home in silence,
Except for Laura who was crying and carrying on.
When she screamed she'd run away again,
Florence turned her horse around,
Got off and whipped her to the ground.
That's when I found my manhood,
Grabbed that whip and threw it down.
My horse trampled it.
When I was finished,
I helped Laura up and she staggered toward home,
As we followed, resigned to our fates,
Masters and slaves, bound to each other
By the iron chains of race.

WHITE MAN

A soldier came up outside of the lodge and called me by name. I got up and went out; he took me by the arm and walked toward Colonel Chivington's camp, which was about sixty yards from my camp. Said he, "I am sorry to tell you that they are going to kill your son Jack."
—JOHN SIMPSON SMITH

The bullet entered below his right breast.
—JIM BECKWOURTH

[When Jack was shot, he] raised up and fell in the fire.
—TEAMSTER CLARK, Sand Creek Massacre, 1864

"Get up!" shouted the voice.
Like always, I did what I was told,
Although it wasn't easy now 'cause I was old and slow.
I shook Maggie and said, "I smell smoke."
She was still asleep, but she said, "I'm woke.
Run get the hose."
"Too late for that," I said, and rose from the iron bed
Where I'd slept nearly fifty years,
Opened a window 'cause I was choking
And saw my cow running down the road.
"There goes Bessie," I said, to the empty room
'cause Maggie was gone. "Lord, woman," I yelled,
"Forget them wedding pictures and save yourself."
"Johnny," she called from the sitting room,
"It ain't nothing. You're hearing things again,"
But I said, "It was fire, it was fire that spoke my name."
"I don't know a thing about it," she called,
"But it's the barn, not the house in flames."
"The children," I cried, for that's what I called my spotted horses,
Maudey and Claude, sometimes,
Then I remembered they were in the corral,
Only Bessie had been in the barn and she was running
Surrounded by a strange orange light
I realized might have been fire.
"Call the sheriff," I told her, "this is struck oil
Destroying our lives," for I knew as certain as death and taxes
I was being impolitely asked to leave my land
With a helping hand and a match.
"They won't catch 'em," I said aloud,
Watching the old barn burn to the ground,
The sound of oil rising through the rig without a thought
To the trouble it brought.
"Help us, Jesus," Maggie prayed.
She was more religious than me.
I didn't see the need for prayers when a bullet would do.
I moved onto the porch with my shotgun
And stood watch 'til the sun came up,

Then I went and found Bessie standing in a pond
Down by the schoolhouse, a little charred, but alive.
Not five minutes after I got home, a man drove up
And offered to buy my house and would not take no,
Until I fired a warning shot over his head.
He got going, red-faced and sweating,
As he backed down the road,
Then got stuck in the rut from the last big storm.
"I didn't mean no harm," he shouted,
So I put down my gun and went to help him.
Neither of us said a word, just grunted and pushed
And got those wheels loose.
"Wanta drop 'a whiskey?" I asked him
And he said, "I knew you was a reasonable man,
Yes I did."
Late afternoon, he staggered down to the truck and drove off
Like a bat outta hell. Oh well, law'd get him for speeding.
Me, I was needing supper, which Maggie had prepared for three.
"Where's that white man?" she asked.
"Gone," I said, "fast."
I said grace as was my place to do.
When I raised my bowed head
I knew what I would do.
"We'll go to Tucson with Ann and Mike.
It can't be worse than Texas."
"We'll be all right," said Maggie, "we'll have the grandkids.
Mike's a good man. Ann married right."
"She married black as night, but I guess it could have been worse.
You know I'm not going because I want to,
I'm just too old to fight now
And I don't want you to get hurt.
First thing tomorrow, we start packing."
I sounded cheerful, but I was fearful.
A man my age is set in his ways.
He can't just change his habits.
He can't just pull a rabbit out of a top hat
And say, That's that and get on with it.
Fact is, he might just rather die
Than say goodbye to his old life.
Mine was peaceful until that fateful day

I let my son-in-law talk me into drilling for oil.
Now I pay the piper for his toil.
"What you say, Johnnie? Talking to yourself I expect
Like no one else is here.
Like I disappeared into thin air,
But I'm right where I've always been,
Since we married in haste
And repent in leisure in the sorry place you brought me."
"Now I seem to recall you were all ready for marriage
The first time I called at your house.
I thought I was just walking out with you for a spell.
I didn't count on settling down then, well, I was cowboying."
"You were gambling and whoring."
"That may well be, but I was happy in my sinful ways,
Raising hell instead of children,
But you made a good wife."
"Yes I am," she sighed, clearing the table,
As I stood and walked outside.
I stared at the stars, which looked like chunks of ice
In a black punch bowl.
I heard a low growl and knew my old dog
Was back from chasing squirrels,
Or girl dogs, or some wild hog,
Anything that could take him on a holiday away from me,
But he'd always come back as if to say
See, you can't escape your destiny.
Remember how we lived a long time ago
As if we'd never known another existence?
Sometimes I think he can speak
And I say something to him in a language I otherwise
Keep to myself, the language of a boy
Who sees a man fall into fire
After he's shot in the chest by a goddamned coward
Who inserted a gun through a hole cut in lodge skins
And murdered him
Just because he was a half—breed.
I still shiver, remembering Sand Creek
When the white trader's Cheyenne wife adopted me.
I was a half-breed too,
But no one was worried about me then.

Later, with my light hair and gray eyes,
There'd be whispers and occasionally, stares that went on too long,
Long enough to make me ride on to the next ranch,
Where I would take my chances
Among the whites who called me Jack,
Which is what the trader called me,
After his murdered son.
Now I'm the one in the white man's gunsights,
The one undone by his greed.
The hell with it, I think. I'll sell the land,
But keep the mineral rights.
I don't need land, but I need my life.
I don't want to end up like Jack.
I don't want a bullet in the back of my head
Because I said no to a "generous offer."
I can't say I don't care,
Or dare ruthless men to shoot me like Jack did the day he died
After he told them, "Go ahead and kill me. I don't give a damn."
I am not that courageous, or am I. "Maggie?" I say,
"Am I a coward to run?"
But she's way up in the front room,
Already packing her precious heirlooms,
I mean the cheap china her mother's people gave her
On our wedding day.
Suffice it to say they weren't yet paid for
And I had to finish what they started,
But I guess in the end for the two of us
It was all about getting to know each other
Like where we joined and where we parted company on things.
Maggie always forgave people,
But not me, I held a grudge,
Judge and jury that's me to a T.
That's why I know I won't be happy moving to Arizona
Even if it's for the best.
I'll never rest in another man's house,
Though I might have once, but now . . .
My noisy thoughts trail off into silence.
The truth is I only heard about Sand Creek
From the man who raised me.
I wasn't alive yet,

Although sometimes I forget
And the story I heard about it becomes so real to me
I think I must be the orphan
Who survived the beginning of the devastation of his tribe.
They told me he was kin of mine,
But I can't find his name among the corpses on the snowy plains
Where I was born one morning four years later
Into the arms of a soldier
Who found my mother dying of a bullet wound
From the gun he fired
As he walked among the fallen, executing the mortally wounded
As if he could achieve forgiveness by his Christian deed.
He wrapped me in the sleeve of a buffalo robe
He'd cut from the body of an old man
And proceeded to shoot a few more heathens,
Then for some reason, he said, his hand started to shake so much
That he dropped the gun,
But the hand holding me was steady,
So he figured it was a sign and deserted,
Yes he did, with me hidden in that sleeve.
He rode hard toward Texas and never looked back
Except to slap his knee sometimes,
Saying, "See what you done to me, boy?"
He'd chew tobacco and spit and tip his chair back
And sigh and tell me what my mother said before she died.
"Your name," he tells me again.
"It isn't my name," I say, "I know what it means."
"White Man. That's your name," he says again,
"You little bastard, ain't you grateful I saved your ass?
Now you sass me," he says, sitting up fast
And slapping me across the mouth.
"Now get out of my house and don't come back."
That time I didn't.
I cowboyed up in East Texas, then I went to Montana
And chopped wood.
I married a Cheyenne girl who died after a year,
Then I came back to find him on his deathbed.
"You're back," was all he said,
Then he took a long raspy breath and died.
I got the house, the horses and one hundred dollars,

Then I got Maggie, eight children
Grandchildren and great-grandchildren,
Now I've got to sell what's mine
And dwell among strangers.
Hell and damnation, that's all I've got to say,
Except I wish sometimes that I'd died
Inside my mother,
Just died like any other poor Indian
And never been an imitation white man,
But it's too late, I think,
Taking out the old man's gun
And lifting it to my head,
But my hand is shaking too,
So I put it back in the buffalo sleeve
And take the steadiness of my hands as a sign
That God's plan to keep me alive is still working.
I just want to know why,
But all I hear are the cries of a dying girl
And a baby who would inherit
The end of the world.

BABY FLORENCE, A.K.A. COMING THROUGH FIRE

*We have come with our eyes shut . . . like coming through fire.
All we ask is that we may have peace with the whites.*

—CHIEF BLACK KETTLE

1.

I lie in a shoebox on the brown leather, high-backed chair
Beside the cast-iron stove where my great-grandmother put me to
keep me warm.
I was born two months premature and weigh barely two and a half
pounds, but I am covered
With hair, "just like a bear," my mother, Stella, whispered the first
time she held me in her arms, then
Handed me back to her grandmother, Maggie, as if to say, That's
that. It was Maggie who rocked me
And hummed Methodist hymns until three a.m. each morning for a
week because I wouldn't go to sleep as

If I knew I wouldn't wake again if I did. I swallowed the hot toddies
   Maggie spooned
Into my mouth to keep my heart beating and between that and
   breast-feeding, it began to seem like I would
Survive despite what the doctor said when he checked "born dead"
   on the birth certificate form and told
Maggie, "She's not going to make it," but Maggie said, "Yes she
   will," and refilled the shot glass
Of whiskey he requested just "to take the chill off" an autumn day
   where Comanches once raided the
Ranches and small nearby towns around Albany, Texas, built after a
   big flood drowned Fort Griffin
When the cavalry was garrisoned there along with Tonkawa and
   Prairie Apache scouts. Even
Doc Holliday and Wyatt Earp as well as a general class of criminals,
   whores and louts found sanctuary
There before the flood closed it down. Once the Indian problem
   was solved by moving them onto
Reservations, there was no need for all the forts anyway, so it was
   bound to close like those others where
All sorts of human vermin once hung on for dear life. Now safe
   from threat of kidnap, rape and death by
Mutilation, gunfights and general act-of-God devastation, I won't
   hasten death but hold it back breath by
Sweet breath that a man breathes into my mouth when Maggie goes
   to sleep at last and he leaves his place in
The photograph above the mantel on the fireplace to tell me his
   story, which is mine too, although if you
Saw him, you'd wonder who he was because he is a yellow-haired
   white man and I am part Southern
Cheyenne as well as black, Irish, German and half
Japanese, which doesn't please him, but when he is close to me, he's
   seized by a love so strong, he wants to
Lean down and kiss my cheek, but must not for his beard might
   scratch me and he fears he'd frighten me,

2.

Although once Maggie saw him and was unafraid, simply saying in
   a loud voice, "Demon, begone,"

But he said, "I'm just Granddaddy. Don't you recognize me?" "Go
   back where you belong," she replied.
"Johnnie, Granddaddy's broke out again," she called to his estranged
   stepson, then Johnnie said something
He couldn't understand and suddenly, he was held captive again, as
   he had held Johnnie's mother and the
Other members of her tribe captive after the Washita battle and took
   her to his bed. She thought she was his
Wife, but he was already wed and when she went to him and said
   she was with child in sign language, he
Sent her back to her people with Johnnie, the son she'd had on the
   march to Camp Supply, but the one
Inside her, that one he claims now, but he is not sure why he came
   to be in Johnnie's house,
Although after years on the mantel where he was used to strike fear
   into naughty children who
Would hear the terrifying words from Maggie, "Granddaddy's going
   to get you if you don't behave," he
Was put in a drawer, where he languished for years until another
   flood washed him away like a sin he
Paid for with his life.

He tells me when Mahwissa, Black Kettle's sister, put the girl's hand
   in his and mumbo-jumboed, he
Didn't know she was marrying them, until Romero, the scout,
   laughed and told him to get ready to take care
Of all her relatives. Politely, he declined, but it seemed it was too
   late and Romero said he'd find himself
Near enslaved by the responsibility of husbandry. "All right, all
   right, all right," he said, his only way of
Cussing, as he led her away, anxious not to offend a pregnant
   woman, then the inevitable happened in spite
Of his best intentions and she conceived. She believed it was his. He
   didn't at the time, because even
His own brother, Tom, partook of her delicacies from time to time.
   He did not mind. Tom called her Sallie
Ann and he turned a blind, winking eye, relieved to be set free,
   especially when his wife joined him, his
Dearest, darling Libbie, who found her own relief when she went to
   see Johnnie and found him undeniably

Indian-looking for she'd heard about an Indian woman who had
    borne him a child, a rumor that drove her
From him and he'd gone after her in hot pursuit and been accused
    of desertion.
He let everyone believe he was just worried about her and an
    epidemic of cholera so he fled his post, but the
Truth was he was trying to save his marriage, but it was only really
    rescued when Libbie held the papoose

3.

And later wrote how it was "a typical bundle of cunning brown
    velvet." Less than nine months later, a
Light-skinned, light-haired boy was born two months premature to
    the girl, Monahseetah (Mona-zee-tah),
The daughter of Chief Little Rock, killed by a gunshot to the head
    as he tried to defend the women and
Children at the Washita and he inherited the daughter, but he wasn't
    there when she gave birth the second
Time, he wasn't anywhere near that occurrence. He was with his
    dear wife in Kansas. Of course, he heard
All about it, but she wasn't his responsibility anymore. The captives
    had all been sent back to the tribe soon
After and his life went on as it had before. Libbie sat beside him as
    he wrote his memoirs. He didn't care
What became of Monahseetah or her sons. Almost anything can
    happen in times of war.

He only found out later she was of the Wotapio, a Sioux name for
    the Cheyenne eater clan,
Known for the cleanliness of their lodges and for stinginess with
    their possessions. A warrior once paid
Eleven horses for her, a price signifying her status and desirability
    which he could see so plainly when
She captured him. Romero told him the man had offended her
    when he demanded that she give in to him
And be an obedient wife before she was ready, so one night, she shot
    him, crippling him. Of course, on
Hearing all the details, her father returned the horses and she was
    divorced. It didn't frighten him, although

He slept with one eye open, almost hoping she'd try it with him,
    although he was nothing but kind to her at
First. It was only after the accursed unfolding of events that he at last
    sent her from him. After all, she wasn't
White; she was a savage who might turn on him, he reasoned. She
    was merely seasoning on the dull meat
Of his days, briefly when he laid her down and found in his
    ravishment a profound peace. The Cheyennes
Were polygamists, a man often marrying sisters, and a man's brother
    was also considered a husband
Substitute, so as his wife, she allowed Tom certain privileges that
    involved elaborate rules and rights of
Kinship. Who was he to try to change the way she lived? Why not
    give her to Tom for a long night of
Oblivion beneath a buffalo robe? He always took what was his
    brother's anyway. He even wore his
Buckskin when he chose. He was rather vulgar at times, but he was
    handsome and single and had won the
Medal of Honor twice. He always said Tom should have been the
    general instead. Sometimes he even
Wondered if he tried to compromise Libbie, then he'd cast the
    thought aside, ashamed of his suspicion.
Who was he to judge, although a physician could and did put him
    on the mercury

4.

Cure? He hoped Tom would be forgiven for his misdeeds like any
    other soldier fighting for his country.
He just needed the right guidance, which Libbie provided. A dyed-
    in-the-wool Presbyterian, she was
Almost disciplinarian in her spiritual ways. She brooked no
    deviation from the path of salvation and if you
Strayed, you paid dearly in the most gentle ways. She made you feel
    ashamed of your weakness, but never
Blamed you for it. In other ways, she was exemplary too, so how
    could he view the closeness they shared
With anything but approval? Tom bared his soul to her; he told her
    everything and she forgave his straying
From her foundation-laying with smiles and encouraging words. He
    heard them declare their love as brother

And sister, yet he was jealous of it and guilty too, more guilty than
    he was when he rutted like a boar with
That poor girl he made a whore in the eyes of her people. He heard
    they said she brought bad luck because
Of what she'd done by becoming his co-wife after he had taken her
    father's life and even blamed her for the
Disappearance of the buffalo. "She gone white," the black
    housekeeper said to describe Monahseetah's transformation.
He wasn't to blame; he only did what soldiers do when they are
    victorious and are considered glorious for a time.

After the flood, when everything that hadn't floated away was caked
    with mud, only Maggie noticed he was
Gone, but Johnnie didn't mind. He'd had mixed feelings about him
    all along, but again, in Cheyenne
Kinship terms, he was his father too, or so he'd heard from his half-
    brother who was the man's blood,
Although you couldn't prove it because the records of his birth had
    disappeared and all who knew the truth
Had either died, or lied to hide the ugly story of the rape of
    several captive women the man allowed
His officers to take to bed, after he had promised them they would
    be safe. He didn't know the value the
Cheyennes placed on chastity, or that they had the reputation for
    being the most concerned with their
Women not giving in to appetite unlike some other tribes. He gave
    Monahseetah the right to choose,
Didn't he, unlike the other women who weren't given any. She
    chose him. They told him she kept silent
About their son because she was a proud woman and doubtless she
    was, although he didn't know her
Well enough to say. He was preoccupied with his command and the
    demands of authority. He'd had a
Few deserters shot. He'd gotten angry looks and was called names
    behind his back, still fame was some
Consolation, although his bank account was in a constant state of
    fluctuation, usually on the debit side. He
Had his pride too. He would not let gossip and rumors ruin him.

5.

After the Little Big Horn, out of respect for Libbie, any mention of
    the boy was expunged from the records.
Some said the grieving widow had been punished enough to
    justify the cover-up and even the Cheyennes
Began to deny the boy ever existed. The belief that it was just
    "squaws' gossip" met little resistance, so the
Years came and went until fate sent him back inside the photograph
    he forgot he'd given Monahseetah as a
Farewell gift. He thought she'd never keep it. He often made fun of
    the old Indian superstition that the soul
Could be captured by such a thing, but now he knows it's true, even
    though his photograph washed away in
The Texas flood, he stayed behind awaiting a time he'd be
    unconditionally set free. Ironic to think it would
Be me who rediscovered him among the trash and debris of my
    exhumation of family history which did not
Lead as I had thought it would to anything good, but to dark secrets
    better left buried upon the Plains,
Surrounded by the mutilated remains of the dead men, women and
    children, red, white and in-between
Along with the corpses of the horses he had shot down that
    November in 1868 when he found Black Kettle
And his people asleep in their lodges one minute and running
    through a foot of snow and bitter cold the
Next, while bullets and arrows, tomahawks and knives pierced their
    bodies as they tried to escape as I do
Now from Custer's luck and failed.

"ELIZABETH TAYLOR HAS CHUBBY FINGERS, YOU KNOW"

Said the designer, celebrating his fifteenth anniversary
Of selling goods on QVC.
But when the host spoke to him in her singsong voice,
Saying, "Really," with such sincerity, I made a gagging face,
Until the designer began to hesitate over each word in response
To her absurd remarks, as if considering the consequences

Of telling the truth. I knew something was wrong with him
And wondered if he'd had a stroke,
When suddenly, the designer almost broke down in tears
And thanked the viewers for their "kind words of support,"
Telling them he would donate ten dollars for each
Specially designed necklace to lung cancer research,
While perched beside him on a stool, his young co-designer
Chimed in soothingly, saying how much they appreciated
The viewers' purchases through the years
And how much it meant to them.
I thought about the designer and how he'd spent his life
Creating baubles for the stars, celebrities and wives of rich men,
But now had descended from the mountaintop of Beverly Hills
To give us all a chance to shop just like the other women
Whose names he dropped as casually as rose petals
Scattered randomly among the ordinary women now,
Who needed a bit of glamour
Perhaps for a wedding, or to revive a marriage,
Or simply to exercise their right
To buy whatever they desired.
I looked closely at the screen for the first time
And saw the pallor of death
Already in residence beneath his skin.
I changed the channel then.
I do not want reality when I am shopping.
I want fantasy and maybe the promise of romance,
If only in one dirty dance.
I do not want to be reminded of my mortality,
But soon, ashamed, I changed the channel back
And nearly bought a piece of jewelry
I didn't want out of my guilt,
Until I caught myself fleeing from my own truth:
I did not care to use my check, debit or credit card
To try to escape the fate awaiting all of us someday
When we must pay for our indulgences with our lives.
I'd wait patiently as a spider for some other prize
I could ensnare in my web of self-delusion
And there surrounded by other ill-considered examples
Of instant gratification,
I could celebrate the occasion of my last breath

As my own not so chubby fingers clutched the remote
In the futile hope of salvation which I know
And the designer knew just how much we all want to believe
We can achieve an imitation of good health and even immortality
Through the purchase of a crystal-encrusted
Silver-toned heart and "included" chain.

DEATHBED SCENES

for Princess Takamatsu (Tokugawa Kikuko)

1.

That I was childless when my granddaughter was born
Is of no consequence,
Nor that she is middle-aged,
For I adopted her, as she cried,
Studying the page
Where my photograph and obituary were displayed
On a website in the United States,
So far from Tokyo and the palace gates,
Closed to all except the Imperial family and regret.
Although I never knew her alive,
She knows me dead
As she imagines herself standing beside the bed where I lie,
Wearing a red kimono
Embroidered with yellow chrysanthemums,
My eyes closed against the sun rising
Through the leafless trees . . .

2.

"I'm right," I whisper, "I'm right,"
A woman can rule Japan again.
The last empress ruled in—
But even she only pays me half the attention
She pays her own musings
On the indignities of death,
As my life's packed up and stored away
To be studied someday by scholars and hobbyists

Who can't resist the pull of the past
As if it's really gone,
But it's only sleeping until the gong of rebirth
Rouses it to the chirping of birds,
The sound of water falling
And the pure, sweet music of a baby calling,
"Obasan, Obasan, wake up and play with me,"
But when I try to rise, a terrible weight holds me fast
And I cannot make the journey back
Down the black corridor lit by torches
To the world of illusion
Emperors, kings and heads of state inhabit,
Although they would not have it so
Where my ancestor, Tokugawa Ieyasu, sits in contemplation
Before the armor he must don
Wondering if he can go on
And startled by the sound of wings,
He sees a falcon on a windowsill before it flies off trilling
As if it's won some victory. A sign, he thinks,
Half rising from the floor where he is kneeling,
Then prostrates himself before his armor, ashamed
That he has wavered, if only slightly
From a life of conquest and strife.
"Will my line end?" he asks aloud.
The silence answers, "Yes."
Troubled, he begins to dress himself
Before remembering he needs his servants' help
And calls gruffly,
Staring at the window, empty now
Except for the sun rising through the leafless trees.
"I'm but a soldier," he mutters to no one in particular,
Understanding at last what Buddhists call
The impermanence of all things,
Yet unready to admit it.
He grasps his sword, stares at it, then feeling restored
Disappears into history
Only to be reborn
In the form of his own descendant,
Thus experiencing life and death simultaneously.

3.

Lord Buddha, if this is enlightenment,
I do not feel it.
I do feel a cold draft about my head
And the soles of my feet are burning.
Am I a ghost now? I wonder,
As I float above the woman reading of my death.
"Granddaughter," I say
And for a moment, she hesitates, then clicks the mouse
Going on to the next page
Which mentions my contributions to charitable institutions.
She is confused by her interest in me,
Although she's used to her own curiosity,
A symptom of her unquenchable thirst for knowledge of all kinds,
But this is different, she thinks, as she finds
More evidence I've left behind
To enlighten and to blind her.
She wonders why she is so drawn to me
But I only sigh, my body starting to rise
And this time, nothing holds me down.
"But who are you? What do you want of me?" she says aloud,
Her questions pulling me back.
You'll know everything in time, I think,
And it won't be important then.
In the end, duty is all that matters,
Or is it honor?
But isn't honor the province of men? I ask myself.
If that is so, are we doomed, I think, rising again.
When I open my mouth to say sayonara,
I swallow a ray of the sun,
But my tongue is strangely cool.
"I'm not the one you should be asking," I cry out finally,
But she doesn't respond. Our conversation of one
Seems to be over as I am spun around and around
By the winds of memory.
She never knew her father, but I did.
He chose to avoid the honor of meeting her
Until it was too late.
Now with her sudden interest in me,

And growing even more confused,
She begins to believe we are related.
Guiltily, I wonder if I should tell her that we are
And expose the scar of truth,
Or leave it as undisturbed as the surface of the pond
In which I once observed a child sitting on a barrel cactus.
Frightened, I cried, "Demon begone,"
Then I decided she was a relative reborn
And called her back,
But she had faded in a storm of autumn leaves.
When I consulted the auguries on that October morning,
They told me she was a message from Heaven.
I said, "But this is nineteen forty-seven
And Heaven and auguries no longer have meaning,"
Warning them to modernize and abandon superstition.
Otherwise, the Japanese would not survive.
Later, I tried to visualize the child,
But she would not come back to me in that form.
Now, of course, she reappears in a storm of words.
She is a poet and words are her way
Of giving shape to shapeless things
And so she begins to build me out of words too,
As though she will know me finally
And by some accidental placement of letters,
Her father will emerge
And let her know him now that he's been purged of desire
And the need for secrecy.
When she begins to write late at night,
I hover above her shoulder, saying, "Yes, that's wrong,"
Or "No, that's right,"
But she just stares through the black letters
To the other side of the world her mother showed her
In a book, titled *Little Pictures of Japan*,
When she was five and began her journey.
It took her fifty-two years to arrive.
Now, we'll take tea beside the pond
Then meditate upon the vanity of "I" and "me," I murmur.
She looks up from her notebook,
Her pen raised for she is about to begin
To handwrite her first draft,

Itself a dying art now that computers
Play a major part in writing
Then stops and goes to put the kettle on.
She won't be long, so I wait,
Letting my thoughts form and evaporate.
When she starts to set the cup down,
She hears a faint sound (is it my breathing? do I breathe now?),
Misses the handle, hitting the cup
And reaches out too late to break its fall,
Watching as the tea spills all over the page
On which the words dissolve
Much like my resolve to tell her everything.
I'll go, I tell myself, knowing I won't
Now that she's trying feverishly to restore
What cannot be restored.
Suddenly, years of frustration erupt from her eyes in yet more tears,
As she cries for her mother, who died a year ago,
Then she blames her absent father for her sorrow,
Calling him a bastard and narrowly misses
Stepping on her cat.
In fact, she catches the tip of its tail with her foot.
Fortunately, the cat's wail seems to calm her
And she gets clean paper, struggling to remember what she wrote,
Then giving up, simply begins a new poem dedicated to me,
As she knows I'm here just beyond her vision.
I know she feels me, feels this collision of life and death as I do.
Expelling one breath,
Then another, she writes line after line,
Ending with the word, "grandmother."
When she laughs out loud in a mysterious change of mood,
I ask, "Granddaughter, may I please sit down?"
"Yes, Full Lotus please," she answers,
Pointing to a cactus plant on her desk,
"While I read a poem I've written in your honor.
It begins, 'The sun is rising through the leafless trees . . .'"

THE CANCER CHRONICLES

Stage 1

She couldn't be sure as she held her arm above her head
Like the pamphlet said she should
To check her breasts for any suspicious signs.
She didn't expect to find anything of that kind
Because it wasn't in her genes.
She'd read somewhere that Japanese women
Had less incidence of the disease
And she was pleased she had less chance of getting it.
She let herself imagine she was free.
And believed her lie to herself,
As she tried to forget the slight swelling
Beside her right nipple.
It didn't hurt. It didn't even show.
It was as though she had dreamed it
And so it seemed reasonable to hide
From the meaning of that lump,
Or was it a bump?
She procrastinated for hours
Over whether or not it was one or the other,
Only to discover it was a mass,
Although she preferred the other terms of the past
For they were more descriptive,
"Poetic" in fact. She could "feel" them.
In time, she grew bored with her musing
And denial restored, she simply ignored the problem
Until one day, as she idly felt in "that" place,
The bump or lump or the mysterious mass was gone
And not wanting to give it power, she left her fear behind,
Until four years later
Perhaps sensing a weakening of defenses,
It had attacked her.
It was more defined this time and harder to the touch,
Visible, but not too much
And impossible to deny,
Although she tried.
She made the decision to hide from herself

The only evidence of the lie of good health
With vitamins and meditation, color therapy,
Prayers to the Virgin Mary
And once in a while, invocations to ancient gods
Who might still inhabit the earth,
But the odds had been against her from birth
And she knew she would die of it,
But she would not give in to it.
She would.

Stage 2

She knew that she should see a doctor,
But she made excuses to herself
For avoiding anything to do with "matters of health."
She preferred a more stealthy method
For getting herself an appointment with certain death.
She was traveling at the speed of light,
Although it took her years
To reach her final destination
And once there, she found she wasn't anywhere in particular.
She was alone on the prairie where she'd been born
To a very young mother
When the howling wind enveloped her in bony arms
And whispered, "What took you so long?"
All that was left of the house
Where she'd made her entrance into existence
Were a few faded bricks.
You played a trick on me, she said aloud,
Although no sound issued from her mouth,
Then as if she'd said the magic word,
She stood before the full-length mirror in her bathroom
And dared herself to look again
At the swelling that was visible now
Where the tumor had settled beside her breast
Like a relative who'd fallen on hard times.
She thought she'd been too kind,
But it was way too late to change her mind,
So she decided to carry on.
I'll feed, clothe and house you,

But I will not allow you to destroy me, she cried
When she was beside herself,
When her fear was so great
She'd feel like taking her own life
Before the other did.
She bought a special knife.
In some misguided hara-kiri fantasy,
She'd imagine plunging it into her stomach
As she kneeled on the tatami mat,
Where her cat, Boo-boo, sat looking up at her
As if to say, "What gives?"
Oh, dear, what would she do about him.
She couldn't just leave him, could she?
He wasn't even two years old.
She'd rescued him from the animal shelter
And had promised to care for him, hadn't she?
She couldn't be that cruel.
She tried to tell herself he would survive.
She'd find a good home
Where he could sleep beside his new mistress,
Unless, unless . . .
Soon, she put the knife away in the utensil tray
And left the mat for him to play upon
When he wasn't using it for scratching to sharpen his claws.
She let the disease proceed at its own pace.
She gave it space until Boo-boo fell ill,
Then she thought maybe it was God's will
When he died of feline leukemia
And marveled at how deliverance had eluded her.
Now she found the will to kill herself was gone,
And she would have to soldier on alone,
But at least she wasn't dead, she thought
As long as she could thrive on pain,
She would remain among the living,
Giving no sign of her struggle.
She resolved to double, even triple her efforts
To cure herself without the questionable help
Of chemo, radiation, tamoxifen
And experimentation of all kinds.
She decided it was still worth being alive,

But that was before the skin tore
Where the tumor adhered to the wall of her chest
As she scrubbed herself in the shower.
This time she thought she really ought to see a doctor
As a trickle of blood ran down her chest,
But she calmed herself
And by the time she finished showering,
The bleeding had stopped.
After that, she felt free and healed
And no longer in need of any kind of shield
Between her breast and the rest of her body.
Two weeks of bliss passed,
Then she noticed a dark spot on her nipple
That got larger and larger,
Until it turned into a scab and peeled off.
Again, she found the courage to ignore the evidence
Of her decay and oddly unafraid,
She let her inner demon loose to roam freely about her body.
To put it plainly, it was strangely exciting
To anticipate the state she'd find herself in on waking each day.
She never knew what to expect from her furtive trysts with death
And much to her amazement,
She realized that had made her husk of a life worth living.

Stage 3

Well what do you know.
She was still alive,
Even though she'd decided she'd die in December.
Now it was February
And she was very anxious instead of relieved
That she had deceived herself
Into believing she'd never be seeing a new year again.
She hadn't made any plans.
She had to admit that she didn't know when anymore,
But she knew how it would end.
Or did she?

Stage 4

She couldn't even drink from a glass.
She sipped through a straw
When she had the strength
To draw the liquid up to the top
And suck at it drop by tortured drop.
The rest of the time, she was just thirsty
And cold to her own touch,
That is when she cared to feel any part of her body.
She consoled herself with thoughts of imminent doom,
Yet she lingered as sometimes the dying must
To further their endless torment
As if it weren't enough that they knew all too well
Life was limited and unjust.
Mere luck had kept her going,
Until it didn't anymore.
Now at death's wide-open door,
She stepped across the threshold
To behold the same old, same old
Where she still lay upon the hospital bed
Among the detritus of what her existence had become,
Her thoughts clattering around in her head like marbles,
Their sound echoing down the long road of suffering
She must have chosen,
Although she couldn't remember doing so.
The marbles' refrain, "Let go, let go,"
Increased as more pain radiated from her body, eased,
Then came back as if released
To attack her again and again
When in one last spasm
Her cataclysm ceased.

INDEX